D0095928

THE ENCYCLOPEDIA OF GOD

Also by Constance Briggs

The Encyclopedia of Angels

THE
ENCYCLOPEDIA
OF
GOD

AN A-Z GUIDE TO THOUGHTS, IDEAS, AND BELIEFS ABOUT GOD

Constance Victoria Briggs

HAMPTON ROADS
PUBLISHING COMPANY, INC.

Copyright © 2003
by Constance Victoria Briggs

All rights reserved, including the right to reproduce this
work in any form whatsoever, without permission
in writing from the publisher, except for brief passages
in connection with a review.

Cover design by Steve Amarillo
Cover art by Steve Amarillo

Hampton Roads Publishing Company, Inc.
1125 Stoney Ridge Road
Charlottesville, VA 22902

434-296-2772
fax: 434-296-5096
e-mail: hrpc@hrpub.com
www.hrpub.com

If you are unable to order this book from your local
bookseller, you may order directly from the publisher.
Call 1-800-766-8009, toll-free.

Library of Congress Catalog Card Number: 2002103101

ISBN 1-57174-248-4
10 9 8 7 6 5 4 3 2 1
Printed on acid-free paper in Canada

*To my husband Ghobad and
my children Kion and Shireen,
the loves of my life.*

Acknowledgments

I offer grateful thanks and appreciation to the following people, without whom this book would not have been possible.

To my husband, Ghobad, for his understanding and unswerving love and support.

To Mimi Malfitano for her assistance and wisdom.

To Terri Franchina and Kathy McGuiness for their loving help and assistance.

To the staff of the San Diego Public Library.

And finally, to my son Kion, for always making me smile, even when things became hectic.

Introduction

How does one go about writing down the thoughts, beliefs, and ideas about God since the beginning of humankind? Initially, it appeared to me that this introduction would be the easiest part of compiling this book. However, as I prepared to write the introduction and thought about the selections, it became obvious that the task was going to be much more complicated.

Who or what is God? Is He one or a trinity? Do we meet Him at death? Did we know Him before we came to the Earth, as many new age thinkers say? There is no one person we can ask questions about God. There is no interviewing God either. What we have are sources such as sacred writings, prophecies, thoughts of philosophers, views on God from ancient cultures, religions, and ancient lore, etc. Although we can't question God, we can evaluate the information contained in these sources and draw our own conclusions about who and what God is.

The idea for *The Encyclopedia of God* came to me a few years ago when I was researching my first book, *The Encyclopedia of Angels*. During that period I realized that it would be worthwhile to chronicle and put into one place the many different beliefs, thoughts, and ideas about God. I wanted it to be a resource that could help people learn all about God, unabashed by all the stigma surrounding religions. As a result, this book includes:

• God's characteristics as seen through the eyes of the various world cultures and religions.

• A chronicle of the acts of God, past and future (such as the parting of the Red Sea, the Flood, and Armageddon).

• God's relationships with the saints, prophets, and other holy men and women.

• God's relationship with the angels.

• Summaries of beliefs in God in world religions.

• Summaries of beliefs in God from ancient cultures.

• new age thoughts about God, and more.

In addition, the book contains quotes, ideas, and thoughts of God from various artists, writers, philosophers, mystics, and notable men and women.

As an aid to the reader, I have highlighted words in the text in bold where they are described in full elsewhere in the book.

It is my desire in writing this book to portray God as a multifaceted spiritual entity whose characteristics have shaped our lives since the dawn of mankind. I hope the reader will walk away with a better understanding of God and feel closer to the truth of God.

Constance Briggs

A

Those who believe that they believe in God, but without passion in their hearts, without anguish in mind, without uncertainty, without doubt, without an element of despair even in their consolation, believe only in the God idea, not God Himself.

—*Miguel de Unamuno y Jugo*

A Mighty Fortress Is Our God

A well-known hymn written by Martin **Luther** (German leader of the Protestant Reformation).

A Se

A Latin phrase meaning "existing of itself." It is used in some philosophical thought when referring to **God.** The belief is that God is the only totally self-sufficient, independent being.

Aaron

The older brother of the **prophet Moses.** He was chosen by **God** to serve as Moses' spokesman, playing a key role in freeing the **Hebrews** from bondage to the **Egyptians.** When Moses declined the mission of delivering the **children of Israel** from slavery because of his being "slow of speech," God appointed Aaron as his spokesman, saying, "What of your brother Aaron, the Levite? I know that he can speak fluently. You shall speak to him and put the words in his mouth; and I will be with your mouth and with his mouth, and will teach you what you shall do. He shall speak for you to the people; he shall serve as a mouth for you, and you shall serve as God for him"

(**Exodus** 4:14-16). In addition, Aaron was chosen by God for the office of priest and was formally consecrated.

At **Mount Sinai,** when Moses and **Joshua** ascended the mountain to receive the stone tablets containing the **Law,** Aaron, along with Hur were left in charge of the **Israelites.** Aaron found favor with God until one day when the people, dismayed at Moses' long absence on the mountain, cried out for a god to worship. To appease them, Aaron fashioned a golden calf (Exodus 32:1-24), thus angering God. He was later pardoned only through the intercession of Moses.

Later, because of their doubts (See Numbers 20), Moses and Aaron were forbidden by God to enter the **Promised Land.** Aaron died on Mount Hor, and his office was passed on to his son Eleazar. According to ancient Hebrew lore, God rewarded Aaron for his faithfulness and service on Earth by making him a great **angel** in **Heaven.** In addition, his descendants became temple **priests.**

Aba

God in **Choctaw (Native Americans)** beliefs. Aba is believed to be a loving God and **father** who grants his **children**

1

eternal happiness after dying. The Choctaw believe that they will reside with Aba in his spiritual home forever.

Abaddon (God's Destroyer)

An **angel** from the **Bible**'s Book of Revelation. According to Revelation, Abaddon is an instrument of **God**. He has been given power and authority by God and is referred to as a king. One of his duties is to watch over the "bottomless pit" or abyss into which **Satan** and his many followers will be thrown and in which they will remain for a thousand years. Revelation 9:11 states, "They have as king over them the angel of the bottomless pit; his name in **Hebrew** is Abaddon."

Abaddon is also in charge of the **locust**-like beings that God sets loose to destroy the wicked people of Earth in the last days. Revelation 9:1-4 states, "I saw a star (angel) that had fallen from **heaven** to earth, and he was given the key to the shaft of the bottomless pit; he opened the shaft of the bottomless pit, and from the shaft rose smoke like the smoke of a great furnace, and the sun and the air were darkened with the smoke from the shaft. Then from the smoke came locusts on the earth, and they were given authority like the authority of scorpions of the earth. They were told not to damage the grass of the earth or any green growth or any tree, but only those people who do not have the seal of God on their foreheads."

Abba

The Aramaic word for "**Father.**" The **Bible** uses the term three times in relation to **God**. At Mark 14:36: **Jesus** says while praying to God, "Abba, father, for you all things are possible." Romans 8:15 states: "When we cry, 'Abba! Father!' it is that very **Spirit** bearing witness with our spirit that we are **children** of God." At Galatians 4:6 it says, "And because you are children, God

has sent the Spirit of his Son into our hearts, crying, 'Abba! Father!'"

'Abd al-Ghani (1641–1731)

Syrian mystic, prose and verse writer whose work reflected the religious ideas of his day. At an early age, 'Abd al-Ghani, joined the Islamic mystical orders of the Qadiriyah and the Naqshbandiyah. Afterward, he spent several years in seclusion studying mystical expressions of divine experiences. A main focus of his work is the theory of the divine existential (pertaining to existence) unity of **God,** the universe, and, ultimately, humankind.

Abel

The second son born to **Adam and Eve.** He was murdered by his older brother **Cain** because **God** favored Abel's **sacrifices** over his. In the **Jerusalem Bible** it states: "Now Abel became a shepherd and kept flocks, while Cain tilled the soil. Time passed and Cain brought some of the produce of the soil as an offering for **Yahweh** (God), while Abel for his part brought the first-born of his flock and some of their fat as well. Yahweh looked with favour on Abel and his offering. But he did not look with favour on Cain and his offering, and Cain was very angry and downcast" (**Genesis** 4:2–6).

Abhir

Ancient **Hebrew** name for **God.** It means "**Mighty One.**"

Abraham (2166 –1991 B.C.)

According to **Genesis**, Abraham was the progenitor of the **Hebrews. Muslims** (who call him **Ibrahim**) regard him as an ancestor of the **Arabians** through his son **Ishmael**. Abraham had a very close and personal relationship with **God**. He was the son of Terah, and was born in Ur. There he married his half-sister **Sarah.** Around 2000 B.C., God told

Abraham to leave Ur with his family and travel to Haran. There, because Abraham was a faithful man, God promised him that he would become a "great nation." As a sign of this **covenant,** Abraham and all his male descendants were to be circumcised. Abraham later moved to Canaan, where he lived as a nomad.

When Abraham and his wife Sarah were very old, God promised them a son. Shortly thereafter, Sarah gave birth to a son whom they named **Isaac.** When Isaac was a young man God tested Abraham's faith and obedience by commanding him to offer Isaac as a **sacrifice.** Abraham obeyed. However, just as he was about to kill Isaac, God sent an **angel** to stop him. God said to Abraham, "Do not put out your hand against the boy and do not do anything at all to him, for now I do know that you are God-fearing in that you have not withheld your son, your only one, from me" (**Genesis** 22:12). God then provided a ram to sacrifice in Isaac's place. Because of his special relationship with God, Abraham became known as **"God's friend."**

Abraxis

In **Gnosticism** the name Abraxis was used for the **Supreme Being,** the source of the **divine** emanations from which all things were created. The Bailidian sects of Gnostics believed that his name contained great mysteries, as it was composed of the seven Greek letters which form the number 365, which is also the number of days in a year. Abraxis was later viewed as the creator and prince of the **Aeons,** a superior order of spiritual beings in Gnosticism that emanated from **God;** also referred to as the "**cycles of creation.**" Abraxis became the intermediary between them and the **Almighty,** as well as humans on Earth. He is also invoked in the magical arts. His name is some-

times found inscribed on talismans and amulets and is used in spells. The famous magic word "abracadabra," is believed to have originated from the name Abraxis. He can also be found in the **Book of Raziel,** and in **Persian mythology.** A variation of the name Abraxis is Abraxas.

Abyss
See Abaddon.

Acosmism

A doctrine denying the existence of a universe distinct from **God.** In philosophy, it is the belief that God is the sole and ultimate reality. As a result, finite objects and events are thought to have no independent existence outside of God.

Adam

According to Judaic, Christian, and Islamic beliefs, Adam was the first human created by **God.** According to **Genesis,** the high point of God's **creation** of all things was the creation of Adam. It is believed that Adam and God had a very close relationship, that of a **father** and son, much like human parents and their **children.** They were so close, in fact, that according to the **Bible,** God communicated with Adam directly.

Adam was so loved by God that according to ancient **Hebrew** lore, God gave him two **guardian angels** to protect him, and three attending **angels** to care for him. In addition, realizing that Adam would be lonely, God gave him a most precious gift, a wife whom Adam called **Eve.** Before the creation of Adam, God had created a beautiful **paradise** for Adam to live in and gave him control of it. **Adam and Eve,** together with their future children were to cultivate this paradise. This was God's gift to his earthly son, and his legacy to future sons and daughters of Adam. Eventually, the paradise was to spread over the entire Earth. Genesis (1:28) speaks of this: "God said to them, 'Be fruitful and multiply, and fill the earth and subdue it.'" Adam and Eve lived happily in this beautiful garden until they ate the **forbidden fruit,** which came from the **Tree of Knowledge.** It was the one thing that God had withheld from them. This one act of disobedience changed Adam's relationship with God forever.

As their punishment, Adam and Eve were banished from their paradise home into a harsh, uncultivated world, where they would one day die. According to Genesis 3:17–19, God said to them, "Cursed is the ground because of you; in toil you shall eat of it all the days of your life; thorns and thistles it shall bring forth for you; and you shall eat the plants of the field. By the sweat of your face you shall eat bread until you return to the ground, for out of it you were taken; you are **dust,** and to dust you shall return."

Afterward, God placed **Cherubim** and a turning, flaming sword at the entrance of the garden to prevent Adam and Eve from reentering, and to guard the way to the **Tree of Life.** Eventually, after living a life of struggle and turmoil and fathering several sons and daughters, Adam died in disgrace, separated from God. See Eve; Tree of Knowledge; Tree of Life; Fall of Man.

Adam and Eve

The first human couple created by God according to the beliefs of **Judaism, Christianity,** and **Islam.** See Adam; Eve.

Adams, John (1735–1826)

Second President of the U.S. and leader in the movement for American independence. He was known for his fascination with Oriental thought, and was a voracious reader of Eastern religious works. Adams preferred to think of **God** as compassionate and sympathetic toward his followers. In a letter to Thomas **Jefferson** written in 1813, he gave his view and ideas on God, referring to him as the "Author of the Universe," and saying that he "adored" Him. In the letter he states: "The **Love** of God and his **Creation;** delight, Joy, Tryumph, Exultation in my own existence, 'tho but an Atom, a Molecule Organique, in the Universe; are my religion."

Adhan (Announcement)

The **Islamic** call to public worship and to *salat* (the five daily hours of **prayer**). The call is made daily and is especially important on Fridays. Adhan is made from a minaret (tower near to, or built into, the structures of a mosque) or a small mosque. The call is made by a *muezzin* (a servant of the mosque chosen for his good and pious character). The customary Sunnite adhan is: "**God** is most great. I testify that there is no god but God. I testify that **Muhammad** is the prophet of God. Come to prayer. Come to **salvation.** God is most great. There is no god but God." The first phrase is said four times, the last phrase once, and the others twice. Worshipers make a set response to each phrase.

Adideva

The original, primordial, supreme **God** in ancient Hindu beliefs.

Adon-Adonai

Ancient **Hebrew** name for **God.** It means "**Yahweh** Our God."

Adonai

A **Hebrew** term for **God.** It means "my **lord**" or "master." From Hellenistic times onward it was used verbally to replace the written **Yahweh.** A variation of Adonai is Adonay.

Adonai Yireh

The **Hebrew** name of the mountain where **God** sent an **angel** to **Abraham** to prevent him from sacrificing his son **Isaac.** Abraham named the mountain **Adonai** Yireh after a ram was found in the bushes, put there by God to be used as a **sacrifice** instead of Isaac. It means "God provides."

Adoration of the Trinity

Artist Albrecht **Dürer** offers his vision of **God** in his early sixteenth-century work entitled *Adoration of the Trinity.* In the composition, he uses beautiful color imagery, portraying God as a heavenly king dressed in royal garments, a large gold crown upon his head, with a long beard representing an ancient existence and wisdom. There, God is holding up **Jesus** who is placed on the **cross.** A **dove** symbolizing God's **Holy Spirit** hovers over him, while **angels** attend them. **Mary** (the mother of Jesus), saints, **prophets,** and saved souls are to the sides and below him. However, God is placed in the center, representing his position in **heaven** and in the universe.

Adversary

In several religions **God** has an adversary. In Zoroastrianism, **Judaism, Christianity, Islam,** and **Buddhism,** the adversary is the principle of evil conceived as a **spirit** person who opposes God. In Zoroastrianism, God's adversary is named **Angra Mainyu.** Angra Mainyu is also called the Lie, and the Destructive Spirit. **Zoroaster** gave Angra Mainyu's followers the name daevas. From daevas comes the word **devil.** Zoroastrians believe that Angra Mainyu resides in a dark **abyss.** He is the creator of **death,** disease, and evil. Zoroastrians hold him responsible for all of mankind's sorrows. Some Zoroastrians believe that God created him and that he eventually turned against God, becoming his chief opponent.

In Christian tradition the adversary is the Devil (also called **Satan**). He was the leader of the **angels** who rebelled against God and were cast out of **heaven.** He and his followers are seen as tempters of humanity and the source of evil in the world.

In Islam, **Iblis** (Satan) is God's adversary. Known as the "spirit of darkness," Iblis is said to have loved God most of all the angels. When God created **Adam,** He told the angels to bow down and worship him. Iblis refused. Because of this disobedient act, God ordered him from His presence. The **Koran** states that when Adam was created, God told the angels to prostrate themselves saying, "Fall ye prostrate before Adam! And they fell prostrate, all save Iblis, who was not of those who make prostration. He said: What hindered Thee that thou did not fall prostrate when I bid thee? [Iblis] said: I am better than he. Thou createdst me of fire, while him Thou didst create him of mud. He said: Then go down hence! It is not for Thee to show pride here, so go forth! Lo! Thou are of Those degraded" (Sura 710).

The Buddhist adversary Mara keeps individuals imprisoned in the cycle of **reincarnation.** It is a cycle that all Buddhist are struggling to be free of. This to the Buddhist believer is the equivalent of **Hell.**

Aeons

Angels in ancient **Gnosticism.** They were believed to be the first beings created by **God,** numbering somewhere around 365. According to ancient lore, some of the Aeons turned away from God when they became fascinated with human sexuality. This belief parallels the story in the **Old Testament** which speaks of angels becoming attracted to women, and coming to the Earth to take them as wives.

Africa

Most African religions recognize a supreme **God** as well as a host of lesser spirits. In the various traditional African beliefs, there are many methods of worship and many names for God. In most African religions, God is the all-encompassing universal power and sustainer. He is known in the various beliefs by such titles as: the Source of All, the Ever-Present One, the Great One Who Determines Fates, and the Mysterious One. As in the traditions of the great monotheistic religions, most African groups acknowledge that there are lesser spirits who dwell on a level lower than God. These spirits are believed to have some influence on the everyday lives of the people, and people most believe they are more apt to have an encounter with one of the lesser spirits than any direct contact with God Himself.

Agape

A term meaning spiritual love. In the **New Testament** the word agape (Greek) was used to denote the fatherly love of **God** for humankind, and mankind's shared love for God.

Agassiz, (Jean) Louis Rodolphe (1807–1873)

Swiss-American naturalist. One of the best-informed and most capable biologists of his day. He believed in **God** and in His special **creation** of every kind of organism.

Age of Enlightenment

An era that stretched from the early seventeenth to the early nineteenth century, especially in England, France, and Germany. Advocates of the Enlightenment, known as the **philosophes,** included such figures as Voltaire, Rousseau, Diderot, and Montesquieu in France; Bacon, Hobbes, and Locke in England; and Kant, Leibniz, Lessing, and Herder in Germany; all of them communicated through correspondence.

These thinkers strove to make reason the ruler of human thinking. They believed that all humans could gain knowledge and freedom by dispelling erroneous systems of thought and by systematizing the various intellectual disciplines. They encouraged people to question values and explore new ideas. The rallying call for the philosophes was the idea of progress. They believed that by mastering both human and natural sciences, humanity could harness the natural world for its own benefit and learn to live peacefully.

Although most of the philosophes did not renounce religion, they held an unfavorable attitude towards any kind of orthodoxy, especially that of orthodox religion. They accepted the existence of **God,** but preferred to view God as a creator who had designed the universe, set its laws in motion, and retreated. They believed the only dependable way to gain knowledge of God's plans was through science, research, and examination, instead of religious doctrines and prophetic revelations. In the Great Ages of Man series by Time-Life Books, Peter Gay, a professor of history at Columbia University and an authority on European intellectual history and political philosophy, comments on the philosophes: "They did not believe in **miracles,** and, if they believed in God at all, thought of Him as the mechanic of the universe—a sort of cosmic watch maker; He had built a superb machine, given it laws to run by and then withdrawn."

Agni

One of the three supreme gods of the Rig Veda. The other gods include Vayu and Surya. These three gods have domain over the earth, air, and sky. Agni has been worshipped in **Hinduism** from the Vedic time through the modern era. His name stands for fire. During fire **sacrifices,** Agni represented all the other gods, linking mankind to the spiritual world. Because of his ability to take on different shapes with fire, he was thought to be an example of the **spirit** world throughout the world of nature on Earth.

Agnosticism

A word coined by Thomas Huxley (English biologist and teacher) as a designation of those who are unsure about whether or not **God** exists. The word is taken from the Greek words *a* meaning "not" and *gnosis* meaning "knowledge." Agnosticism is a form of skepticism that holds that the existence of God cannot be logically proved or disproved; that no one has knowledge of God or the origin of the universe. Agnosticism is not to be confused with **atheism,** which denies the existence of God. Agnostics avoid the charge of being complete atheists by admitting that theoretically, there is a chance that God exists.

Ahaitin

See Angra Mainyu.

Ahmad, Ghulam (1839–1908)

Indian **Muslim** scholar who founded an important Muslim sect known as the Ahmadiyah. Ahmad was from a wealthy family and received an education in **Arabic** and **Persian**. Although his family insisted that he go into law or join the British government, he chose instead to enter into a life of **meditation** and religious contemplation. In 1889, he received a revelation from **God.** He claimed that God told him that he was entitled to receive *bay'at* (an oath of allegiance). He later claimed that he was *mahdi* (a figure expected by some Muslims at the end of the world), the

Christian **Messiah,** an incarnation of the Hindu god **Krishna,** and a reappearance *(buruz)* of **Muhammad.**

About God he once said: "I believe in **Allah** (God), the **angels,** the apostles, the revealed Books, **paradise** and **hell** and the Day of Resurrection." He taught that God established two structures for the operation of the universe; the visible and the invisible worlds. He held that no part of the visible world could operate without the guidance of God's angels in the invisible world. He believed that God made angels administrators of the universe, and that it is because of them that there is change and progress.

Ahmadiyah

See Ahmad, Ghulam.

Ahriman

See Angra Mainyu.

Ahura Mazda (Wise Lord)

The supreme **God** in Zoroastrianism. He is the overseer of **Heaven** and Earth; the possessor of knowledge and immortal powers; the source of all that is **light,** joyful, beautiful, and good. In art he is portrayed with a beard and wearing a robe adorned with stars. In Heaven, myriad **angels** continually sing praises to him. His **adversary** is **Ahriman,** the **spirit** of darkness with whom he is continuously locked in battle. It is a struggle between good and **evil,** one in which Ahura Mazda will be victor.

In the heavens, he is assisted by six angels referred to as the **Amesha Spentas.** He and these six angels represent seven fundamental moral ideas. They include: Ahura Mazda (**Holy Spirit**); Vohu Manah (Wisdom); **Asha** Vahishta (Truth); Armaiti (Devotion); Khshathra Vairya (Desirable Dominion); Haurvatat (Wholeness); and Ameretat (Immortality). A song (Yasna) written by **Zoroaster** (founder of Zoroastrianism) says, "When I conceived of Thee, O Mazda, as the very First and the Last, as the most Adorable One, as the Father of Good Thought, as the Creator of Truth and Right, as the **Lord** Judge of our actions in life, then I made a place for Thee in my very eyes" (Yasna, 31-4). Another name for Ahura Mazda is Ohrmazd.

Akashic Records

A spiritual library of knowledge said to hold a complete record of **God's** memory. It is also said to hold the history of the universe from **creation** to the present day and the history of every **soul** since the dawn of creation. The records are believed to be located somewhere within the spiritual realm. **Prophets,** mystics, and psychics have talked about the Akashic Records for centuries. Some claim to be able to tap into these records for information. One such example is Edgar Cayce (called the sleeping prophet), who first brought the term "Akashic Records" to general use. Cayce claimed that he could retrieve information from the Akashic Records for health diagnoses while in a trance state. In addition, the **angels** are said to use the Akashic Records to provide humans with needed information to help with difficult problems. The records are also thought to contain insight into the future of mankind. Most importantly, they are believed to hold the answers to questions about God.

Akedah

A **Hebrew** term which refers to the **Old Testament** story of the **"Binding of Isaac."**

Alcott, Louisa May (1832–1888)

Popular American writer, born in Germantown, Pennsylvania. She was raised in Boston and was tutored by the great American writers Ralph Waldo Emerson and Henry David Thoreau. She is best known for her works, *Little Women,* an autobiographical novel of her childhood, and its sequels, *Little Men* and *Jo's Boys,* which are considered classics.

Alcott had an informal, relaxed attitude toward religion and **God** in general. In her writings, however, she seemed interested in and rather close to God. In one journal entry in particular, she gave an experience of feeling close to God. It was a memory that she wanted to keep forever. The entry read: "I had an early run in the woods before the dew was off the grass. The moss was like velvet, and as I ran under the arches of yellow and red leaves, I sang for joy, my heart was so bright and the world so beautiful. I stopped at the end of the walk and saw the sunshine out over the wide Virginia meadow. It seemed like going through a dark life or grave into **heaven** beyond. A very strange and solemn feeling came over me as I stood there, with no sound but the rustle of the pines, of one near me, and the sun so glorious, as for me alone. It seemed as if I felt God as I never did before, and I prayed in my heart that I might keep that happy sense of nearness all my life." In a letter she once wrote, "God is enough for me, and all the **prophets** are only stepping stones to him."

'Alenu (It is Our Duty)

The expression found at the beginning of an ancient **Hebrew prayer.** The 'alenu has been spoken at the conclusion of the three periods of daily prayer since the European Middle Ages. The first part of the 'alenu is a prayer of gratitude for **Israel** having been chosen from the **nations** to do God's work. The second part, removed by those who follow the Sephardic (Spanish) custom, conveys a hope for the approaching age of the **messiah;** a period when all the nations will worship the one true God. The 'alenu ends with the expression: "And the **Lord** will become king over all the Earth; on that day the Lord will be one and his name one" (**Zechariah** 14:9).

Aleph to Taw
See Blessings from Aleph to Taw.

Alfadir (All-Father)
One of the epithets of **Odin**, the creator god of ancient Norse beliefs.

Alighieri, Dante (1265–1321)
Noted Italian poet. He is best known for writing *The Divine Comedy*, a magnificent three-part narrative poem. It is considered one of the greatest masterpieces ever written. In *The Divine Comedy*, Dante portrays visions of **hell,** purgatory, and **heaven,** giving a case-by-case study of the eternities to be endured by several celebrated people of his day. At the end of the poem, Alighieri is privileged to see the Beatific Vision (**God**).

All, The
In some **Wiccan** beliefs there is a **god** and **goddess,** and above them is a genderless mass of energy called, "the All" from which all life emanates.

Allah (The God)
God the **Almighty** in **Islam.** The word Allah means God in **Arabic.** It is used in Islam when referring to God. Allah comes from the Arabic words *Al* which means "the" and *Elah* which means god. The term Allah, meaning "the God," was originally created to refer to the true God, separating Him from the gods that were worshipped prior to Islam. Allah, the God of Islam, is the same as the God of the **Jews** and the Christians. Because many Westerners are not familiar with the

Arabic language or Islam, they mistake the word Allah for a name for God, or a different God all together.

Surah 35 of the **Koran** states "Praise be to Allah, Who created [out of nothing] the heavens and the earth, Who made the **angels, messengers** with wings. He adds to **Creation** as He pleases: for Allah has power over all things." In the Koran, angels are seated around the great throne of Allah ministering to Him and paying homage to Him. These angels ask Allah to pardon sinners and act as **mediators** between Him and humankind.

Allah is believed to reside in **paradise** (another word for Heaven). It is the will of Allah that all humankind enjoy eternity with him in paradise. According to the Koran, angels watch over humankind and record their deeds. The records of these deeds are used at the time of judgment in the afterlife. When a person dies, Allah sends an angel to guide the **soul** to the afterlife. The good go to a fabulous paradise home where there are lavish meadows, streams of honey, and *houri* (beautiful virgins who dwell in paradise and reward the faithful with sensual pleasures). Those who do not worship Allah, or who cannot pass certain tests in Heaven will be cast into **Hell.**

All-Knowing
The phrase "**God** is All-Knowing" is inspired from the **Bible.** The scripture is found at 1 John 3:20, where it states, "God is greater than our hearts, and he knows everything."

Almighty, The
A title applied to **God.** It means, "God, who is all powerful."

Almond Tree
In the **Old Testament** Book of **Jeremiah** (1:11-12), **God** showed

Jeremiah an "almond" rod *(shoqed* in Hebrew*),* to illustrate the point that God was "watching over" *(shaqad)* his own Word to perform it. There Jeremiah writes: "The word of God came to me, saying, 'Jeremiah, what do you see?' And I said, 'I see a branch of an almond tree.' Then God said to me, 'You have seen well, for I am watching over my word to perform it.'"

Alpha and Omega

The first and last letters of the Greek alphabet. The term is used to mean "the **first and the last.**" In the **Bible, God** referred to Himself as the Alpha and Omega. The term "the Alpha and Omega" is used three times in Revelation, referring to God the **Father** (twice) and the Son (once). The phrase "I am the Alpha and the Omega" means "I am the beginning and the end." At Revelation 1:8 it states: "I am the Alpha and the Omega, says the **Lord** God, who is and who was and who is to come, the **Almighty.**"

Alphabet, The

An ancient **Hebrew** tale tells how each letter of the alphabet asked **God** to create the world using a word that began with it. However, starting with the end of the alphabet, each letter was disqualified, because an unappealing word began with it. This disqualification continued until *beth,* the second letter of the alphabet was reached. *Beth* was given the privilege of being used. The word *bara* ("to create") begins with *beth.* The first letter of the alphabet *(aleph)* was given the privilege of beginning the **Ten Commandments.**

Altar(s)

A special, flat surface set aside for honoring **God** or the gods. In **places of worship,** altars represent the holiness of God. In biblical days it was a table or other structure where **sacrifices** were offered to God. Altars vary in size, shape, and construction. People as early as at the time of **Noah** used altars. Noah, who survived Earth's biggest catastrophe—the **Flood**—decided to honor God and built an altar to Him. There he sacrificed burnt offerings. According to the **Bible,** God smelled the pleasing aroma rising from the altar and said in His heart: "Never again will I **curse** the ground because of humankind, even though every inclination of the human heart is **evil** from childhood. And never again will I destroy all living creatures, as I have done" (**Genesis** 8:21).

During ancient times, the **Hebrews** offered sacrifices on altars as **atonement** to God, when the **Tabernacle** did not exist. Those altars served as a bridge for speaking with God. At the Burnt Offering Altar of the Tabernacle, the **priests** sacrificed various offerings to God. The offerings were for their own sins as well as for the sins of the people. The Bible speaks of a magnificent **golden altar** that stands before the **throne of God.** Around it **angels** gather listening to the **prayers** of the saints that are being offered up to God. In Revelation 8:3 we read: "An angel with a **golden censer** came and stood at the altar; he was given a great quantity of **incense** to offer with the prayers of all the saints on the golden altar that is before the (God's) throne." In the Jewish synagogue and in the Roman Catholic, Christian Orthodox, and Anglican churches, the altar is of great importance. In these religions, only the priest may approach the altar, which symbolizes God's holiness. Note: Some churches have done away with altars and priests seeing **Jesus** as the only **mediator** to God.

Altea, Rosemary (c. 1935–)

Internationally renowned English psychic medium, healer, and best-selling author who won international acclaim with the publication of her first book, *The Eagle and the Rose,* her autobiography. In addition, she has been featured on *The Oprah Winfrey Show, The View, PrimeTime Live with Diane Sawyer, Larry King Live,* and *Maury Povich.* She has also been featured in *Vanity Fair, Entertainment Weekly, People, Elle,* and the *New York Times.* She is the founder of RAAH (The Rosemary Altea Association of Healers), a nonprofit organization based in England with patients worldwide.

She is known as "The Voice of the **Spirit** World," having obtained this title by traveling extensively around the world demonstrating that we don't die, and by helping thousands make contact with their loved ones on the Other Side. In her book *Proud Spirit,* Rosemary shares her insights on **God.** "To learn to love ourselves is to come to the awakening, the realization of the fact that we, each individual, is of God, part of God, and of his **light.** And how can we not love God? And how can we not give to God? And how can we not like God, and the light which is God? Be careful here to understand. I am not saying that each of us is God, only that all of us have God within, and if we deny ourselves love, we deny God."

Am

To exist or be. "**I AM** WHO I AM," the reply to **Moses'** request for the name of **God,** indicates that God makes himself present as he wills (**Exodus** 3:14).

Amazing Grace

See Newton, John.

America

Gallup polls indicate that 92.5 percent of the United States population profess belief in **God.** They believe in the adage: "One nation, under God." This statement, from the Pledge of Allegiance, describes how most Americans view our relationship with God as a country.

American Indians

See Native Americans.

Amesha Spentas

See Ahura Mazda.

Amidah

The main section of the morning, afternoon, and evening **prayers** in **Judaism.** The *amidah* is first recited by each person as a silent prayer. This gives those who have sinned a chance to atone in private. The prayer is then repeated aloud. All Jewish services include an *amidah.*

THE AMIDAH

Blessed are you **God**

You are our God, and the God of our **fathers**.

The God of **Abraham,** the God of **Isaac,** and the God of **Jacob,**

The **Almighty,** great powerful and awesome. God who is supreme

Who does loving kindness

Who possesses everything, He remembers the kindness of the **Patriarchs**

And He brings a redeemer to their children's **children**

For the sake of His name, with love. King, who helps, saves, and shields (protects us). Blessed are you God who shields Abraham.

Amos

A **Hebrew Prophet** that was called upon by **God** to give **Israel** a warning. During the reign of Jeroboam II, Amos was a herdsman and a dresser of fig trees in the village of Thecua, located in the Southern Kingdom, twelve miles south of Jerusalem. Thecua was a shepherd's town, and it was while attending his flock in the wilderness that God called upon Amos to speak to the northern kingdom of Israel and admonish them for their breaking of God's laws, a difficult task for a simple man with no prophetic training.

Amos condemned the nation for their many crimes against humankind including violence and war. He warned that they would suffer punishment from God for abandoning God's laws. He roared against Israel for their extravagant self-indulgence and their cruel and callous treatment toward the poor. He accused them of appearing to love God while, in his words, they turned "justice into poison and the fruit of righteousness into wormwood" (Amos 6:12). According to Amos, Israel had trampled over their **covenant** with God and become corrupt in every way. Amos warned that if they did not repent, they would suffer punishment from God. Israel, however, ignored his words and the warning he had brought them from God.

Amun

Ancient **Egypt**ian deity who was venerated as king of the gods. Variations of the name Amun are Amon, Amen, and Ammon.

Amun-Ra

Amun-Ra was the greatest of the **Egypt**ian gods. Known as "King of the gods," he was a combination of the god **Amun** and the sun god Ra. In art he was usually portrayed as a man crowned with two tall plumes. Variations of the name Amun-Ra are Amun-Re and Amen-Re.

Anabaptists

The name Anabaptists is taken from the Greek word *anabaptizein,* which means "to baptize again." It was originally used in scorn for certain Christian sects found in Europe during the six-

teenth century. The Anabaptists held that infant **baptism** is not authorized in Scripture, and that baptism should be given only to adult believers. The Anabaptists believed in the paramount importance of personal **faith** in **God,** as opposed to rituals, and to the right of independent personal judgment which they believe is a God-given right. They advocated nonviolence and were in opposition to state **church**es as a part of God's will. In the sixteenth century, Anabaptism appealed most strongly to the poor and to uneducated peasants and artisans.

Analogy of Being

Thomas Aquinas' theory that there is a correlation between the **Supreme Being** and the created order resulting from the **divine** creatorship.

Analogy of Faith

A hypothesis made by Karl Barth that any connection between the created order and the Supreme Being is founded on the self-revelation of God.

Ancient of Days

A title associated with the **Hebrew** and Christian **God.** It is taken from **Daniel** 7:9–10. There, God is described in great detail from a vision of Daniel. The account says, "I kept on beholding until there were thrones placed and the Ancient of Days sat down. His clothing was white just like snow, and the hair of his head was like clean wool. His throne was flames of fire, its wheels were a burning fire. There was a stream of fire flowing and going out from before him. There were a thousand thousands **(angels)** that kept ministering to him, and ten thousand times ten thousand that kept standing right before him." In some translations of the **Bible** the term "Ancient of Days," is replaced with **"Ancient One."**

Ancient One

See Ancient of Days.

Andreasi, Osanna (1449–1505)

Catholic Saint who in her life claimed to have been embraced by **God** Himself. Born in Mantua, Italy, in 1449 to Italian aristocrats Agnes and Nicolaus, she reportedly began to have visions of **heaven, angels,** the **Trinity, Christ** on the **cross,** and **paradise** at the tender age of 5. It was in one of these visions that she was held by God. She felt called by God to enter into a religious life, and she became a Dominican tertiary at 17. However, her parents died during her childhood and she became responsible for her siblings. Because of this responsibility, she waited thirty-seven years to complete her vows. She also experienced the stigmata as red marks, but had no bleeding.

Angel of God

The equivalent of the **Angel of the Lord.**

Angel of Mount Moriah

The **angel** sent from **God** to save **Abraham's** son from being **sacrificed.** See Mount Moriah.

Angel of the Lord

God's personal **spokesman.** He is also referred to as "the **Angel of God.**" He has no individual characteristics except that he is a **mediator** for the **Almighty.** In the **New Testament** he is personalized as both **Gabriel** and the **Holy Spirit.** In various parts of the **Bible** he has different roles. He judges and destroys disobedient people, delivers the righteous ones from harm, and brings important announcements. When he appears to men, he is sometimes mistakenly addressed as "God." (Note: It is a misconception to think that the Angel of the Lord is one **angel.**

God has myriad angels to perform various deeds and functions for Him. Therefore, the Angel of the Lord more than likely is several different angels that God calls on to represent Him.)

Angel(s)

A spiritual being found in **Judaism, Christianity,** Zoroastrianism, and **Islamic** beliefs. They are generally portrayed as winged beings who serve as **messengers** of **God.** See Angel of the Lord; Angels of Judaism and Christianity; Angels of Islam; Angels of the Presence; Angels of Zoroastrianism; Apostate Angels; Archangels; Bene Ha-Elohim; Cherubim; Dominations; Fallen Angels; Gabriel; Guardian Angels; Israfel; Michael; Ministering Angels; Powers; Principalities; Raphael; Seraphim; Thrones; Uriel; Virtues; Watchers.

Angelolatry

The adoration and worship of **angels.** Throughout history it has been debated whether or not it is appropriate to revere angels. Many believe that attention given to angels is **idolatry** and takes away from worship due only to **God.** The worship of angels is addressed in Revelation and the **Apocalypse** of **Zephaniah.** Revelation 22:8-9 shows John, after being given a vision from an angel, kneeling at the angel's feet in an act of worship. The angel stops him, saying, "You must not do that! I am a fellow servant with you and your comrades, the **prophets,** and with those who keep the words of this book. Worship God!" In the Apocalypse of Zephaniah 6:15, Zephaniah prostrates himself before an angel named Eremiel. Eremiel tells him, "Take heed. Don't worship me. I am not God **Almighty.**"

Angelou, Maya (1928–)

Maya Angelou was born April 4, 1928, as Marguerite Johnson. While growing up in rural Arkansas, Angelou regularly attended a Baptist **church** where she enjoyed listening to the sermons and spirituals. There she became fascinated with the words behind the music. It was the first poetry that she ever experienced. It was during those early days that Angelou first contemplated the existence of **God.** Today she is a writer, poet, historian, actress, playwright, civil-rights activist, producer, and director. She also lectures throughout the U.S. and abroad. Her best-selling books and numerous magazine articles have earned her Pulitzer Prize and National Book Award nominations. Of God, Angelou says: "I believe in God. I believe in whatever people call God." "I have a great attachment, a gratitude for the presence of God." "We are a community of **children** of God, whether we admit it or not, whether we call it God or the Creator or the Source of Nature. We're a community."

Angels of Islam

In **Islam, angels** are **messengers** of God who also praise Him. There are four **archangels** in Islamic beliefs. The **Koran** lists only two, **Jibril (Gabriel),** the "faithful servant," and **Mikhail (Michael),** "who provides men with food and knowledge." The other two are Azrael, the **angel** of **death,** and **Israfel,** the angel of music who praises God in many languages. It was Jibril who revealed the Koran to **Muhammad.** He also took Muhammad on a tour of **paradise (Heaven).** There are also the **El-Karubiyan (Cherubim),** the Hafazah **(guardian angels),** the Huri (a group of female angels who inhabit paradise), the Al-Zabaniya (nineteen guardians of **Hell),** and the Malaika (angels who record mankind's deeds). Other angels include Harut and Marut (angels who gave in to sexual temptation).

According to early **Muslim** lore, the El-Karubiyan were created from the tears of Mikhail when he cried over the sins of the faithful. In Islam, angels are said to sit in the mosques listening to and recording the **prayers** of men. The archangels of Islam are believed to record the good and bad deeds of humankind. In ancient Islamic lore, there is an elite class of angels called the Abdals, who were chosen by God to preside over the operation of the universe. There are seventy angels of this order.

Angels of Judaism and Christianity

In **Judaism** and **Christianity,** God's purpose and destiny for mankind is communicated through celestial **messengers** whose primary function is to serve the **Almighty** and do His will. These heavenly beings are known as **angels.** The word "angel" is a generic term that is generally used for all spiritual creatures that dwell in the heavenly realm with God. The word angel means **messenger,** and was derived over a period of time from several languages, including the **Hebrew** word *malakh* which originally meant the shadow side of God, but later came to mean messenger; the **Persian** word *angaro* meaning courier; and the Greek word *angelos* which also means messenger.

Angels act as intercessionaries between God and humankind. This is because God is too overwhelming a force for Man to come face-to-face with. According to the **Bible** no man can see God's face and live (**Exodus** 33:20). Therefore, angels are thought to be a necessary link between God and humans.

ORDERS OF ANGELS. There are nine orders of angels in the angelic hierarchy. These include 1) **Seraphim;** 2) **Cherubim;** 3) **Thrones;** 4) **Dominations;** 5) **Virtues;** 6) **Powers;** 7) **Principalities;** 8) **Archangels;** and 9) Angels.

The Seraphim and Cherubim are nearer to God while the others are moving out and away from God.

PRAISES TO GOD. One of the many functions of the angels is to praise God. Praising God is believed by some to be the sole purpose of God's creating the angels, while others contend that the angels do not praise God out of duty, but out of love for their creator. In addition, the word angels also refers to the angels of the angelic hierarchy. They are the last order of angels (also known as Angeloi), standing only one stage higher than mankind. They work more with humans than any other class of angels. The **guardian angels** are from this class.

Angels of the Presence

In **Judaism** there are twelve **angels** who were given the privilege of existing in the presence of **God**.

Angels of the Soul

According to ancient **Hebrew** lore, there are five **angels** who lead the **souls** of man to the judgment of **God**. They include: Araqiel, Aziel, Rumael, Samiel, and **Uriel**.

Angels of Zoroastrianism

In Zoroastrianism there are six **archangels** who assist **God (Ahura Mazda)**. These archangels are referred to as **Amesha Spentas**. God and the Amesha Spentas represent seven fundamental moral ideas: God (Holy Spirit); Vohu Manah (Wisdom); **Asha** Vahishta (Truth); Armaiti (Devotion); Khshathra Vairya (Desirable Dominion); Haurvatat (Wholeness); and Ameretat (Immortality). God and the Amesha Spentas protect specific aspects of **creation**. God—Mankind; Vohu Manah—Cattle; Asha Vahishta— Fire; Armaiti—Earth; Khshathra Vairya—Sky; Haurvatat—Water; Ameretat—Plants. They are also referred to as Amshashpands and Amshaspendas.

Angra Mainyu

The spirit of darkness in Zoroastrianism. He is **Ahura Mazda's (God) Adversary.** He is also called "the Lie," "the Destructive Spirit," "Leader of the Demonic Hordes," and "**Demon of Demons.**" His followers were given the name *daevas* by **Zoroaster**. From *daevas* comes the word **devil**. Zoroastrians believe that Angra Mainyu resides in a dark **abyss** in the North. When he manifests, he takes on one of three forms, a lizard, snake, or a male youth. He is the creator of **death**, disease, and **evil**. Zoroastrians hold him responsible for all of mankind's sorrows. Some Zoroastrians believe that he was created by God himself and that he eventually turned against God and became His chief opponent. Another name for Angra Mainyu is Ahriman.

Animal Sacrifices

See Sacrifices.

Animals

Genesis tells us that **God** created animals before humans, that He gave humans authority over the animals, and that **Adam** named them. Genesis 1:16 reads, "Then God said, 'Let them have dominion over the fish of the sea, and over the birds of the air, and over the cattle, and over all the wild animals of the earth, and over every creeping thing that creeps upon the earth.'" Genesis 2:19 says, "Out of the ground God formed every animal of the field and every bird of the air, and brought them to the man to see what he would call them; and whatever the man called every living creature, that was its name."

After the **Flood**, in speaking with **Noah**, God speaks again about man's authority over the animals, stating, "The fear and dread of you shall rest on every animal of the earth, and on every bird of the air, on everything that creeps on the ground, and on all the fish of the sea; into your hand they are delivered" (Genesis 9:2). Originally, humans were vegetarians, but after the Flood, God gave animals for food to humans as well, saying, "Every moving thing that lives shall be food for you; and just as I gave you the green plants, I give you everything" (Genesis 9: 3).

ANIMALS AND GOD. Many people believe that animals as well as humans go to **Heaven** to be with God after **death,** citing the scripture at Psalms 36:6 which says, "Your righteousness is like the mighty mountains, your judgments are like the great deep; you save humans and animal alike, O **LORD.**" Among some facets of **Christianity**, the word "saved" denotes a forgiveness of sins and going to dwell in heaven with God after death. Some cite the account found in 2 Kings 2:11 where God takes the **prophet Elijah** from Earth into Heaven in a chariot drawn by horses. "As they continued walking and talking, a chariot of fire and horses of fire separated the two of them, and Elijah ascended in a whirlwind into Heaven." It is believed that the horses entered heaven along with Elijah, thereby supporting the idea that animals as well as humans go to Heaven.

Annunciation, The

The term Annunciation refers to **God's** announcement to **Mary** that she would give birth to the **Messiah.** Mary, the young virgin, was engaged to Joseph, a descendant of **Abraham** and **David.** During this time, God sent the Archangel **Gabriel** to Nazareth with the message. Gabriel told Mary not to be frightened and announced to her that she would become pregnant; she would have a child, a son, who would be called Son of the **Most High,** and that he would inherit the throne of David and

reign forever. Mary wondered how this could happen since she was not yet married and still a virgin.

Gabriel explained to her that she would become pregnant by the power of God's **Holy Spirit.** Mary believed what the **angel** told her and accepted it as God's will. The **Bible** reads, "God sent the angel Gabriel to Nazareth, a village in Galilee, to a virgin, Mary, engaged to be married to a man named Joseph, a descendant of King David. Gabriel appeared to her and said, 'Congratulations, favored lady! The Lord is with you!' Confused and disturbed, Mary tried to think what the angel could mean. 'Don't be frightened, Mary,' the angel told her, 'for God has decided to wonderfully bless you! Very soon now, you will become pregnant and have a baby boy, and you are to name him "Jesus." He shall be very great and shall be called the **Son of God.** And the **Lord** God shall give him the throne of his ancestor David. And he shall reign over **Israel** forever; his Kingdom shall never end!' Mary asked the angel, 'But how can I have a baby? I am a virgin.' The angel replied, 'The Holy Spirit shall come upon you, and the power of God shall overshadow you; so the baby born to you will be utterly **holy**—the Son of God.' Mary said, 'I am the Lord's servant and I am willing to do whatever he wants. May everything you said come true.' And then the angel disappeared" (Luke 1:26-38).

Anointed One

The title of the one whom **God** chose and appointed as Savior and **Lord (Jesus Christ).**

Anselm, Saint (1033–1109)

Theologian, archbishop (of Canterbury), philosopher, and Doctor of the **Church,** who proposed an argument for **God's** existence that is still being debated. Saint Anselm was an

Italian-born gifted teacher and avid defender of **Christianity.** He is best known for his **ontological argument** for the existence of God. This argument has been debated for centuries among many great **philosophers,** theorists, and truth-seekers alike. In his book *Faith Seeking Understanding,* Anselm argued for the existence of God saying: "Men believe God to be the Being than which none greater can be thought. It is greater to exist in reality and in the understanding than to exist in the understanding alone. Therefore, it is contradictory to hold that God exists only in the intellect, for then the being than which none greater can be thought is one than which a greater can be thought, namely, one that exists both in reality and in the understanding." In *Christian Philosophy Made Simple,* by P. Weiss, this complex argument is simplified in eight points.

St. Anselm's ontological argument for God's existence, point by point:

1) God is defined as the being in which none greater is possible.

2) It is true that the notion of God exists in the understanding (your mind).

3) And that God may exist in reality (God is a possible being).

4) If God only exists in the mind, and may have existed, then God might have been greater than He is.

5) Then, God might have been greater than He is (if He existed in reality).

6) Therefore, God is a being which a greater is possible.

7) This is not possible, for God is a being in which a greater is impossible.

8) Therefore God exists in reality as well as the mind.

Anthropomorphism

The attributing of human features (such as hands or arms) or other human characteristics to **God.** Anthropomorphites argue that man is made in the likeness of God (**Genesis** 1:26-17) and point to verses of the **Bible** that refer to God having a body, such as "strong right arm of God," "the eyes of God," etc.

Antinomianism

The word is taken from the Greek word *anti* (against) and *nomos* (**law**). It is the belief that **faith** in **God** and trusting in God's **grace** frees Man from the obligation to observe moral law. In the **Bible's New Testament,** Paul speaks against the concept of antinomianism in Romans 6:1-2: "Are we to continue in **sin** that grace may abound? May it never be! How shall we who died to sin still live in it?"

Anu

Sky god in **Mesopotamian** beliefs. He was the highest of the gods, although he played a small role in the **mythology,** hymns, and cults of the period. He was the **father** of all the gods as well as the evil spirits. In addition, he was the god of kings and of the calendar. He was usually portrayed wearing a headdress with horns, a signature of his might.

Apocalypse

The period of cataclysmic events that will precede the ending of the world and the coming of **God** to sit in judgment upon all humankind. The word is taken from the Greek *apokalypsis,* which means "revelation." The term is also associated with literature regarding the prophecies about that period. The Biblical Revelation is considered to be a book of the Apocalypse.

Apocalypticism

The belief in **God's destruction** of the world as we know it, and eschatological views surrounding the revelations about a sudden end of the world brought on by God. During this period there will be judgment of all people who ever lived, **salvation** for the righteous, and the eventual rule of God's Kingdom in a renewed **Heaven** and Earth. Belief in apocalypticism first arose in Zoroastrianism. It was developed to a fuller extent in the **eschatology** of **Judaism, Christianity,** and **Islam.**

Apocrypha

Old Testament books that are included in the **bibles** used by Roman Catholic and Orthodox Christians, but not in the bibles used by most Protestant Christians and **Jews.** The word was coined by the fifth-century Christian scholar Saint Jerome for the biblical books received by the **church** of his time as part of the Greek version of the Old Testament but which were omitted from the **Hebrew Bible.** The word Apocrypha is derived from the Greek *apokryphos* which means "hidden." The Apocryphal books were given this name because they were thought to have been hidden from the public, unknown by the public, or because they were believed to contain "secret" teachings that were to be reserved for the specially selected or the initiate. In the Authorized, or King James, Version of the Bible, the books are either printed as an appendix or are omitted altogether; they are not considered canonical by Protestants.

The writings were originally rejected by the Hebrews as Old Testament writings for a number of reasons. One reason was because of their doubtful authorship, but more importantly, the books were viewed by the rabbis as dangerous to their **faith** and beliefs about **God.**

They also worried about their apocalyptic hysteria, which could be viewed as detrimental to the Jewish state of mind during the troubled years following the **destruction** of the **Holy** Temple in the year 70 A.D. In addition, they felt that the physical **attributes** of God described in the books were disrespectful of the idea of God's incorporeality, which had been for so many centuries a central pillar of the Hebrew faith.

The rabbis of the period also took issue with the many **angels** in the writings. They believed that the many listings of angels and their functions in nature bordered on **paganism.** In those days of **polytheism,** in which the Greeks and Romans associated a god with every aspect of nature, the rabbis believed that the idea of the true God being a monotheistic God was threatened and felt that the angels given in the books nearly overwhelmed the Creator Himself. Because of these reasons, and perhaps for more that remain undisclosed, the rabbis suppressed and condemned all of the writings in this genre. The exclusion of the Apocrypha from the Hebrew Bible resulted in their gradual disappearance from the Jewish scene. It is because of their translation into Greek and the preservation of many of them as an important part of the Bible of the Catholic Church that these writings have survived.

Today, the apocryphal writings are considered somewhat problematic within **Judaism** and **Christianity.** This is because they threaten the generally accepted traditions and religious teachings. Many within the more conservative branches of Christianity reject any notion that some of the biblical writings may have been lost or hidden away. It is unthinkable to them that the present Bible might be somehow incomplete. Some have even argued that God would never allow His word to be incomplete. They reject the writings as lost books and deny that they are inspired by God as the rest of the books of the Bible are believed to be.

The Apocrypha include many types of literature, including wisdom, history, and visionary writing. The writings that make up the books of the Apocrypha include: 1 Esdras, 2 Esdras, Tobit, Judith, Wisdom of **Solomon,** Ecclesiasticus or Sirach, **Baruch** and the Letter of **Jeremiah,** the Prayer of Manasseh, 1 Maccabees, and 2 Maccabees. There are Greek additions to Esther and several additional sections of **Daniel,** including the **Prayer** of Azariah, the Song of the Three Young Men, Susanna, and Bel and the Dragon. Orthodox Christians also include 3 Maccabees, 4 Maccabees, and Psalm 151. The Catholic position was set at the Council of Trent (1546), which proclaimed that the Apocrypha was sacred scripture, inspired by God. See also Pseudepigrapha.

Apokatastasis

Term for universal **salvation,** meaning that eventually all humans, lost souls as well as **Satan** and his **demons,** will find redemption in God. This line of thought was taught by **Origen** as well as St. Gregory of Nyssa.

Apostate Angels

Angels who have turned against **God's** laws. They are also called **fallen angels** and **demons.** The first apostate angel was **Satan.** He became an apostate angel when he told the first lie to **Eve** in the **Garden of Eden.** The angels who followed him also became apostates. Others include the **Watchers** who left their positions in **Heaven** to come to Earth to have sexual relations with women (**Genesis** 6:2). Since this was a forbidden act, they too became apostate angels. In regard to these angels, the **Bible** states, "Remember the angels who did not stay within the limits of their proper authority, but abandoned their own dwelling place: they are bound with **eternal** chains in the darkness below, where God is keeping them for that great Day on which they will be condemned" (Jude 6).

Apostles' Creed

A creed used in Western **Christianity** in daily **prayer,** worship, and as a **baptism**al confession. It has received this title because of its great antiquity dating back to early times in the **Church,** a half-century or so from the last writings of the **New Testament.** It is also called, "a faithful summary of the apostles' **faith.**" It is one of the best-loved prayers of the Christian faith. Within the Apostles' Creed, believers state their beliefs in **God** and his son **Jesus Christ.** It includes insights into their belief in the nature of God's **Heaven,** pointing out that God resides in Heaven and that His Son is beside him. It has maintained in modern times its distinction as the most widely accepted and used creed among Christians.

THE APOSTLES' CREED

I believe in God, the Father almighty, creator of heaven and earth. I believe in Jesus Christ, God's only Son, our Lord. He was conceived by the Holy Spirit and born of the Virgin Mary. He suffered under Pontius Pilate, was crucified, died, and was buried. He descended to the dead. On the third day he rose again. He ascended into heaven, and is seated at the right hand of the Father. He will come again to judge the living and the dead. I believe in the Holy Spirit, the holy catholic Church, the communion of saints, the forgiveness of sins, the resurrection of the body, and the life everlasting. Amen.

Apple of His Eye

A phrase found in the **Bible.** It refers to the value a person had for another person or an object. In **Deuteronomy, God** refers to **Israel** as, "the apple of His eye."

Aquinas, Saint Thomas (1225–1274)

Dominican priest, theologian, and philosopher. Called the *Doctor Angelicus* (the Angelic Doctor), Aquinas is considered one of the greatest Christian **philosophers** who ever lived. Aquinas had a brilliant theological life. His works made him the most important figure in Scholastic philosophy and one of the leading Roman Catholic theologians. He wrote more than forty books and several beautiful hymns, all attesting to his love and devotion to **God.** Two of his most famous works, the *Summa Theologica* and the *Summa Contra Gentiles,* are the finest examples of his work on Christian philosophy. For centuries his works have helped people to understand God better.

In *Summa Theologica* (Summary of **Theology**), Aquinas formed logical proofs of the existence of God, coming up with five (see **Causality Argument**). In addition, Aquinas explained the relationship between God and humankind. He clarified how humans and other creatures were fashioned by God as derivations of His perfection. He explained how we could once again return to God, becoming one with Him, by means of His power to join with us and through our great need and yearning for Him.

In addition, Aquinas was the first person to promote the ideas of **classical theism,** which taught that God is unchanging, impassable, **eternal,** and without parts. At the end of his life, Aquinas was blessed with a vision of **Heaven.** The beauty and magnitude of this vision compelled him to realize that everything he had ever written, thought, argued, and defined was "like straw." Afterward he refused to continue writing. He died three months later, on his way to see the Pope. He was canonized in 1323 and named a Doctor of the **Church** in 1567. His teachings were sanctioned by Christendom and have influenced generations of religious scholars.

Arabia

The Arab world, especially the Arabian peninsula, has been the cradle of the greatest of cultures and dynasties. The Islamic religion, which originated in the western Arabian peninsula in the seventh century, predominates in most Arab nations, where forms of both major divisions of **Islam**—the Sunni and the various Shiite sects—can be found. It was in the Arabian Desert that **God** sent an **angel** to the **prophet Muhammed** with a revelation that later became the **Koran** and the start of one of the greatest religions in the world.

Arabot

According to ancient Jewish lore, Arabot is the name of the Seventh **Heaven.** It is where **God** and the highest orders of **angels** (such as the **Seraphim** and **Cherubim**) are said to dwell. It is also where the Court of Heaven convenes and where God will judge the souls of men on **Judgment Day.**

Archangels

The archangels are high-ranking **angels** who act as **messengers** for **God.** They are said to be the most important **mediators** between God and humans. The word "archangel" is often misapplied, as it is used as a generic term referencing all angels above the order of angels. In the angelic hierarchy, archangels are one step above the angels. **Judaism** and **Christianity** recognize seven archangels, which are believed to be the seven angels standing in the presence of God in Revelation (8:2). The four most well known are **Gabriel, Michael, Raphael,** and **Uriel.** The names of the other three are uncertain, and have been a source of debate by theologians for centuries. In **Islam** there are only four archangels. They are Azrael, **Israfel, Jibril,** and **Mikhail.** See Gabriel, Israfel, Jibril, Michael, Raphael, and Uriel; Angels.

Archives

See Heavenly Archives.

Archons

The Archons are powerful spiritual beings of ancient Gnostic beliefs. Archon is a Greek term meaning "ruler." The Archons traditionally are believed to have been created by the **Demiurge** (the creator of the universe). Although they were originally considered **evil,** they later became equated with the great **angels** who assist **God** in the running of the world.

Argument from Design

An argument for **God's** existence. William **Paley,** an eighteenth-century English Anglican priest and philosopher, argued for the existence of God using this rationale. He surmised that living creatures are far too complex to have come into being by chance, and argued that the universe and all creatures were the product of an intelligent designer. Paley looked at the presence of design in such things as watches, using the analogy that someone finding a watch but having no prior knowledge of what watches are would deduce that there was a watch designer. He reasoned that such things as the human eye have also been designed. If natural objects such as human eyes are designed, then they must have a designer, this designer being God.

Arguments for the Existence of God

See Ontological Argument; Causality Argument; Argument from Design; Teleological Argument.

Arianism

A major early Christian theological position, founded by Arius (Libyan theologian) in the fourth century. As a cleric in Alexandria, Arius taught that **God** created, before all things, a son who was the supreme of God's creatures, but who was neither equal to nor coeternal with the **Father,** thus denying **Jesus' divine** status. Arius taught that God could not appear on the Earth, that Jesus was not **eternal** and therefore could not be God. In addition, Arius taught that there was only one person in the Godhead, the Father. Arius' opinions created a controversy which ended in his being accused of heresy. His teaching was condemned by the Council of Nicea in 325. The Arian controversy came to be of major importance in the development of Christology during the fourth century.

Aristotle (384–322 B.C.)

Greek philosopher and scientist, who, besides **Plato,** is the most famous of ancient philosophers. He is one of a succession of Greeks who changed the world of ideas in ancient times. Aristotle was a brilliant student in Plato's Academy, remaining there for twenty years and earning the nickname of the "Intellect" of the school. He later conducted his own school, called the Lyceum, in a spot sacred to Apollo in Athens.

In his metaphysics, Aristotle argued for the existence of a **Divine** Being, the Prime Mover, who is responsible for the unity and purposefulness of nature. It is a being with **everlasting** life, and perfect blessedness, engaged in neverending contemplation. Aristotle believed that **God** is perfect and the aspiration of all things in the world because all things desire to share perfection. The Prime Mover, or God, described by Aristotle is not very suitable for religious purposes, as many later philosophers and theologians have observed. This is because, to Aristotle, God was devoid of all qualities such as **mercy**, love, and sympathy. It was through this explanation of God that Aristotle could explain the cause and effect of the universe and the goal of universal progress.

Ark

A ship of wood built by **Noah** as instructed by **God** before the great **Flood.** God gave specific directions as to how the ark was to be built as well as its dimensions. It housed Noah and his family, seven pairs of every kind of "clean" animal and one pair of every "unclean" animal; that is, animals revealed by God to be suitable and unsuitable to eat. The entire account can be found in **Genesis** (6:11–8:22). See Noah, Flood.

Ark of the Covenant

The sacred chest that held the Tablets of the **Law (Ten Commandments)** given to **Moses** from **God.** It was the **Hebrews'** most **holy** object and was very important to God. It served as a dwelling for God. To touch the Ark meant **death.** It was carried into battle, as its presence implied victory, and it was once captured by the Philistines. Restored many years later, it was placed in **Solomon's temple.** In **Exodus** 25:8, God gives his reason for building the Ark: ". . . and let them make me a sanctuary; that I may dwell among them." He instructs this sanctuary to be built after the pattern of the **tabernacle.** In this way, in battle, the

Hebrews actually carried God before them. During the wilderness period, it was kept in the Tabernacle, and after King **Solomon** built the Temple in Jerusalem, it was kept in the **Holy of Holies,** the inner shrine.

It is described as a gold box, measuring two cubits and a half in length, a cubit and a half in breadth, and a cubit and a half in height. Made of setim wood (an incorruptible acacia), it was overlaid within and without with the purest gold, and a golden crown or rim ran around it. At the four corners, most likely towards the upper part, four golden rings had been cast; through them passed two bars of wood overlaid with gold to carry the Ark. These two bars were to remain always in the rings, even when the Ark was placed in the temple of Solomon. The Ark had two large **Cherubim** forming the foundation of the **Mercy Seat** from which God communed with the **children of Israel.** The Ark was lost in the destruction of the Temple in 586 B.C.

It was known also as the Ark of the Law, the Ark of the Testimony, the Ark of God, or the **Covenant** Box. It is further described in Exodus 25:10–22. "And you must make a cover of pure gold, two and a half cubits its length and a cubit and a half its width. And you must make two cherubs of gold. Of hammered work you are to make them on both ends of the cover. And make one cherub on this end and one cherub on that end. On the cover you are to make the cherubs at its two ends. And the cherubs must be spreading out their two wings upward, screening over the cover with their wings, with their faces one toward the other. Toward the cover the faces of the cherubs should be."

The Cherubim symbolized God's protective spirit over the Hebrews and God's sacred knowledge written on the tablets. The Ark is believed to have been either destroyed or carried off, in

925 B.C. during an **Egypt**ian invasion on Jerusalem, or in 586 B.C. by the Babylonians when they devastated Jerusalem prior to the Jewish captivity during that period.

Armageddon

In Christian beliefs it is traditionally the name of the great war between the forces of **God** and **Satan.** Some refer to it as "God's righteous war." It is the final war between good and **evil,** and it will prepare the way for God's Kingdom. It is believed that God will judge and destroy the wicked during this time. Afterward, the good will reside in God's Kingdom forever. According to lore, the Archangel **Michael** will lead the heavenly army against Satan and his **demon**s. It is prophesied in Revelation that the **angels** will win in the war and will lock Satan and his followers away for a thousand years in the **Abyss** (Revelation 16:14, 16). A variation of Armageddon is Harmagedon. See Judgment Day.

Armies

Another name for the celestial army, which is **God's** army of **angels** in **Heaven.** It was these angels who at the command of the Archangel **Michael,** cast **Satan** and his **demon**s out of Heaven. The Book of **Job** 25:3 asks, "Is there any number to his (God's) armies?"

Arya Samaj

A Hindu religious group founded in 1875 by Swami Dayandana Sarasvati. According to the Arya Samaj, they follow the "true knowledge" sent by **God** at "the beginning of this Universe," namely the Vedas. Followers believe that the Vedas are the only true revelation from God and the basis of all science. There are four Vedas: the Rigveda, Yagurvedas, Atharvaveda, and Samaveda. The Aryas believe that the law and knowledge of the universe was given to them by God Himself at the beginning of the universe.

Aryans, The

Semi-nomadic warriors who came to Pakistan and northwest **India** in two-wheeled, horse-drawn chariots. They were a harsh race, strong, fierce, and warlike. Their beliefs in **God** reflected who they were as a people. "God" to the Aryans was male and took on many forms. Their major gods were connected to the sun, the most important were **Agni, Indra,** and Varunai. Their main god was Dyeus **(Sky God).** Aryan **priests** composed hymns in praise of the gods. These hymns were sung during fire **sacrifices** to appease the gods.

Ascension, The

In some religious and spiritual beliefs, the word ascension is associated with souls rising to **Heaven** to dwell with **God** after **death.** In Christian beliefs, the Ascension is the departure of **Jesus** from the Earth forty days after his resurrection from the dead. It is one of the key beliefs of the Christian **faith.** He is believed to have ascended to Heaven to be with God, his **Father,** and to share the glory of Heaven. It is believed by many that he now reigns over the entire universe, and represents his followers before God. During his ascension, Jesus was escorted to Heaven by two **angels.** The **Bible** describes them as "two men in white garments" (Acts 1:10–11). As the Apostles watched Jesus ascend, the angels informed them that Jesus would return in the same manner. One way that the Ascension has been portrayed in art is showing Jesus ascending upon clouds toward the outstretched **hand of God.** Christians believe that all saved souls will one day have glorified bodies like that of the risen **Christ** and will dwell forever in Heaven with God the Father.

Aseity

One of **God's divine attributes**. It means "complete independence." It is believed that God is completely independent of anyone or anything for His existence.

Asha

An **angel** of Zoroastrianism who works on behalf of **Ahura Mazda (God)**. Asha is the Angel of Truth, and the Protector of Fire. Considered to be the most beautiful of all the **Amesha Spentas,** Asha represents **divine law,** order, and morality. Those who follow him are called Ashavan. Those who do not follow him cannot enter **Heaven.** Godly people pray to see Asha so that they may follow him to **Paradise** where they will live forever in peace and righteousness. He fights **death,** the wicked, sickness, and all that is in opposition to the goodness of Ahura Mazda (God). In **Hell,** he makes certain that the good are not disciplined beyond what their **transgression** merits. **Indra,** the spirit of apostasy, is his opponent. This is because apostasy lures men away from God. He is also called Asha Vahishta.

Asian Religions

In the great religions of Asia, the use of the word **God** in a religious context may be misleading because it usually carries the suggestion of a personality. A broader expression that would include both the idea of a personal God and the idea of an impersonal or suprapersonal absolute, is **Holy** Being. In Asian religions the **immanence** and impersonal nature of Holy Being are stressed.

Askr and Embla

The first **man** and woman in Norse **mythology.** Like **Adam and Eve,** they were the parents of the human race. Legend has it that three gods (**Odin,** Hoenir, and Lodur) created them from tree trunks found near the ocean. Odin breathed life into them, Hoenir gave them wisdom, and Lodur gave them their senses and physical beauty.

Assumption of Mary

The belief that **Jesus'** mother, **Mary,** was transported bodily to **Heaven** by **God** and thus did not experience **death.**

Assyria

See Mesopotamia.

Astrology

In the Cro-Magnon period, **Man** looked to the signs of nature and signs in the movement and positions of the stars for guidance from **God.** That ancient practice eventually spread throughout the ancient civilizations and is still popular in modern times. It is believed by some **new age** thinkers that God reveals Himself in a number of ways—often through the belief system of the individual and not always through orthodox religious systems. Therefore, there are some who still look to the stars, via astrology, for guidance from God or "the universe."

Aten

A prominent **Egyptian** sun god during the reign of pharaoh Amenhotep IV (1367–1350 B.C.) during Dynasty 18. Aten was depicted as a disk with rays, each ray terminating in a human hand and bestowing symbols of life upon those below. Amenhotep, who later assumed the name Akhenaten, attempted to establish a monotheistic religion with Aten as the sole deity. However, after his **death,** Egypt was returned to **polytheism** by Amenhotep IV's successor Tutankhamen. A variation of the name Aten is Aton.

Athanasius, Saint
(c. 293–373 A.D.)

Christian theologian, bishop, and Doctor of the **Church** who was one of the most illustrious defenders of the Christian **faith** in the fourth-century struggle against **Arianism**. Athanasius formulated the homoousian doctrine, which states that **Christ** is of the same substance as the **Father**. Arianism held that the Son was of a different substance from the Father altogether and was simply a creature, no more perfect that any other creature, and was used by God in his succeeding acts of **creation**. On God, Athanasius states: "God, however, being without parts, is Father of the Son without division and without being acted upon. For neither is there an effluence from that which is incorporeal, nor is there anything flowering into him from without, as in the case of men. Being simple in nature, he is Father of one only Son."

Atheism

The denial of the existence of **God**. The word is taken from the Greek words *a* which means "not" and *theos* which means "God." Most atheists have concluded that there is no real evidence of the existence of God. They believe that the entire universe, including Earth and its life, evolved through natural courses, and without the involvement of a supernatural being.

Athenagoras

A Christian apologist who flourished in the second half of the second century A.D. No more is known of him than that he was an Athenian philosopher and a convert to **Christianity**. Two extant works, *Plea on Behalf of Christians* and *On the Resurrection of the Dead,* have traditionally been attributed to him. Of **God** Athenagoras states: "I have sufficiently demonstrated that we are not atheists, since we acknowledge one God, unbegotten, **eternal,** invisible, incapable of being acted upon, incomprehensible, unbounded, who is known only by understanding and reason, who is encompassed by **light** and beauty and **spirit** and indescribable power, by whom all things, through his word, have been produced and set in order and are kept in existence."

Atman

The individual **soul;** the real self that continues to exist after one's life on Earth is complete. It is the part of the individual that returns home to **God.** In some **new age** thought, it is the supreme and universal soul from which all individual souls arise. Some call this supreme, universal soul God.

Atonement

An act performed by humans that reconciles their relationship with **God** after they have committed an act of wrongdoing or **sin**. Atonement compensates for the sin and allows the individual and God to once again have harmony and unity between them. In biblical times, atonement was made to God through the use of **sacrifices**. In fact one of the first stories of the **Bible** speaks of this. **Cain,** the eldest son of **Adam,** atoned for his sins to God by offering produce of the soil, while **Abel** offered the first-born of his flock.

JUDAISM. In **Judaism,** the **Day of Atonement** is a day of **fasting** and praying for forgiveness of the past year's sins. In ancient Jewish lore, on the Day of Atonement it is said that a scapegoat was thrown off the cliff at Haradan, plummeting to its **death** below. It was believed that the goat transferred the sins of the **Jews** to the fallen **angel** Azaz'el, who was believed to be trapped beneath a huge pile of boulders at the bottom of the cliff.

CHRISTIANITY. In **Christianity,** atonement is the payment for sin and appeasement of God through the life, sufferings, and death of **Jesus Christ.** The two main ideas used in explaining atonement are (1) that the atonement exists in Christ's sacrifice for the sins of all humankind; (2) that God, through the **incarnation,** entered into humanity to eradicate sin through Jesus' life and death, and to unite humans with Himself. Of this last explanation, the German theologian Martin **Luther** once said: "**Mystery** of mysteries, God forsook God."

Attiq Yomin

Ancient **Hebrew** name for **God.** It means: "**Ancient of Days.**"

Attributes

See Divine Attributes.

Augustine, Saint (354–430)

Early **church** father, Doctor of the Church, Bishop of Hippo. Born on November 13, 354, in Tagaste, North **Africa,** he was originally named Aurelius Augustinius. Augustine was one of the greatest theologians in the history of **Christianity** and is considered to be one of the most prolific geniuses that humanity has ever known. He was a main influence on the development of Western culture and thought. His two most celebrated writings include his spiritual autobiography, *Confessions* (a detailed account of his conversion, addressed to **God**), and *City of God*.

Augustine drew from his own experience when devising ideas about God. To Augustine, God is **spirit,** power, and majesty. He completely rejected the popular view that matter is **evil,** believing instead that all God's creations are innately good since they reflect their **maker.** He believed that those on Earth should emulate the behavior of the **angels,** and he taught that humans

should spend more time in **prayer,** contemplation, and worship of God just as the angels of **Heaven.** He believed this to be the goal of all humankind.

Of God, Augustine says, "Our God is everywhere present, wholly everywhere; not confined to any place. He can be present unperceived, and be absent without moving; when He exposes us to adversities, it is either to prove our perfection or correct our imperfections; and in return for our patient endurance of the sufferings of time, He reserves for us an **everlasting** reward."

Avatar

A physical manifestation of **God,** or a god on Earth. For example, **Jesus Christ,** who is believed by some facets of **Christianity** to be God in the flesh, would have been, according to that belief, an avatar of **Yahweh** (or **Jehovah**). The Hindu god **Krishna** was an avatar of **Vishnu.**

Averroes (1126–1198)

Spanish-Arabian Islamic philosopher, born in Córdoba, Spain. Averroes made significant contributions in philosophy, logic, medicine, music, and jurisprudence. His greatest works were his commentaries on **Aristotle** which exerted considerable influence for centuries. Averroes held that the areas of **faith** and reason did not conflict, and that philosophic truth stems from reason rather than faith. He held that both **God** and the world are **eternal,** but that the world is dependent on God. He believed God to be the prime mover, the self-moved force that stimulates all motion, that transforms the potential into the actual. Averroes stated: "Anyone who studies anatomy will increase his faith in the **omnipotence** and oneness of God the **Almighty.**" He said that **Islam** aims at true knowledge, which is knowledge of God and of His creation. In addition, he compared spiritual laws to medicine in their effect on human beings physically and spiritually, pointing out that spiritual health is termed *Taqwa* in the **Koran** which means "righteousness and God-fearing."

Avesta, The

See Zoroaster.

Avicenna (980–1037)

Persian Islamic philosopher and physician. Avicenna was born in 980 A.D. at Afshana near Bukhara in Uzbekistan. He was the most renowned philosopher in medieval Islam and the most influential name in medicine from 1100 to 1500. Even at a very young age, Avicenna displayed signs of a brilliant intellect. He received his early education in Bukhara. At the age of ten he knew the **Koran** by heart. Before he was sixteen he had mastered physics, mathematics, logic, and metaphysics. At sixteen, he began the study and practice of medicine; and before he had completed his twenty-first year, he wrote his masterpiece, *Canon of Medicine*. Avicenna's best-known philosophical work is *Kitab ash-Shifa* (Book of Healing), a monumental work, embodying a vast field of knowledge from philosophy to science.

Avicenna's personal philosophy was based on a mixture of Aristotelianism and Neoplatonism. Contrary to traditional Islamic beliefs, Avicenna rejected the idea of personal immortality, **God's** interest in individuals, and the **creation** of the world in time. His unorthodox views made him the primary target of an assault on such philosophy by the **Muslim** philosopher al-Ghazali. Nonetheless, Avicenna's views continued to be influential throughout the Middle Ages.

He viewed God as originating the universe from Himself in a series of triads formed of mind, **soul**, and body. He also laid the foundation for later thinking among Muslim and Christian groups about the connection of God to creation. Avicenna viewed individuals in the universe as being necessary in relation to God, but reliant on themselves. He believed that God eternally creates the world; therefore, the world is **eternal** but dependent on Him.

B

The operations of God are various, but his essence is simple.
—Basil the Great

Baal

Canaanite **High God.** The name Baal can be found numerous times in the **Old Testament** for the god and gods of the land of Canaan. In the beginning, the name was used for a variety of local gods. However, Baal eventually became known as the "Ruler of the Universe," carrying such lofty titles as "Rider of the Clouds," "The **Almighty**," and "**God** of the Earth.**"** Closely associated with thunderstorms, Baal was seen as the most forceful of the gods, the one humans called most often upon and relied upon. In 1978, Israeli archaeologists digging at an eighth-century B.C. site in the eastern part of the Sinai desert, uncovered numerous **Hebrew** writings with the names Baal and El (another name for Baal) in the form of **Elohim,** a name used to refer to the Hebrew God.

Ba'al Shem (Master of the Name)

A title in **Judaism,** given to men who purportedly performed wonders and were able to heal through the secret knowledge of the unutterable names of **God.** During the seventeenth and eighteenth centuries there are said to have been many ba'al shem in Eastern Europe. These men were said to have cured illnesses through such items as herbs and old remedies, and predominantly through the use of God's Name. The **Tetragrammaton** (four **Hebrew** letters signifying the ineffable Name of God) was largely used as well as other unpronounceable references to God. In addition, they used sacred formulas, magic spells, and talismans with the Names of God written on them to aid in their healing. They were continuously ridiculed and scorned by the rabbis of the period. Variations of Ba'al Shem are Baalshem, or Balshem, plural Ba'ale Shem, Baaleshem, or Baleshem.

Babbage, Charles (1792–1871)

British mathematician and inventor, the founder of computer science. Babbage was a Christian with strong beliefs in **God,** so much so that he wrote an important book defending the **Bible** and **miracles.**

Babel

See Tower of Babel.

Babylon/Babylonia

See Mesopotamia.

Baha'ism

Religion founded by **Baha'u'llah.** Baha'ism originated in **Persia** during the nineteenth century. Baha'ism teaches a "Oneness" of **God** and the Oneness of religion. Followers believe that God is constantly revealing Himself to humankind through revelations from His **divine prophets.** Some of these prophets have included: **Moses, Abraham, Krishna, Zoroaster,** Buddha, Confucius, **Christ, Muhammad,** the Bab, and Baha'u'llah. The Bahai believe that each of these **messengers** fulfilled predictions regarding His own coming and in turn left predictions concerning the next **messenger** of God.

Baha'u'llah (Splendor of God)

Founder of **Baha'ism.** Originally named Mirza Husayn Ali Nuri, Baha'u'llah was one of the first disciples of Babism (**Persia**n sect, an outgrowth of Shiite **Islam**). In 1850, upon the martyrdom of the Bab, he became the leader of one of the Babi divisions. Previously, in 1844, the Bab had foretold that in nineteen years a **divine** figure would appear from **God.** Later, in 1863, in Baghdad, Iraq, Baha'u'llah proclaimed himself to be that divine manifestation. Baha'u'llah's followers, called Baha'is, believe that he was the latest divine figure to bring the world a new revelation from God. Other divine figures include: **Moses, Abraham, Krishna, Zoroaster,** Buddha, Confucius, **Christ, Muhammad,** and the Bab. See Baha'ism.

Balaam

In the **Bible,** Balaam was a diviner who was famous for the curses he put on people. Numbers 22 tells the story of Balaam and his encounter with **God.** Balaam was sent by the King of Moab to put a **curse** on the **Hebrews.** He hesitated at first, because he feared the Hebrew God. However, he decided to go after God gave authorization to his trip, with a condition that he only spoke what God Himself told to him to say. However, God was angered when, during the trip, Balaam started thinking about the rewards that Balak the King had promised him if he would put a curse on the Hebrews. God then sent an **angel** with a drawn sword to prevent him from continuing on the journey.

Unbeknownst to Balaam, the donkey he was riding saw the angel standing in the middle of the road. The donkey, frightened, turned off the road to avoid the angel. Balaam, unable to see the angel, beat the donkey in order to make her turn back onto the road. The angel spoke through the donkey to Balaam, and finally opened Balaam's eyes so that he could see him. When Balaam saw the angel standing before him, he prostrated himself on his face, and confessed his sin. He offered to return home. However, the angel instructed him to continue on the journey, but told him not to say anything except what God told him.

Baptism

The word Baptism is derived from the Greek word, *bapto,* or *baptizo,* "to wash or to immerse." The use of lustral water is found among the Assyrians, Babylonians, **Egyptia**ns, Greeks, Hindus, Romans, and others. In religion, baptism is a rite of purification by water, invoking the **grace** of **God** to regenerate a person and cleanse him or her from **sin.**

JUDAISM. Well before the first century A.D., converts to **Judaism** were required to bathe (or baptize) themselves as a symbol of entering the **covenant** with God. Some of the later **prophets** envisioned that Jewish exiles returning home would cross the Jordan and be sprinkled with its water to cleanse them of sins prior to the establishment of the **Kingdom of God.** Says **Ezekiel** 36:25, "I will sprinkle clean water upon you, and you shall be clean from all your uncleannesses, and from all your idols I will cleanse you."

CHRISTIANITY. Today, in **Christianity,** baptism is a sacrament and is done in the name of the **Father** (God), the Son, and the **Holy Spirit,** or in the name of **Christ.** The act of baptism is the total or partial immersion of a person in water or the wetting of the head. **Jesus** was baptized by **John the Baptist** at the beginning of his ministry (see Mark 1:9–11). After his resurrection, Jesus told his disciples to preach and baptize the **nations** (Matthew 28:19) as the sign of God's coming rule.

Both the Baptists and the modern descendants of the **Anabaptists** practice adult baptism, but most other **church**es prefer infant baptism. **Origen** (one of the most brilliant Christians of his time) believed that during a baptism, there are really two baptisms taking place at the same time. The person's physical body is being baptized with water, and the person's **soul** is being baptized by God's Holy Spirit by **angels.**

Barth, Karl (1886–1968)

Swiss Protestant theologian, considered one of the leading Christian thinkers of the twentieth century. The son of the Swiss Reformed minister and **New Testament** scholar Fritz Barth, Karl Barth was born in Basel, May 10, 1886, and was reared in Bern, where his father taught. He studied theology at the Universities of Bern, Berlin, Tübingen, and Marburg. Popular writings by Barth include: *Epistle to the Romans, The Word of God and the Word of Man, Credo,* and *Evangelical Theology, an Introduction,* along with the monumental multivolume *Church Dogmatics.*

In his teachings, Barth placed emphasis on **God's** absolute transcendence, and the belief that humans are incapable of knowing God except through divine revelation. He regarded the **Bible** not as the actual revelation of God but as evidence of His revelation, believing that God's only revelation of Himself is found in **Jesus Christ.** In addition, Barth viewed God as the "wholly other," completely different from humans. Barth believed that the mission of the **church** was to make known the word of God, calling it a "place of encounter" between God and humans. Says Barth in his discourse on Romans (1919), "God is the wholly other; he is known only in his revelation; he is not the patron saint of culture, but its judge." He held that religion is humanity's effort to take hold of God and as a result is completely opposed to revelation, in which God has come to humans through Jesus Christ.

Baruch

A book in the **Old Testament** of the Roman Catholic **Bible** and the Protestant **Apocrypha** (it was left out of the **Hebrew Bible**). It was traditionally ascribed to Baruch, a trusted friend, disciple, and secretary of the **prophet Jeremiah.** The book was written partly in prose and partly in poetry. The prose section consists of a confession of **sin,** a promise of deliverance after repentance, and a **prayer** asking **mercy** and praising **God.** The poetry section contains verses in praise of wisdom and of God's commandments and of verses encouraging the exiles to be brave and comforted. The Letter of Jeremiah, which is addressed to the exiles in **Babylon,** expands on the thought from the Biblical Book of Jeremiah (10:11), which speaks of the reality of God and the unreality of idols. The three parts of the book are thought to be written at different periods. Baruch may have been compiled as late as the first or second century A.D. by an Alexandrian editor using original **Hebrew** manuscripts. It has been preserved in a Greek version. It is considered by the Roman Catholic **Church** to be a sacred and canonical writing inspired of God.

Basque Proverb

"**God** is a busy worker, but He loves help."

Beatific Vision

The term "beatific vision" refers to seeing the full vision of **God** in all His glory. It is the joy of seeing God face to face, a time when the human **soul** is united and, in some beliefs, reunited with God. It is a belief held by many **faiths**, including **Judaism, Christianity, Islam,** and some Asian religions. Christians believe the vision is the reward for living out our lives on Earth, our destiny. Some facets of Christianity believe that only the spiritual **elect** will have the privilege of seeing God. Others believe that all righteous souls will dwell with God in **Heaven** after their **death.** In some metaphysical ideologies, the soul resided with God in the beginning and will return to dwell with God after completing its life on the Earth.

The Catholic Encyclopedia defines the beatific vision this way: "The immediate knowledge of God which the angelic spirits and the souls of the just enjoy in Heaven. It is called 'vision' to distinguish it from the mediate knowledge of God which the human mind may attain in the present life. And since in beholding God face to face the created intelligence finds perfect happiness, the vision is termed 'beatific.'" Some writers, such as Thomas **Aquinas,** taught that certain pious individuals—such as **Moses** and Paul—were allowed this vision while still on Earth. He also taught that the chief happiness of a saved person would be to see God.

Beatitude

Supreme Blessedness. In his *Summa Theologica,* St. Thomas **Aquinas** expressed his thoughts on **God** and the subject of beatitude, asking the question whether beatitude belongs to God. Aquinas answered with this: "I answer that, Beatitude belongs to God in a very special manner. For nothing else is understood to be meant by the term beatitude than the perfect good of an intellectual nature; which is capable of knowing that it has a sufficiency of the good which it possesses, to which it is competent that good or ill may befall, and which can control its own actions. All of these things belong in a most excellent manner to God, namely, to be perfect, and to possess intelligence. Whence beatitude belongs to God in the highest degree." See Beatitudes, The.

Beatitudes, The

The Beatitudes are eight **blessings** spoken by **Jesus** at the beginning of the Sermon on the Mount (Matthew 5:3–12). In his discourse, Jesus promised blessings from **God** to those who accept his teachings and who exercise such **virtues** as **mercy,** humility, patience, and purity of heart. The eight beatitudes are:

Happy are those who know they are spiritually poor; the **Kingdom of Heaven** belongs to them!

Happy are those who mourn; God will comfort them!

Happy are those who are humble; they will receive what God has promised!

Happy are those whose greatest desire is to do what God requires; God will satisfy them fully!

Happy are those who are merciful to others; God will be merciful to them!

Happy are the pure in heart; they will see God!

Happy are those who work for peace; God will call them his **children!**

Happy are those who are persecuted because they do what God requires; the Kingdom of Heaven belongs to them!

Beerlahairoi

In the **Old Testament,** Beerlahairoi is the well in which the pregnant **Hagar** (the handmaid to **Abraham's** wife, **Sarah**) was visited by an **angel** sent from **God** to speak with her. After fleeing into the wilderness to escape the wrath of Sarah, Hagar came upon a well. There an angel appeared to her, and told her that she would give birth to a son, and that she should call him **Ishmael.** He informed her that God would multiply her seed by many. Awed by this experience, Hagar called the well Beerlahairoi, which means, "the well of him who lives and sees me" (**Genesis 16:1–14**).

Beersheba

At his wife **Sarah's** request, the **prophet Abraham** sent the handmaid **Hagar** and their son **Ishmael** away. Eventually, Hagar wandered into the wilderness of Beersheba. Exhausted and dehydrated, she put her son Ishmael under a bush and walked away, asking **God** not to let her see it when he died. God, who heard the boy crying from **Heaven,** sent an **angel** to speak with her. The angel called out to her saying: "What are you troubled about, Hagar? Don't be afraid. God has heard the boy crying. Get up, go and pick him up, and comfort him. God will make a great nation out of his descendants." Then God opened her eyes, and she saw a well (**Genesis 21: 17–19**).

Belshazzar

According to the **Old Testament,** Belshazzar was a **Babylon**ian King, mentioned in **Daniel,** chapter 5, who had a direct encounter with **God.** He was the son of Nebuchadnezzar and the last King of Babylon. During his reign he decided to host a great banquet at his palace. During the gala he ordered that the **holy** cups from the Jewish temple be brought in so that he and his guests could drink from them. As soon as he did this profane act, a disembodied hand appeared and wrote a message on the wall. In fear, Belshazzar ordered an interpretation of the message from his advisors and diviners. However, the only person that could interpret the supernatural handwriting, was the **prophet** Daniel.

The message was from God and directed to Belshazzar. It was a message of doom. Daniel informed Belshazzar of what God was saying to him. The message said that his days were numbered, that he had been weighed and found wanting, and that his kingdom would soon be divided. That same night Belshazzar was killed, and Darius the Mede seized the royal power.

Bene ha-Elohim (God's Children)

Angels who sing praises to **God** both night and day. In some writings they are equated with the **Grigori.** Other writings refer to them as **"sons of God."** A variation of Bene ha-Elohim is Bene Elohim.

Benediction

An asking for **God's** blessing, as by a clergyman or priest at the conclusion of a religious service.

Berkeley, George (1685–1753)

Brilliant **Irish** philosopher and bishop. He is generally regarded as the founder of the modern school of idealism. Born in county Kilkenny, Ireland, March 12, 1685, he was educated at **Trinity** College, Dublin, where he became a fellow in 1707. According to Berkeley, **God** is the only other person or thing (other than **souls**) that exists. Berkeley believed that even though humans cannot immediately perceive God, we can tell that He exists based on the way our thoughts and ideas hold together. Berkeley considered God and souls to be the reality behind sense impressions. He believed that there must be a mind in which all ideas exist, that mind of course belonging to God.

Bernard of Clairvaux, Saint (1090–1153)

One of the most memorable Christian teachers and representatives of monasticism in the Middle Ages. Bernard was born in 1090 at Fontaines, near Dijon, in Burgundy. He was the son of a knight and vassal of the duke of Burgundy who perished in the first Crusade. Feeling the calling towards a life of **meditation** and study, he joined the monastery of Citeaux in 1113 when he was twenty-two years of age. As a child he was said to have been "marvelously cogitative." As an adult his intellectual abilities and powers of persuasion could be seen in his writings and also his preaching work, as he was said to have converted his four brothers—two of whom were in the military and at least one of whom was married and had **children.** His writings are numerous, consisting of epistles, sermons, and theological treatises. His most memorable work is titled *Sermons of the Canticle of Canticles,* said to be a love song to **God.** He states, "The **Father** is never fully known if He is not loved perfectly." One of Bernard's favorite **prayers** states the following, "Whence arises the love of God? From God. And what is the measure of this love? To love without measure." This, he believed, was the key to serving God.

Bethel (House of God)

In ancient times, Bethel was a town twelve miles north of Jerusalem. It had an honorable standing in **Israel's** early days. **Abraham** offered a **sacrifice** there, and **Jacob** had his legendary dream there. During the era of the judges, it was a key center for worship.

Bhagavad-Gita (Song of God)

The Bhagavad-Gita is a Hindu poem composed around 200 B.C., forming part of the *Mahabharata* (one of the classics of **Hinduism**). It is the most popular and beloved text of the Hindu tradition. It consists of 700 verses divided into eighteen chapters. The Gita is regarded by most Hindus as their most significant text and is the essence of their spiritual beliefs. So sacred is it to the Hindus that it corresponds to the **New Testament** in the Christian world. The Gita consists of a dialogue between the incarnate god Krishna and Prince Arjuna on the eve of the battle of Kurukshetra. Arjuna expresses his anguish at going to war against his friends and relatives. Krishna's reply is an exhortation for Arjuna to do his duty as a warrior which is to fight and kill. Krishna persuades him to fight by instructing him in spiritual wisdom and the means of attaining union with God through selfless action, knowledge, and devotion. The Gita incorporates many doctrines, such as the immortality of the **soul (atman)**, its identity with the supreme godhead (Brahman), the process of **reincarnation,** and the need to renounce the fruits of one's actions and the proper way to reach God.

Bhagavan

A Hindu epithet for **God.** A **Bhagavata** is a person dedicated to Bhagavan.

Bhagavata

The word Bhagavata means "One who is devoted to **Bhagavan**" (a Hindu epithet for **God**). Sacred writings of the Bhagavatas include the Bhagavad-Gita and Bhagavata-Purana. Contemporary scholars suggest that the cult of the Bhagavata was specifically monotheistic, promoting one god with several names including: **Vishnu,** Vasudeva, **Krishna, Hari,** and Narayana.

Bhakti Yoga

A discipline of **Hinduism** that encourages the direction of one's love to **God.**

Bible, The

Considered to be the greatest book ever written, the Bible contains the collected books of the **Old Testament** (**Hebrew** scriptures) and the **New Testament** (Christian Scriptures). The word Bible comes from the Greek *biblia* which means "little books." The Bible is made up of sixty-six "little books" which were written over a period of 1,600 years, from 1513 B.C. to 98 A.D. Some forty men shared in the writing of the Bible, which is believed to be inspired by **God.** The writing of the Bible began around 3,500 years ago in the Hebrew language, and about 2,200 years ago, translation into the various languages was undertaken. Today the Bible can be read, in its entirety or in part, in more than 1,700 languages.

The first book, **Genesis,** tells of the **Creation** and how humans lost their **paradise** home because they rebelled against God. The last book, Revelation, tells of God's plan for His Kingdom. It is believed that the Bible was given to humankind from God to provide knowledge and answers to questions that humans might have about God and His purposes. Some believe that God created the Bible because it was the easiest way for God to get His message to humans on all parts of the Earth and at different periods of time. The first thirty-nine books of the Bible were written primarily in Hebrew, with some small parts in Aramaic; the last twenty-seven books were written in Greek, the common language of the people when **Jesus** was on Earth. These two major sections of the Bible are entitled the "Hebrew Scriptures" and the "Greek Scriptures." The Greek Scriptures quote from the Hebrew Scriptures more than 365 times, and make about 375 additional references to them.

GOD IN THE OLD TESTAMENT. The theme of the Old Testament is that there is only one true God **(Yahweh)**, who is God of the **Hebrews** and of the entire Earth, and that He alone must be worshipped. He is all-powerful but concerned for His people. He is known to reveal himself in various ways— through events, through the **law,** and through **prophets** and **priests.**

GOD IN THE NEW TESTAMENT. The God of the New Testament is creator of all life and sustainer of the universe. He is the source and final end of all things. He takes the initiative to seek with love all humankind, behaving toward those who respond and worship Him with justice and **mercy,** with judgment and forgiveness. In addition, the words and activity of Jesus were understood as bringing followers into the presence of God. The New Testament speaks of Jesus as being God's only son, and declares that only he can point the way to the **Father.**

Biblical Inspiration

The idea that writers of the **holy** books were inspired by **God** to write. In the **Hebrew** Scriptures, God is believed to have put the words directly into the mouths of his **prophets**, servants, and appointed **messengers**, often instructing them to write the words down exactly as they were given. Christian writers of the **New Testament** acknowledge that the Hebrew scriptures were divinely given, and they took the position that the books of the Christian Greek Scriptures were inspired of God. In **Islam, Muhammad** also wrote down the entire **Koran** which was dictated to him from God. Some sources liken the giving of information from God to the writer, prophet or messenger to that of a boss to a secretary who writes what is dictated to her word-for-word.

Binding of Isaac, The

As a test of his **faith, God** commanded the **Hebrew** patriarch **Abraham** to offer his son **Isaac** as a sacrifice. Obediently, Abraham took Isaac to the designated spot, built an **altar,** bound him and placed him on the altar. When he picked up the knife to slay him, God called to him from **Heaven** saying, "Abraham, Abraham, do not hurt the boy or do anything to him. Now I know that you honor and obey God, because you have not kept back your only son from Him" (**Genesis** 22:12). Abraham looked up and saw a ram caught in a thicket by its horns. He then took the ram and offered it as a sacrifice instead of his son.

Bird of God

A term sometimes used when referring to the **angels.** Throughout history birds have been a symbol for angels. In addition, various birdlike beings can be found in religious beliefs around the world. Native North Americans worshipped a god they referred to as Thunderbird, symbolized by the eagle and the hawk. In Etrurian beliefs there was Charon, the winged god of the dead.

He had huge wings and a large crooked nose resembling the beak of a bird. He carried the souls of the dead to Hades. In Judaic lore there is the Phoenix, a bird who resides in **Heaven.** He is charged with protecting the Earth from the rays of the sun. In **Egypt**ian **mythology** there was the Bennu, the sacred bird of Heliopolis which was usually depicted as a heron. In Heliopolis, the Bennu bird played a major role in Egyptian mythology, living on the benben stone within the sanctuary and was worshipped alongside Ra and **Osiris.** The Bennu was later referred to as the Phoenix by the Greeks. In addition, Bird of God is a term used in Dante's *Divine Comedy* when referring to angels. The task of this angel is to act as pilot of the ferry transporting the souls belonging to purgatory.

Bismillah (Bismillah arrahman arrahim)

An Islamic **prayer.** In **Islam** every chapter (Sura) of the **Koran** opens with Bismillah (Bismillah is short for "Bismillah arrahman arrahim," which states, "In the name of **God,** the Merciful, the Compassionate"). **Muslims** use Bismillah to call on God for all important aspects and events in their lives. This would include asking God to bless their actions, calling on God in all legal procedures, and when introducing all formal documents. Magicians also use the Bismillah in talismans, believing it to have been written on **Adam's** side, **Gabriel's** wing, **Solomon's** seal, and **Jesus'** tongue.

Blake, William (1757–1827)

English poet, artist, visionary, and mystic. At the young age of eight Blake saw a tree filled with **angels.** Afterward, and for the rest of his life, he continued to have mystical visions. For the most part, as evidenced by his great work, William Blake was a spiritual person.

He believed in the **divine,** he believed in an almighty, and he believed in **Heaven.** However, he despised traditional religions such as **Christianity** and **Islam** and their version of **God,** depicting Him as controlling and disallowing humans to use their imaginations and explore their passions. Yet, Blake believed his work to be guided by God's angels, and credited his creative genius to them. In fact, Blake once wrote, "It is not because angels are holier than men or **devils** that makes them angels, but because they do not expect holiness from one another, but from God alone."

During his lifetime he created a large number of memorable drawings revolving around spirituality and the divine. Among the most famous paintings are: *Elohim Creating Adam, Satan Smiting Job with Sore Boils, The Good and Evil Angels, The Simoniac Pope, A Father's Memoirs of His Child, The Meeting of a Family in Heaven,* and *What Gleams for Joy.* His books of poems, the texts of which he engraved and illustrated, were influenced by his unorthodox religious and political beliefs and by such mystics as Boehme. As an artist his imaginative watercolors for the Book of Job and Dante's *Divine Comedy* were inspired by his visions, gothic sculpture, and engravings after **Michelangelo.** He died in London, August 12, 1827, leaving uncompleted a cycle of drawings inspired by Dante's *Divine Comedy.*

Blessings from Aleph to Taw

In **Hebrew** tradition, **God** blesses the **Jews** from "aleph to taw." These are the first and last letters of the Hebrew alphabet, therefore the expression means "God blesses the Hebrews completely."

Blood

The life-giving fluid of the body. In the **Old Testament,** it is considered to be the seat of life. Since shed blood means **death,** the word "blood" refers to both life and death. **New Testament** writers speak of the blood of **Christ** as a symbol for **atonement** or **reconciliation** with **God.**

Bodhisattvas (Enlightenment-Being)

The Bodhisattvas are spiritual beings in **Buddhism,** sometimes referred to as "Buddhas-to-be." Once mortal beings on Earth, the Bodhisattvas have reached Nirvana, but have put off their own **salvation** in order to become emissaries of the Buddha. In their enlightened state, they return to Earth to help humans on Buddha's behalf. They act as healers, spiritual guides, and teachers. In addition, they act as guides for the **soul** of those who are near **death.** In **Heaven,** they are privileged beings who receive all the rewards of those who have reached salvation.

Body of God

It is commonly believed that **God** is spiritual, and as such is bodiless and formless. Yet, there were some cases in scripture where the **prophets** saw God embodied in their visions. Daniel (7:9–10) states, "I kept on beholding until there were thrones placed and the **Ancient of Days** (God) sat down. His clothing was white just like snow, and the hair of his head was like clean wool. His throne was flames of fire, its wheels were a burning fire. There was a stream of fire flowing and going out from before him. There were a thousand thousands that kept ministering to him, and ten thousand times ten thousand that kept standing right before him."

In another passage from the **Pseudepigraphal** Book of 1 **Enoch** (8–25), Enoch in describing a vision, wrote, "And behold I saw the clouds: And they were calling me in a vision, and in the vision, the winds were causing me to fly and rushing me high up into **heaven**. And I observed and saw inside it a lofty throne—its appearance was like crystal and its wheels like the shining sun. And the **Great Glory** (God) was sitting upon it—as for his gown, which was shining more brightly than the sun, it was whiter than any snow.

"None of the **angels** was able to come in and see the face of the Excellent and the **Glorious One**; and no one of the flesh can see him—the flaming fire was round about him, and a great fire stood before him. No one could come near unto him from among those that surrounded the tens of millions that stood before him. Until then I was prostrate on my face covered and trembling. And the **Lord** called me with his own mouth and said to me, 'Come near to me, Enoch.' And he lifted me up and brought me near to the gate, but I continued to look down with my face."

It is believed that God uses typology in these visions to convey His **divine attributes**. Anthropomorphites argue that **Man** is made in the **image of God** (Gen. 1:26–17) and reference **Bible** verses showing God having human features. Early theologians, however, held that God is a **spirit** having no body parts.

Boethius, Anicius Manlius Severinus (480–525)

Roman senator. Boethius was born in or near Rome around the year 480 A.D. He was orphaned at a young age and raised in the home of an aristocrat named Symmachus. He grew into an extremely intelligent, well-educated man, making contributions to logic, religion, and music theory in addition to his role of senator. His book, *The Consolation of Philosophy,* was of great importance during the Middle Ages. It was modeled upon the books of **Job** and Wisdom and upon the Platonic dialogues of Socrates while he was awaiting execution in Athens. It presents arguments that the universe is run by a perfect **God** and that suffering has its recompense. A line from the *Consolation* reads: "You [God] who are most beautiful produce the beautiful world from your **divine** mind and, forming it in your image, You order the perfect parts in a perfect whole."

Bonaventure, Saint (1217–1274)

One of the greatest mystical philosophers of all time, Saint Bonaventure held such prestigious titles as Doctor of the **Church**, Cardinal-Bishop of Albano, Minister General of the Friars Minor, Seraphic Doctor (a title given to him because of his interest in **angels**), and Doctor Devotus. Bonaventure wrote theological doctrines on **God**, the angels, the spiritual world, and **Heaven**. His works show that he had an all-absorbing love for God. In fact, God's presence pervades all of his writings.

His basic position on God is nicely expressed in his work entitled *On the Reduction of the Arts to **Theology**.* There he states: "The manifold wisdom of God, which is clearly revealed in sacred scripture, lies hidden in all knowledge and in all nature." In another famous work, *The Mind's Journey Unto God,* he states: "relative to our life on earth, the world is itself a ladder for ascending to God." In metaphysics, Bonaventure supports **exemplarism** (the belief that all **creation** is patterned after exemplar causes or ideas in God's mind). He suggests that it is through such ideas that God knows all of His creatures. In addition, Bonaventure adopts the emanationist belief that creation stems from God's goodness.

Of God, Bonaventure says, "Whoever loves this **death** can see God because it is true beyond doubt that **man** will not see God and live. Let us, then, die and enter the darkness; let us impose silence upon our cares, our desires and our imaginings. Let us rejoice with **David** saying: My flesh and my heart have grown faint; You are the God of my heart, and the God that is my portion forever. Blessed be the **Lord** forever and all the people will say: Let it be; let it be. Amen."

Book of Certitude (Kitab-i-Iqan)

A book of the Baha'i **faith.** The Book of Certitude is **Baha'u'llah's** explanation of the basic doctrines of the Baha'i faith. On **God's messengers** and the unity of God, it states: "If you call them all by one name, and ascribe to them the same attribute, you have not erred from the truth. Even as He has revealed, 'No distinction do We make between any of His Messengers!' For they one and all summon the people of the earth to acknowledge the unity of God."

Book of Death

In ancient Jewish tradition, the Book of Death is the book in which **God** writes the names of the unrighteous.

Book of Life

In **Judaism** and **Christianity,** the Book of Life (also referred to as the **Book of Records**) is sacred, the book in which **God** inscribes the names of the righteous. It is the basis from which God's Judgment is formed. On Rosh Ha-Shanah (the Jewish New Year), the Book of Life is open for the righteous and the **Book of Death** for the unrighteous. During the ten days of Repentance between Rosh Ha-Shanah and **Yom Kippur,** extra **benedictions** are said during the *amidah* (the main section of the morning, afternoon, and evening **prayers** in Judaism) for inscription in the Book of Life. In Christianity,

in Revelation, those whose names are found written in the Book of Life will escape God's **everlasting** Judgment.

According to the **Pseudepigrapha's** 3 **Enoch,** God is assisted with the Book of Life (referred to here as the Book of Records) by Radweri'el **YHWH,** an **angel** who acts as the heavenly archivist. He is the angel who is responsible for maintaining the heavenly archives in which the Book of Life is kept. There is a passage in 3 Enoch (27:1–2) that talks about Radweri'el YHWH's role as the heavenly archivist. There it says, "He takes out the **scroll** box in which the book of records is kept, and brings it into the presence of the **Holy** One (God). He breaks the seals of the scroll box, opens it, takes out the scrolls and puts them in the hand of the Holy One. The Holy One receives them from his hand and places them before the scribes, so that they might read them out to the Great **Law** Court."

Book of Mormon

The **holy** book of the Mormons. It is a volume of sacred writings comparable to the **Bible.** The **prophet** Joseph **Smith** called the Book of Mormon "the most correct of any book on earth, and the keystone of our religion" and said that a person "would get nearer to **God** by abiding by its precepts, than by any other book." To members of the **Church of Jesus Christ of Latter-Day Saints,** the Book of Mormon forms the doctrinal foundation of the **Church** and speaks the **word of God** to all the world. It was translated from text taken from golden tablets hidden away for centuries until an **angel** named Moroni revealed them to Joseph Smith (founder of the Church of **Jesus Christ** of Latter-Day Saints). In 1823, Moroni appeared to Joseph Smith and led Smith to a place where the golden tablets were buried. The tablets included inscribed text that was foreign to Smith. With the help of Moroni, the text was translated, and it eventually became known as the Book of Mormon.

The Book of Mormon reveals the story of a **Hebrew** family, who in 600 B.C. fled from the desolation of Jerusalem. The family boarded a ship, which later ended up in North America. The offspring of this family are thought to be the forefathers of **Native Americans.** Family records from an elder named Mormon reported that Jesus appeared to them after his Crucifixion. Mormon's son Moroni buried the records of his father around 400 A.D. Those were the tablets to which the angel Moroni later lead Joseph Smith. After his death Moroni was transformed into an angel and became the revealer of the Book of Mormon. Smith later founded the Church of Jesus Christ of Latter-Day Saints. Today, a statue of the angel Moroni stands on a hill in Palmyra, New York, where Moroni first led Smith to the tablets. See Mormonism.

Book of Raziel

According to Jewish legend, the Book of Raziel is an ancient text written by the **angel** Raziel. It is said to have contained information on heavenly and earthly mysteries. It also had more than a thousand keys to unlock those mysteries. Legend has it that **God** took compassion on **Adam** and sent Raziel to give him a book so that he might look into the mirror of existence and so see the **Divine** Face and himself as Adam so illuminated as an **image of God.** Adam later passed the book to **Enoch;** Enoch gave it to **Noah,** who later built the **Ark** from the instructions laid out in it. The book is also said to have contained medical information to aid humankind with information taken directly from the heavens. It was later given to King **Solomon** who kept it for a short time.

The book turned up during medieval times under the ownership of Eleazer of Worms, a writer who was given credit for authoring the book.

Books of Enoch

The Books of **Enoch** are a collection of apocalyptic writings, and are the lengthiest work included in the **Pseudepigrapha.** Scholars have concluded that the original collection was written either in **Hebrew** or in Aramaic. Composed during the second and first centuries B.C., the Books of Enoch relay the **prophet** Enoch's experiences and conversations with **God,** the **angels,** and his travels through the **seven heavens.** The books speak of God's coming Judgment and the places of final punishment and reward; it predicts the coming of the **Messiah,** and describes the future heavenly **kingdom of God.** The writings of Enoch were not included in the **holy** canon because the rabbis of the period doubted their authorship. The books were at one time well read by the **Jews,** and were considered by earlier rabbis to be scripture inspired of God. Note: The books are often ascribed, perhaps erroneously, to the Hebrew patriarch Enoch.

Booth, William (1829–1912)

Extraordinary English religious leader who labored tirelessly on behalf of the poor, and who considered himself a missionary of **God.** He, along with his wife Catherine Booth, founded the **Salvation** Army. He has been called "God's General." Originally a local preacher for the Wesleyan Methodists, Booth went to London and entered the ministry of the Methodist New Connexion **Church.** However, in 1861, he began independent evangelistic work. Traveling widely, he won recognition wherever he went. At the age of eighty-two and nearly blind, Booth had these final words to say to an audience of ten thousand at Royal Albert Hall in London: "While women weep as they do now, I'll fight; While children go hungry as they do now, I'll fight; When men go to prison, in and out, I'll fight; While there is a drunkard left, I'll fight; While there is a poor girl left on the streets, I'll fight; While there remains one dark soul without the light of God, I'll fight. I'll fight—I'll fight to the very end."

Borysenko, Joan (1945–)

American medical scientist, psychologist, clinician and teacher, and a pioneer of mind-body health, and one of the leading authorities on women's spirituality. Her brilliance in these areas has placed her on the leading edge of the mind-body revolution, and she has become a world-renowned spokesperson for this new approach to health. In addition, she is president of Mind/Body Health Sciences, Inc.; a nationally known lecturer; and author of several books including *The Ways of the Mystic: Seven Paths to God,* and *A Woman's Journey to God*. In *A Woman's Journey to God,* Borysenko writes: "God is beyond gender, a strange and paradoxical mystery that is big enough to contain the world in all its beauty and ugliness, cruelty and grace."

Bradstreet, Anne (1612–1672)

One of the greatest poets of the seventeenth century, and the first important American poet. She is best known for *The Tenth Muse Lately Sprung Up in America,* a collection of her poems. This work was the first volume of original poetry written in the American Colonies; it was published in London in 1650. Bradstreet later won critical acceptance in the twentieth century as a writer of enduring verse, particularly for her sequence of religious poems "Contemplations," written for her family and not published until the mid-nineteenth century. Bradstreet emigrated to the New World as part of John Winthrop's party of colonists. Upon arriving in the New World, she found herself sad and homesick. It was her faith in God that sustained her. Realizing that it was God's will, she came to accept her life in the New World and became a practicing Puritan. Her strong faith in God was evident in her writings.

Brahma

The first god represented in the Hindu triad (the other two are Vishnu, the Sustainer, and Shiva, the Destroyer). He is the creator of the universe and all living beings are said to have evolved from him. It is believed that life exists on Earth as long as Brahma stays awake. When he sleeps, everything except the saints and gods in Heaven perishes. One Day of Brahma equals 4.32 billion years. He appears seated on a lotus (a symbol of glorious existence), has four heads (five heads were originally assigned to him, but one was destroyed by Shiva), and four hands. Each hand is holding a sacrificial tool *(sruva)*, the Vedas (knowledge), a water pot *(kamandalu)*, and a rosary. He rides upon a swan and the goddess Sarasvati, the goddess of learning, is his consort. In Hindu religion today, Brahma plays almost no part at all, while Vishnu and Shiva are more popularly worshipped.

Brooks, Phillips (1835–1893)

American Protestant Episcopal minister. Brooks was a dynamic speaker and an independent thinker. His sermons and ideas on doctrine made him popular with people of all denominations. He authored the popular Christmas hymn, *O Little Town of Bethlehem,* and several volumes of sermons. Wrote Phillips, "**Prayer** is not the overcoming of **God's** reluctance, but the taking hold of God's willingness."

Browne, Sylvia (1936–)

World-renowned psychic and spiritual leader. She is the author of such books as: *Journey of the Soul; Conversations with the Other Side; Astrology through the Eyes of a Psychic; Adventures of a Psychic; God, Creation, and Tools for Life; Life on the Other Side: A Psychic's Tour of the Afterlife;* and the best-selling: *The Other Side and Back: A Psychic's Guide to Our World and Beyond.* In addition, she has created an organization entitled Society of Novus Spiritus, meaning "new spirit," based upon a Christian Gnostic **theology.**

It is Browne's aspiration to prove that the human soul survives **death** and that God is a real and loving being. Through her teachings and organization, Browne hopes to establish a spiritual community, one that loves God without the guilt found in many of the world's religions. In *The Other Side and Back: A Psychic's Guide to Our World and Beyond,* Browne writes: "I know that God is alive and well. He created us. He loves us constantly, eternally, and unconditionally, and He is as much a part of us as our parents, grandparents, and everyone else in our ancestry."

Bruno, Giordano (1548–1600)

Italian philosopher, he was considered a forerunner of modern philosophy. Bruno was born at Nola, near Naples. Originally named Filippo, he took the name Giordano when he joined the Dominicans (a Roman Catholic religious order founded in 1214 by Saint Dominic) in 1565. He was later accused of heresy, left the order, and became a wandering scholar. For a short period he studied and taught in Geneva, but later left because of problems encountered with the Calvinists. Afterward, he taught in France, Czechoslovakia, England, and Germany; in 1591 he returned to Venice. He was later arrested by the Venetian Inquisition and given over to the Roman Inquisition, which burned him to **death** for heresy. His best known works include: *Ash Wednesday Supper; On the Infinite Universe and Worlds;* the dialogue *On the Cause, Principle, and Unity;* and *The Expulsion of the Triumphant Beast.* In *Glieroici Furori,* he praised a kind of Platonic love that joins the **soul** to **God** through wisdom. Bruno believed that the universe is infinite and that God is the universal world-soul. He held that human ideas are mere shadows of **divine** ideas, and that God is transcendent and hence incomprehensible.

Bruyere, Jean de la (1645–1696)

French essayist and moralist. "I feel that there is a **God,** and I do not feel that there is none. For me that is enough."

Buber, Martin (1878–1965)

Jewish theologian and philosopher, born in Vienna, Austria. He is best known for his religious philosophy. He studied philosophy at Vienna, Berlin, and Zürich, then became attracted to **Hasidism** and the Christian existentialism of Kierkegaard. He taught Jewish philosophy and religion in Germany until he was forced to leave the country in 1938 in order to escape the Nazis. He later settled in Jerusalem where he became a professor of social philosophy. His major works include: *The Tales of Rabbi Nachman* and *The Legend of the Baal-Shem.*

Buber's most widely known work was *I and Thou* which posited a personal and direct dialogue between **God** and the individual; it has had a great impact on contemporary Christian and Jewish beliefs. Buber describes God as the ultimate Thou, the Thou who can never become an It, and concluded that God is reached not by inference but by a willingness to respond to the concrete reality of the divine presence. Buber argued that religion means talking to God, not about God. He believed that **Man** becomes conscious of being spoken to by God in every situation if he remains open to God and ready to respond with his entire **soul.** On God, Buber wrote: "When God rewards our good works he is rewarding his works and gifts in us, rather than our own works."

Buddhism

Buddhism was founded by Siddhartha Gautama, an Indian prince born in Kapilavastu, **India,** who grew up living a sheltered life of luxury. It wasn't until he grew up and went out into the world that he was able to see the world as it was and witness the pain and suffering experienced by others. Desiring to help others, he became a teacher and devoted himself to religion. He later became known as the Buddha which means "Enlightened One."

Unlike most religions, Buddhists do not believe in **God,** a **Supreme Being,** or a **Divine** Entity that created the world or that rules the World. In fact, the emphasis in Buddhism is not on having **faith** in an unknowable God or afterlife, but lies within the knowledge that focuses on transcending the self. Buddhists don't concern themselves about God or gods. They concern themselves with the Dharma, which is neither a god or gods. It is "truth" or "reality." While **Jews,** Christians, and **Muslims** believe in a personal God,

Buddhists feel that this is an unreligious idea and prefer to speak of an ultimate but indescribable reality. Buddhism is an attitude of accepting the inevitable changes of life, and of being thankful for every moment we are alive.

Burnham, Sophy (1936–)

An award-winning author who is known for her speaking and writing on **angels** and the spiritual dimension. She has published such popular works as *A Book of Angels: Reflections on Angels Past and Present and True Stories of How They Touch Our Lives, Angel Letters,* and *The Ecstatic Journey: Walking the Mystical Path in Everyday Life.* About **God,** Burnham says in her popular book entitled *A Book of Angels,* "We are put here with blinkers on our eyes, to play a game of blind man's bluff with God for reasons we do not understand, and I suppose it would ruin the game if we cheated and knew the reward. We'd never be afraid. We'd know there's always more. We'd want to sling ourselves into the sea of love that's God."

Burning Bush

It was through a burning bush that **God** first spoke to the **prophet Moses,** instructing him to go to **Egypt** and free the **Hebrews** from Pharaoh's rule. While tending his flock one day, Moses drove the herd into the wilderness and came upon **Mount Horeb,** the **mountain of God.** Nearby, he noticed a bush that was on fire; however, the bush was not consumed by the flames.

Exodus (3:2–10) tells the story: "Now Moses was tending the flock of Jethro his father-in-law, the priest of Midian, and he led the flock to the far side of the desert and came to Horeb, the mountain of God. There the **angel of the Lord** appeared to him in flames of fire from within a bush. Moses saw that though the bush was on fire it did not burn up. So Moses thought, 'I will go over and see this strange sight—why the bush does not burn up.' When the **Lord** saw that he had gone over to look, God called to him from within the bush, 'Moses! Moses!' And Moses said, 'Here I am.' 'Do not come any closer,' God said. 'Take off your sandals, for the place where you are standing is **holy** ground.' Then he said, 'I am the God of your father, the God of **Abraham,** the God of **Isaac,** and the God of **Jacob.**' At this, Moses hid his face, because he was afraid to look at God.

"The Lord said, 'I have indeed seen the misery of My people in Egypt. I have heard them crying out because of their slave drivers, and I am concerned about their suffering. So I have come down to rescue them from the hand of the Egyptians and to bring them up out of that land into a good and spacious land, a **land flowing with milk and honey**—the home of the Canaanites, Hittites, Amorites, Perizzites, Hivites, and Jebusites. And now the cry of the Israelites has reached Me, and I have seen the way the Egyptians are oppressing them. So now, go. I am sending you to Pharaoh to bring My people the Israelites out of Egypt.'"

C

Do not say "This is a stone and not God." God forbid! Rather, all existence is God, and the stone is a thing pervaded by divinity.

—*Moses Cordovero*

Cagn

Supreme god of the Kalahar Bushmen of Southern **Africa.**

Cain

The first son born to **Adam and Eve.** Cain became a farmer, while his brother **Abel** (the second child born to Adam and Eve) became a shepherd. When the day came to make an offering to **God,** Cain and Abel brought their tributes. Abel brought the very finest from his flocks, while Cain brought an average offering from his crops. God favored Abel's offering, and rejected Cain's. Angered by God's rejection, Cain called his brother to go with him into the fields and killed him. When God asked Cain, "Where is your brother Abel?" Cain responded with, "Am I my brother's keeper?" (**Genesis** 4:2–10) God then cursed Cain and banished him, saying "You will be a homeless wanderer on the earth." In the **Bible,** it says a mark was placed on Cain's forehead by God after the murder of Abel to prevent Cain from being killed (Genesis 4:15).

Call

A summons by **God** to an individual to carry out a particular function on his behalf.

Calvin, John (1509–1564)

See Calvinism.

Calvinism

The **theology** created by John Calvin (1509–1564), emphasizing **predestination** and **salvation.** Calvin's teachings were based on a strong contrast between **God's** power and enormity, and the corrupt state of humanity. He taught that God's magnificence fills the entire universe and that all is sacred to God. Calvin believed that everything that happens is because of God's **divine** will, from the tiniest incidents in life to great events, everything that occurs is due to God's grand scheme and His desire. Humankind was believed to be in rebellion against God. God however, allows this so that humans will know that He is merciful. In addition, Calvin stressed what is termed unconditional **election,** meaning that God's favor to **Man** is completely by God's free choice and has nothing to do with Man's deeds, service, or devotion to God as taught in other facets of **Christianity.**

In his work, *Institutes of the Christian Religion,* Calvin spoke of the natural tendency of humans to seek and worship God. He states, "That there exists in the human minds and indeed by natural instinct, some sense of Deity, we hold to be beyond dispute, since God himself, to prevent any man from pretending ignorance, has endued all men with some idea of his Godhead, the memory of which he constantly renews and occasionally enlarges, that all to a man being aware that there is a God, and that he is their Maker, may be condemned by their own conscience when they neither worship him nor consecrate their lives to his service. Certainly, if there is any quarter where it may be supposed that God is unknown, the most likely for such an instance to exist is among the dullest tribes farthest removed from civilization. But, as a heathen tells us, there is no nation so barbarous, no race so brutish, as not to be imbued with the conviction that there is a God."

Canite

Member of a Gnostic sect that flourished in the second century A.D. They are thought to have lived in the eastern section of the Roman Empire. **Origen** (a Christian theologian) believed that the Canites had completely abandoned **Jesus.** The Canites believed that the **Hebrew God (Yahweh)** was inferior to the **Demiurge,** and **evil** because his **creation** of the world seemed designed and intended to hinder the uniting of the **divine** nature in **man** with the mysterious perfect God.

Carlyle, Thomas (1795–1881)

Scottish essayist and historian, who was an influential social critic. About **God,** Carlyle wrote, "Time and space are not God, but creations of God; with God, as it is a universal Here, so is it an **everlasting** Now."

Carmichael, Amy (1867–1951)

Amy Carmichael was an accomplished missionary and gifted writer,

who said she lived for one reason, and that was to make **God's** love known to those living in darkness. Carmichael, born in northern Ireland in 1867, was the oldest of seven **children.** Her father's **death** when she was eighteen had a profound effect on her, leading her to think seriously about her future and God's plan for her. That plan, as it turned out, was to be a missionary, a **call** to which she responded joyfully, first traveling to Japan, then China, and Ceylon.

In 1895, she was commissioned by the **Church** of England Zenana Missionary Society to go to Dohnavur, **India,** where she would eventually serve fifty-six years. There Carmichael saw five- and six-year-old girls being sold to pagan temples for prostitution. She began to purchase these girls hoping to raise them and teach them about God. This conflicted with the policies of her denomination but did not stop her from obeying God and rescuing these children. She founded the Dohnavur Fellowship, a refuge for children in mortal danger. More than a thousand children were rescued from neglect and abuse during Amy's lifetime.

Carmichael was also a prolific writer with thirty-five books published to her credit. Her book *If* was a bestseller and beloved classic on the message of the **Cross.** This simple **prayer** was specially written for a new convert who knew very little English. Says Carmichael, "If you have never been hurt by a word from God, it is probable that you have never heard God speak."

Carver, George Washington (1864–1943)

American educator and outstanding innovator in the agricultural sciences. Carver was a **man** of great **faith** in **God,** and a man whom God empowered to become one of the most influential men of his time and some say the most remarkable American who has ever lived. An agricultural chemist, Carver developed crop-rotation methods for conserving nutrients in soil and discovered hundreds of new uses for crops such as the peanut, which created new markets for farmers, especially in the South.

Born of slave parents in Diamond Grove, Missouri, Carver left the farm where he was born when he was about ten years old and eventually settled in Minneapolis, Kansas, where he worked his way through high school. He grew to manhood during Reconstruction, the time of the South's most intense racial hatred and violence against her former bondsmen. It was Carver's trust in God that saw him through times of great adversity. As a boy, he trusted in God and became a Christian. Many years later, in describing his childhood conversion, Carter said, "I was just a mere boy when converted, hardly ten years old. God just came into my heart one afternoon while I was alone in the loft of our barn." Later, while in his sixties, he wrote of that time, "That was my simple conversion, and I have tried to keep the faith." Through his trust in God, Carver triumphed over misfortune, becoming a friend to three presidents, a confidant of millionaires, and a scientist of world renown.

The magnitude of his accomplishments as a botanist are only rivaled by his success in teaching students to know God by studying nature. He wrote of his students: "How I long for each one to walk and talk with the Great Creator through the things He has created." Carver credited his ideas for the peanut to God. He says that he asked God, "Mr. Creator, why did You make the peanut?" Carver later shared that God led him to his laboratory and worked with him to discover some 300 marketable products from the peanut. Carver's inventive genius and close relationship with God made him a success.

Catholicism
See Roman Catholics.

Causality Argument
One of the arguments for the proof of **God's** existence. Thomas **Aquinas** is thought to be the first to use the Causality Argument as published in his *Summa Theologica.* He held that unaided human reason (philosophical reason) could demonstrate that God exists. He believed that only nothing comes from nothing—everything comes from something and everything leads back to a more original form.

He gave logical proofs to the existence of God, conceiving five in total, which include: the Argument from Motion, Causation of Existence, Contingent and Necessary Objects (Beings), the Argument from Degrees and Perfection, and the Argument from Intelligent Design.

Celts
The Celts of ancient times relied more on memory than the written word. Therefore, understanding the Celtic view of **God** is difficult because of the lack of resources. However, scholars have been able to piece together some information through data from Europe as well as from the islands of Britain and Ireland. It appears that Belenus was the most widely worshipped Celtic god. He was the god of light known as "The Shining One." He was married to Belisama and was believed to have been overseer of sheep and cattle. In some stories he corresponds with the **Irish** God Bile. Belisama, his wife, was the **goddess** of light and fire, forging and craft. She corresponds to the classical Roman goddess Minerva.

Centering Prayer
A type of **contemplative prayer**. It is a Christian form of **meditation** that

has been practiced for centuries. It is thought to be a way of offering oneself to **God,** based on the belief that God is not absent but fully present inside us. Centering **prayer** is practiced once or twice a day for twenty to thirty minutes. The participant sits in a relaxed position opening herself to the interior presence of God through silence, releasing all notions and ideas that we are separate from God. Silence plays a major role in centering prayer. Outward silence keeps one free from distractions. Interior silence helps the participant move past conversing with God and to simply enjoy God's presence. Centering prayer benefits practitioners by helping them to develop a capacity to let go of things that are negative and hurtful. It is believed that it opens the participant to the joy of experiencing God's presence in one's life.

Cghene

Supreme and creator god of the Isoko people of southern Nigeria.

Characteristics

See Divine Attributes.

Chariots of the Sun

Worship of the sun god was common in the ancient Near East. Many cultures portrayed him as a charioteer streaming across the heavens pulling the sun behind him. In the **Bible,** King Josiah removed from the entrance to the Temple the horses that the kings of Judah had dedicated to the worship of the sun, and burned the "chariots of the sun" used in this worship, in an effort to rid **Israel** of foreign gods so it could follow the one true **God** (2 Kings 23:11).

Chavez, Cesar (1927–1993)

Cesar Estrada Chavez became a voice for the migrant workers of California. In his fight to gain rights for the workers, he eventually founded and led the first successful farm workers' union in U.S. history. In his battle to gain rights for the workers, he used purely nonviolent means of protest such as strikes, demonstrations, and boycotts. This faith in nonviolence was related to his deep **faith** in **God.** Regarding this, Chavez once stated, "The non-violent technique does not depend for its success on the goodwill of the oppressor, but rather on the unfailing assistance of God." Commenting on his deep spiritual beliefs, Chavez states, "I find that, if I provide time and silence for God, He will make His presence known to me."

Cherubim

The name Cherubim means "Fullness of **God's** Knowledge." In the Zohar we read, "Come and see. When the sun sets the cherubim . . . beat their wings above and stretch them out, and the melodious sound of their wings is heard in the realms above." The Cherubim are brilliant and mighty **angels** who dwell close to God. They are the second-highest order of angels in **Heaven.** They are sometimes referred to as Cherubs, but are not to be mistaken with the baby angels, also called Cherubs.

According to the **Books of Enoch,** they are majestic and very beautiful. The name Cherubim originated in Assyria and is derived from the word *karibu,* which means "one who prays." They emanate a subtle vibration of knowledge and wisdom that they receive from God. They are also the keepers of the celestial records, and are said to praise God night and day continuously. In **Islam** they are called *el-karubiyan,* which means those "brought close to **Allah** (God)." Originally they were portrayed as mighty guardian figures which appeared in the Near and

Middle East. In Assyrian art, Cherubim were depicted as winged creatures with faces of either a lion or a human set on bodies of sphinxes, eagles, and bulls. In the Book of Psalms (18:10), God rides upon a Cherub.

The Cherubim are sometimes referred to as living creatures, winged creatures, **Holy** Beasts, and "many-eyed ones," a phrase used in scripture. Revelation describes the Cherubim as being full of eyes. "And the four living creatures, each of them with six wings, are full of eyes all around and inside" (Revelation 4:8). The many eyes symbolize God's all-seeing power.

Children

Children are believed to receive visitations from **God** by means of **angels** more often than adults. This is thought to be due to their innocence and openness. In some **new age** beliefs it is thought that children are closer to God because they recently came from God. However, their memory of God diminishes as they get older. According to Judaic lore, as a baby is growing inside of the mother's womb, an angel instructs it on the wisdom of the **Torah.** Just before the child is born, an angel touches the mouth of the baby, so that it will forget what it learned. However, the impression of the wisdom is said to remain with the child during his earthly life.

In other thought, it is believed that God protects children with angels because they are so young and careless. As they grow and are better able to look after themselves, they require less angelic protection. However, when children are very little, it is believed that they have many **guardian angels.** In Catholicism children are taught that they have two angels, one sits on each shoulder: a good angel and a bad angel. Legend has it that guardian angels of children dwell in a privileged place in

Heaven, close to God. This belief stems from the scripture in the Book of Matthew 18:10, where **Jesus** says, "See to it that you men do not despise one of these little ones; for I tell you that their angels in heaven always behold the face of my **Father** who is in heaven."

Children of Israel

Another name for the **Hebrews,** who, according to the **Bible,** were God's chosen people.

Chinmoy, Sri (1931–)

Peace Run Founder. Sri Chinmoy has dedicated his life to world peace. He enthusiastically spreads the universal message that all will be united someday as a world-family in the pursuit of peace. In his book *God Is . . .*, Chinmoy writes: "**Man** and God are one another's supreme necessity. Man needs God for his highest transcendental realisation and God needs man for His absolute earthly manifestation. Man needs God to realise his highest truth, his highest existence. God needs man to manifest Him here on earth totally, **divinely** and supremely."

Chiuke

Ibo (Nigeria) creator god. He is believed to be the source of all that is good.

Choctaw Indians

Native Americans of the bayous of Louisiana. In Choctaw religious beliefs **God** is named **Aba.** Aba is a loving God and **father** to his earthly **children.** Upon **death,** Choctaws believe that they go to **Heaven** to be with Aba where they will live in **paradise** forever.

Chopra, Deepak (1947–)

Renowned physician and author. Deepak Chopra, M.D., is one of the world's greatest leaders in the field of mind-body medicine. His work is changing the way the world views physical, mental, emotional, spiritual, and social wellness. In his book, *How to Know God*, Chopra comments: "God is the infinite, unbounded, **eternal** intelligence that constantly projects itself as the Universe—through the **creation** of space, time, matter, and infinite energy."

Chosen Ones

A term used when referring to the **Israelites** (also called **Hebrews** and **Jews**). According to the **Bible, God** chose Israel as the people who would know Him and carry His laws and learn and receive His moral and spiritual guidance. Their being the chosen ones is referred to numerous times in the Bible. In **Deuteronomy** 7:6, it states: "You belong to the **Lord** your God. From all the peoples on earth he chose you to be his own special people." It was considered a privilege to be the chosen people, but with that privilege came a huge responsibility. The Israelites had to live up to God's moral and spiritual **law,** something which proved difficult for them at times. When they broke God's laws, they were severely punished.

Christ

The word Christ is Greek meaning pure, perfect, or the **anointed one.** It is the equivalent to the **Hebrew Messiah** *(Meshiach)*. The Messiah was the chosen one of **God;** he was to be the only begotten **Son of God.** See Jesus.

Christ Consciousness

A phrase used to denote the spiritual and mystical knowledge of the unity of the entire universe. To achieve **Christ** consciousness means to see the universe as **God** and God as the universe. Everything else is a part of this whole.

Christian Science

A **faith** based on the life and teachings of **Jesus Christ,** in particular the healings ascribed to him in the **New Testament.** Officially called "**Church of Christ,** Scientist," it was founded by Mary Baker **Eddy** in Boston, Massachusetts. Eddy believed sickness to be an illusion, something unknown to **God,** who created a perfect human in His image. Members of the church believe that matter is unreal; and that **evil, sin,** sickness, and even **death** are erroneous beliefs that can be overcome through God's power, **prayer,** and the power of Truth.

Christianity

Christianity is the religion that traces its origins to **Jesus of Nazareth,** whom it affirms to be the Chosen One **(Christ)** of God. Acceptance of Jesus as the **Messiah,** the **Son of God,** is central to the **faith.** It is the most widely distributed of the world's religions, practiced by one-third of the population of Earth.

BELIEFS IN GOD. Christianity is a form of monotheism, believing in one God. It began as a Jewish sect and thus took over the **Hebrew** God **Yahweh** (also **Jehovah**). The Jewish Scriptures eventually became for the Christians the **Old Testament.** In Christianity, the humanity of God is the chief significant point. There is still an emphasis on God as a creator and judge; however, the God of the Christians was a loving, compassionate, merciful God who was called "**Father.**" He was a God that was different from the one portrayed in **Judaism.** The God of Judaism was all-powerful yet wrathful, whereas the God of Christianity encouraged loving one's neighbor. In Christianity, love for your neighbor is equal to love for God.

In addition, He is a forgiving God. All can be forgiven through Jesus Christ. Christianity did not change the importance of being obedient to God; however, Christians believe that God provided an easier way of gaining **salvation** through Jesus. In addition, Jesus represented the fulfillment of God's plan and **covenant**, which was established with the followers of Judaism. Some Christians also believed that Jesus was God made flesh to fulfill this covenant. In this way, God was born to do what **Man** could not, and thereby bring both God and Man closer together.

The Christian God differs from the gods of the world's religions in terms of His nature and existence. Most of the world religions describe their god as existing within the universe, whereas the Christian God is believed to exist and operate in dimensions of space and time other than those to which humans are confined. Christians believe that God could not have created the universe if He were a part of it. In addition, this thought is supported by scriptures such as 1 Kings 8:27 which reads, in speaking about God, "Even **heaven** and the highest heaven cannot contain you."

Christina, Saint (1150–1224)

Saint Christina had an extraordinary near-**death** experience at the age of twenty-two. In her experience she visited **hell**, purgatory, and finally **heaven**, where she had the privilege of seeing **God** in all His glory. After her near-death experience, God gave her the choice of staying with Him in glory, or returning to Earth to work for the **salvation** of other **souls**. After witnessing the souls in hell and purgatory, she chose to resume her life on Earth and help others. She later became a nun and dedicated herself to the work of saving souls.

Church (House of God)

The word church has two meanings: 1) House of **God**, a place where people go to worship God; 2) a term used in **Christianity** meaning a group of people. Specifically, the church is made up of those destined to inherit the **Kingdom of God**. The word church is derived from the Greek *kyriokon*, which means "House of God."

Church of Jesus Christ of Latter-Day Saints

See Mormonism.

Circular Argument

An argument used in proving the existence of **God**. The Circular Argument uses as evidence the very thing it is trying to substantiate. In the case of God, the argument is used this way: It is obvious that there is a God, because one look at His **creation**, the cosmos, the Earth, and the creatures in it shows that He is all-powerful, all-mighty, and all-loving. Many arguments for God's existence are circular.

Circumcision

As a sign of **God's covenant**, **Israel**ite boys were required by God to be circumcised eight days after they were born (**Genesis** 17:9–14). This rite symbolized obedience to the covenant that God had made with His people.

City of God

A treatise by Saint **Augustine** considered to be his best work and hailed as a masterpiece, written from 413 to 422. It is a large work of twenty-two books. The work itself has had a huge impact on **Christianity**, with some scholars suggesting that it not only influenced Christianity, but formed the basis of its beliefs. In *City of God*, Augustine offers his viewpoint of **Heaven**. It is a city in which Heaven and Earth are separated by only the thinnest of veils. The book began as a reply to the charge that Christianity was responsible for the decline of the Roman Empire. Augustine produced a wealth of evidence to prove that **paganism** bore within itself the seeds of its own **destruction.**

In *City of God,* Augustine describes Heaven as a perfect spiritual community, a **paradise** where there is peace and ultimate satisfaction, with **God** at its center. He writes about **creation,** the fall of **Adam and Eve,** and the advancement of human events since then. He concludes that governments and whole societies rise and fall, but that God is a continuous and never-changing God. People should therefore consider themselves a part of God's heavenly home first and members of their earthly home second, because our place on Earth is temporary. However, God's home in Heaven, God's city, is **eternal.** Says Saint Augustine, "These two cities were made by two loves: the earthly city by the love of self unto the contempt of God, and the heavenly city by the love of God unto the contempt of self." See Augustine, Saint.

Civil War (American)

In his second inaugural address, Abraham **Lincoln** spoke of the Civil War, **God,** and the paradox of opposing sides praying to God, saying: "Both read the same **Bible,** and pray to the same God; and each invokes his aid against the other. It may seem strange that any men should dare to ask a just God's assistance in wringing their bread from the sweat of other men's faces; but let us judge not, that we be not judged. The **prayers** of both could not be answered—that of neither has been answered fully."

Classical Theism

A term denoting the main idea of **God** in Western philosophy. Under this definition, God is impassable, immutable, simple, and **eternal.** He is the creator of the universe, having created all things out of nothing, and is therefore the ultimate cause and source of meaning for all of **creation.** Classical theism achieved definitive statement in the *Summa Theologica* of Saint Thomas **Aquinas.**

Cleanness and Uncleanness

The **Hebrew** ceremonial **law** went to great lengths to differentiate between the realms of cleanness and uncleanness, even prescribing rituals of cleansing. Sources of uncleanness included unclean **animals,** skin diseases, bodily secretions, and corpses. The main purpose for this was to remind the Hebrews of the large chasm between them and **God.** The people needed to prepare themselves in order to meet with God, and they needed to do so respectfully and with care.

Cloud of Unknowing

Written by an unknown author thought to have been a monk or a priest around the year 1375, *Cloud of Unknowing* is a guide to **contemplative prayer,** advocating an apophatic spirituality. In the guide, the writer explains the advantage of putting all of one's thoughts under a figurative "cloud of forgetting" in the mind, and then singleheartedly seeking to love **God,** hidden from our finite consciousness by a "cloud of unknowing." In order to penetrate that cloud, readers are directed to send "sharp darts" of "longing love." The *Cloud of Unknowing* is remarkable in its encouragement of monologistic **prayer,** prayer using a short word such as "God" or "love" repetitively while praying to help expel any extraneous thoughts and find that place of inner calmness and quiet where one may "be still and know God."

Cohen, Alan (1950–)

Inspirational author. Says Cohen, "When you love what you are doing, you are **God** in action."

Columbus, Christopher (1451–1506)

Italian-Spanish navigator. Columbus embarked on a journey west across the Atlantic Ocean looking for a route to Asia, but achieved widespread fame by making landfall in the Americas instead. Columbus first set sail on his famous voyage guided by the **Bible** and a **prophecy** of **God.** He believed that his journey across the Atlantic was in fulfillment of a prophecy from God found in **Isaiah** (46:11). There God says, "I am calling a **man** to come from the east; he will swoop down like a hawk and accomplish what I have planned. I have spoken, and it will be done." Later, after his third trip to the New World, in his work entitled *A Book of Prophecies*, Columbus wrote the he was convinced that he had fulfilled Isiah's prophecy as well as a number of other Bible prophecies.

Contemplative Prayer

A type of **prayer** that is a way of spending time with **God.** The term is derived from the Latin word *contemplare* which means "with time." It is a way for individuals to spend time with God just as one would spend time with any other loved one. The practice of contemplative prayer requires only a commitment to spend time quietly, offering time to God.

Cornelius

A captain in the Roman army who found favor with **God.** God sent an **angel** to tell him this very thing. The account is found in the **Bible's New Testament** in the Book of Acts (10:3–4). Cornelius found favor in God's eyes because of his **prayers** and help that he gave the **Jews.** One afternoon an angel appeared to him and said, "Cornelius! God is pleased with your prayers and works of charity."

Court of Heaven

According to ancient Judaic lore the Court of **Heaven** convenes in **Arabot,** the **Seventh Heaven. It** includes **God, Jesus, Metatron** (King of **Angels),** the great princes of Heaven, the throne angels, the saints and the **prophets,** the **ministering angels,** and the angels of destruction. The **Bible** speaks of the Court of Heaven. There God is seated on his throne, and angels are gathered in front of Him. Daniel 7:9–10 tells us: "As I watched, thrones were set in place, and an **Ancient One** took his throne, his clothing was white as snow, and the hair of his head like pure wool. A thousand thousands served him, and ten thousand times ten thousand stood attending him. The court sat in judgment, and the books were opened."

Those books that are being opened and read by the Court have been interpreted as being the books where the good and **evil** deeds of mankind have been recorded by God. While the Court is in session, only the great princes of Heaven that carry the name of God **(YHWH)** are allowed to speak. However, it is the seventy-two princes of the kingdoms of the world who read the deeds of humankind from the books. After the books are read, the angels of punishment go forth to execute judgment against the wicked.

Covenant(s)

A binding agreement, involving promises from **God** to **Man.** God made a covenant with **Noah (Genesis** 9:8–17) and with **Abraham** (Genesis 17:1–8), but in the **Old Testament,** the term usually refers to the covenant made between God and the people of **Israel (Exodus** 24:4–8). The covenant between God and Israel was made at **Mount Sinai** during the time of **Moses.** The tablets on which the **Ten Commandments** were written were referred to as "the tablets of the covenant" (**Deuteronomy** 9:11). The chest in which the tablets were kept was called "the **ark of the covenant**" (Numbers 10:33; Deuteronomy 31:9).

The **Bible's New Testament** speaks often about the new covenant that God made with His people. Even the term "New Testament" means "new covenant." The new covenant was promised in **Jeremiah** (31:31) where it is the only mention in the entire Old Testament (many other Old Testament passages speak of this covenant in indirect terms). In Jeremiah 31:31 it states: "Behold, the days are coming, says the **Lord,** when I will make a new covenant with the house of Israel and the house of Judah."

The old covenant is not annulled however. The new covenant was a continuation of the original covenant made to Abraham by God. The new covenant was superior to the old because it is confirmed by the oath of God (**Hebrews** 7:22). God swears more than once in the Old Testament to keep His covenant (Deuteronomy 4:31). By calling the promised covenant new, God made the first covenant obsolete. The old covenant actually continued on for nearly 500 years after Jeremiah, but with the promise of the new, attention was taken away from the old covenant and directed toward the new one that was coming. It was considered a better covenant, because it was established on improved promises. The first covenant had its laws written on tablets of stone; the new covenant was one that requires God's laws be written in people's hearts. God states, "I will put My laws in their mind and write them on their hearts." **Jesus** became **mediator** of the new covenant.

Cowper, William (1731–1800)

English poet. He wrote about the simple pleasures of country life and produced spiritual hymns that expressed a deep concern with human cruelty and suffering. Throughout his life Cowper suffered from bouts of depression, some of which was rooted in religious doubts and fears that plagued him all his life. After a stay in an asylum, he retired to the country, taking refuge with the family of Mrs. Mary Unwin, who took care of him, encouraged him to write poetry, and helped him to recover. Most of his country life was spent at Olney, where he met John **Newton,** who became his pastor and friend. It was John Newton who helped him through his illness, even preventing him from committing suicide on several occasions. Cowper contributed several poems to Newton's *Olney Hymns* (1779) including the two commencing *Oh for a closer walk with* **God** and *Light Shining Out of Darkness*. In his poems he addresses many social issues, such as **African** slavery and spreading the Gospel.

LIGHT SHINING OUT OF DARKNESS
(God Moves in a Mysterious Way)
by William Cowper

God moves in a mysterious way,
His wonders to perform;
He plants His footsteps in the sea,
And rides upon the storm.

Deep in unfathomable mines
Of never-failing skill,
He treasures up His bright designs,
And works His sovereign will.

Ye fearful saints, fresh courage take,
The clouds ye so much dread
Are big with mercy, and shall break
In blessings on your head.

Judge not the Lord by feeble sense,
But trust Him for His grace;
Behind a frowning providence,
He hides a smiling face.

His purposes will ripen fast,
Unfolding every hour;
The bud may have a bitter taste,
But sweet will be the flower.

Blind unbelief is sure to err,
And scan his work in vain;
God is His own interpreter,
And He will make it plain.

Creatio ex Nihilo (Creation from Nothing)

A belief found in **Judaism, Christianity,** and **Islam.** The doctrine is that **God** created all things out of no pre-existing material. He created the universe *ex nihilo* (Latin meaning "from nothing").

Creation

The act of **God** in making the heavens and the Earth and bringing forth life. The understanding that all living things came into existence by means of an **Almighty** God who designed and made the universe and all the basic kinds of life upon the Earth. Many wonder why God created the universe and humankind. In **Islam,** God explains why through the mouth of the **Prophet.** God said, "I was the hidden treasure. I wanted to be known. Therefore I created the world so that I would be known." By creating the Earth, and placing humans in it, God manifested the hidden treasure. His created beings are reflections of that treasure.

Throughout the various cultures and religions of the world, there are many creation stories. There are creation stories involving sky gods, stories of creation through emergence, from a childbearing woman, or creation by the marriage of two parents representing earth and sky. There are also stories of creation via a cosmic egg from which protohumans emerge, a feature of some Hindu, **African,** Greek, and Chinese myths. In other beliefs, the Earth is brought up from the primordial waters by a diver, or is formed from the dismembered body of a preexisting being. Perhaps the most famous story is the one most of us know best, that is stories of Creation by a **Supreme Being.** In these tales the Creator is usually **eternal,** existing outside of time and his creation. Also, the Creator exists alone and the act of creation is conscious planning and deliberation. Last, the Creator chooses freely whether to relate to his creation or not.

The most famous creation story is found in **Genesis.** It reads, "In the beginning when God created the heavens and the earth, the earth was a formless void and darkness covered the face of the deep, while a wind from God swept over the face of the waters. Then God said, 'Let there be light' and there was light. And God said, 'Let there be a dome in the midst of the waters, and let it separate the waters from the waters.' God called the dome Sky. And God said, 'Let there be lights in the dome of the sky to separate the day from the night and let them be for signs and for seasons and for days and years, and let them be lights in the dome of the sky to give light upon the earth.' And God said, 'Let the waters bring forth swarms of living creatures, and let birds fly above the earth across the dome of the sky.' And God said, 'Let the earth bring forth living creatures of every kind: cattle and creeping things and wild **animals** of the earth of every kind.'

"Then God said, 'Let us make humankind in our image, according to our likeness; and let them have dominion over the fish of the sea, and over the birds of the air, and over the cattle, and over all the wild animals of the earth, and over every creeping thing that creeps upon the earth.' So God created humankind in his image, in the **image of God** he created them, male and female he created them. God saw everything that he had made, and indeed, it was very good" (Genesis 1: 1–31).

The apostle Paul once stated, "Ever since God created the world, His invisible qualities, both His eternal power and His **divine** nature, have been clearly seen; they are perceived in the things that God has made" (Romans 1:20). In other words, if we know anything about His creation, we have learned something of God. That is, creating is what God does.

Creationists

A person who believes in a **God** who created the universe or who acknowledges the theory or rationale of **creation.** Many times, scientists are on the opposite end of the spectrum. However, there are many who support the belief in God, even though their work is deeply ingrained in scientific theory. Some famed creationists who work in the field of science but who had a strong belief in God include:

Albert **Einstein** (1879–1955)
Bernhard Riemann (1826–1866)
Blaise **Pascal** (1623–1662)
Carolus Linnaeus (1707–1778)
Charles **Babbage** (1792–1871)
Georges Cuvier (1769–1832)
Gregory Mendel (1822–1884)
Isaac **Newton** (1642–1727)
James Joule (1818–1889)
James Simpson (1811–1879)
Johann **Kepler** (1571–1630)
John Ambrose Fleming (1849–1945)
John Dalton (1766–1844)
John Ray (1627–1705)
Joseph Clerk Maxwell (1831–1879)
Joseph Henry Gilbert (1817–1901)
Joseph Lister (1827–1912)
Louis **Agassiz** (1807–1873)
Louis **Pasteur** (1822–1895)
Matthew **Maury** (1806–1873)
Michael Faraday (1791–1867)
Nicolaus Steno (1631–1686)
Robert Boyle (1627–1691)

Thomas Anderson (1819–1874)
Wernher **von Braun** (1912–1977)
William Mitchell Ramsay (1851–1939)
William **Petty** (1623–1687)
William Thompson (1824–1907)

Cronus

In Greek **Mythology,** Cronus was the elder of the gods, the ruler of the Titans. He ruled the Earth before **Zeus** (who later became the supreme god) overthrew him.

Crosby, Frances Jane "Fanny" (1820–1915)

American hymn writer and poetess. Blinded by an illness at the age of six weeks, Crosby is said to have never become bitter. At the age of fifteen, Crosby entered the New York Institute and afterward taught history and English. As a pupil and as a teacher, Fanny spent thirty-five years at the school. Her first book of poems entitled *The Blind Girl and Other Poems* was published in 1844; in 1858, she published a book called *A Wreath of Columbia's Flowers.*

She was most famous for her hymns, which were used in evangelical missions and revivals. She wrote over 9,000 hymns during her life. Her mission in writing hymns was to bring people to **God.** Her hymns are said to have changed **sinners,** encouraged Christians, and inspired countless others. In addition, Crosby was known for her selfless dedication to the poor and needy, often using money earned from her writing to help those in need.

One memorable poem written by Crosby, and kept for several years as a personal tribute to God, lingers in the minds of those who admire her work:

Someday the silver cord will break,
And I no more as now shall sing;
But oh, the joy when I shall wake
within the palace of the King!

And I shall see Him face to face,
and tell the story—saved by grace!

Cross

An upright pole with a bar across it near the top on which the ancient Romans fastened convicted persons to die. **Jesus** was executed on a cross as a result of false criminal charges against him. According to the **Bible**, he was called to this painful but **sinless death** by **God** to compensate for the sins of humankind. Christians believe that through Jesus' death on the cross the world could see God's great love for His **children** of the Earth. Through Jesus' death and **sacrifice**, people could then be brought back into a relationship with God (which was originally sullied by **Adam and Eve**) and enjoy a clean standing before God.

Curse

To call on **God** to punish someone.

Cycles of Creation

Another name for the **Aeons**, a superior order of spiritual beings in **Gnosticism** that emanate from **God.** See Aeons.

Cyrus the Great (580–529 B.C.)

The first Achaemenian Emperor. He established **Persia** by merging the Medes and the Persians. It was the largest empire the world has ever seen. Although he was known to be a great conqueror, he is best remembered for being a tolerant, merciful ruler towards those he defeated. Significant among his deeds was his granting of permission to the Jews to return from their exile in **Babylon** to their native **Israel** to rebuild the Temple of **Solomon.** His famous decree to the **Jews** is preserved in Ezra 1:2,3. There Cyrus states, "The **Lord,** the **God of heaven,** has given me all the kingdoms of the earth and he has charged me to build him a house at Jerusalem. Whoever is among you of all his people, may his **God** be with him, and let him go up to Jerusalem . . . and rebuild the house of the Lord, the God of Israel—he is the God who is in Jerusalem."

D

God is the source of Light and Life and yet He is above
and beyond all these. God is conscience.
—*Mahatma Gandhi*

Dagda

Irish-Celtic god of the Earth and death. Dagda, or the Dagda is one of the most prominent gods and the leader of the Tuatha De Danann. He is called the "Good God" (not in the moral sense, but in the sense of being omnicompetent, skilled in many trades); he was also called Eochaid Ollathair ("Eochaid the All-Father") or Ruad Ro-fhessa ("**Mighty One** of Great Wisdom"). In Celtic beliefs he was one of the leaders of a mythological Irish people, the Tuatha De Danann. The Dagda is portrayed as possessing both super-human strength and appetite and having many powers. He had a great cauldron which provided an inexhaustible source of food, fruit trees that were always ripe with fruit, and two pigs—one live and the other which he was continually roasting. He owned an enormous club which could both kill and restore men to life. Another possession was a magic harp that played by itself, with which Dagda was said to summon the seasons of the year. His mate was the war **goddess** Morrigan.

Daimon

In Greek lore, a daimon is a supernatural being who intercedes between **God** and mankind. It was the Greek word from which the word "**angel**" was originally derived. The people of **Greece** believed that each person had his own daimon which acted as a spiritual guide, offering encouragement, advice, and protection when needed. The belief in **guardian angels** was adopted from the belief in daimons. A variation of daimon is daemon.

Daniel (God has Judged)

A biblical **Hebrew prophet** and visionary of **God,** whose story is told in the Book of Daniel in the **Bible's Old Testament.** Daniel was the fourth of "the greater prophets." During the exile of the **Jews,** God used Daniel to bring comfort and hope to the people. In the Book of Daniel he is portrayed as a man who loves God and has great **faith** despite extreme pressures. Nothing is known of his parentage or family. However, he appears to have been of royal or noble descent, and possessed considerable personal endowments. The first six chapters of the Book of Daniel tell how Daniel and his friends were taken captive from Judah to **Babylon,** and how they grew in wisdom and remained faithful to God. Within these chapters we find the familiar stories of Daniel's interpretation of Nebuchadnezzar's dreams, his three friends in the fiery furnace, **Belshazzar's** feast, and God's deliverance of

Daniel from the **lion's den.** The second part of the Book of Daniel gives an account of Daniel's visions about the future. The common thread between both parts of the book is the idea of God's control of the world's **empires** and His vindication of His people.

Dark Side

That **God** has no dark side is the common belief. Most, if not all, religions teach that God resides in the **light** of **everlasting** pure love. However, there are spiritual beings that do have a dark side or reside in darkness. These are **spirits** who reject God and His pure love. In some religious beliefs these are called **demons.** However, demons, according to some sources, are **angels** who have turned away from God and therefore do not comprise all the spirits who have a dark side. Other names for those on the dark side are dark spirits or lost **souls.** Those with a dark side can be members of the human population as well.

Daughters of Men

A term used in the **Bible** referencing the women whom the **angels** came to Earth to marry, leaving their lofty positions in **Heaven** with **God.** The account in **Genesis** 6:2 reads as follows: "Now it came to pass, when men began to multiply on the face of the earth, and daughters were born to them, that the **sons of God** saw the daughters of men, that they were beautiful; and they took wives for themselves of all whom they chose." See Watchers.

David (Beloved) (?–961 B.C.)

A **Hebrew** king who had a very special relationship with **God.** The **Bible** speaks of him as "a **man** after God's own heart" (1 Sam. 13:14). He was the King of Judah and **Israel** (1000–961 B.C.), and founder of the Judean dynasty. There are several accounts of King David and his accomplishments in the **Old Testament,** primarily in the books of Samuel, Kings, and Chronicles. King David had a deep and passionate love for God. The son of Jesse and a descendant of Ruth, David became king of Israel after the death of the defiant Saul, and thus began the golden age of Israel. He skillfully ruled the tribes of Israel, fashioning them into a united nation.

God had blessed him with many talents and abilities. David was a brave soldier, a great military strategist, a skilled administrator, a diplomat, a composer, a musician, and king. As a very young man, David displayed an unswerving love, **faith,** and loyalty to God in several instances. However, it was during the battle between the Israelites and the Philistines that David displayed his bravery and loyalty in defending God and his army against the giant Philistine Goliath. Before defeating him, David (at the tender age of seventeen) said to him: "You are coming against me with sword, spear and javelin, but I come against you in the name of the God **Almighty,** the God of the Israelite armies, which you have defied. This very day God will put you in my power; I will defeat you and cut off your head. And I will give the bodies of the Philistine soldiers to the birds and animals to eat. Then the whole world will know that Israel has a God, and everyone here will see that God does not need swords or spears to save his people. He is victorious in battle, and he will put all of you in our power" (1 Samuel 17: 45–47).

David was close to the heart of God, and from his line the promised **Messiah** was to come. David later became king, and reigned for many years in Israel from his capital, Jerusalem. The City of David remains to this day and the old buildings can be seen as a reminder of King David and his love for God.

Day of Atonement

In **Judaism,** the Day of **Atonement** is a day of **fasting** and praying for forgiveness of the past year's sins. It is believed that through atonement people can recover their original sinless relationship with **God.** According to ancient Jewish lore, on the Day of Atonement a scapegoat was thrown off the cliff at Haradan, plummeting to its **death** below. It is believed that the goat transferred the sins of the **Jews** to the fallen **angel** Azaz'el, who was believed to be trapped beneath a huge pile of boulders at the bottom of the cliff. See also Yom Kippur.

Day of Judgment

See Judgment Day.

Day of the Lord

In the **Bible,** the day of the **Lord** is a day when **God** will punish **evil.** It is a day of universal disaster and darkness. The **Old Testament** has several scriptures referencing this day. In **Amos** 5:18–20 it states: "The day of the Lord will bring darkness and not light; it will be a day of gloom, without any brightness." **Isaiah** 2:11,12 states: "A day is coming when human pride will be ended and human arrogance destroyed. The Lord alone will be exalted. On that day the Lord **Almighty** will humble everyone who is powerful, everyone who is proud and conceited." Isaiah 13:6 says: "The day of the Lord is near, the day when the Almighty brings **destruction.**" **Zephaniah** 1:7 states: "The day is near when the Lord will sit in judgment," and 1:14 says: "The great day of the Lord is near. It will be a day of fury, a day of trouble and distress, a day of ruin and destruction, a day of darkness and gloom." In the **New Testament** we read that this day of the Lord will come as a surprise. At 1 Thessalonians 5:2 we read: "The day of the Lord will come as a thief comes at night."

Death

Death means different things to different cultures and religions. To the materialistic thinker, death means complete annihilation. For the Hindu and the Buddhist, death means **reincarnation,** while Shiite Muslims believe that death will bring incomparable pleasures in **paradise.** In **Christianity** the word "death" has two meanings. First, it is used to describe the end of life. In many religious beliefs this constitutes the physical separation of the **soul** from the body. Second, it is believed that there is a far worse death, that is, spiritual death which is an **eternal** separation from **God** as a result of **sin.**

Death, Angel of

An **angel** assigned by **God** to slay His enemies. In many religions around the world, there is a common belief that God uses a helper in His **destruction.** This helper is often referred to as the Angel of **Death.** It is the Angel of Death who swiftly acts at God's command and carries out God's orders when it comes to death and destruction, often aimed at the enemies of God or **sinful** and disobedient humans.

According to several religious traditions, the Angel of Death is also the angel that escorts the **souls** of the dead to the spiritual realm. This can be either **Heaven** or the Underworld. Azrael is the Angel of Death in **Islam.** In Judeo-Christian lore **Gabriel,** Sammael, and Sariel have all been called the Angel of Death. In Zoroastrianism the Angel of Death is Mairya. In **Babylon** it was Mot. In rabbinical lore there are fourteen angels of death: Yetzer-hara, Adriel, Yehudiam, **Abaddon,** Sammael, Azrael, **Metatron,** Gabriel, Mashhit, Hemah, Malach ha-Mavet, Kafziel, Kesef, and Leviathan.

The Angel of Death destroyed 90,000 people during the time of David at God's command. It slaughtered 185,000 people in the camp of the Assyrians who were fighting against the **Jews.** It was the Angel of Death whom God sent to destroy the first-borns of **Egypt** as the last and final plague of the Egyptians before **Israel** was set free. The Viking's Valkyries were known as angels of death. The Greeks had Thanatos, the god of death, who performed all of the functions of an angel of death. Thanatos came to humans when their life spans were completed and carried them off to Hades. The angel of death is sometimes referred to as the Grim Reaper. The Etruscan **god of the dead** was named Charon. He had huge wings and a large crooked nose resembling the beak of a bird. Charon carried the **souls** of the dead to Hades, and was the overseer of the cities of the underworld.

Deism

Deism is the philosophical idea that **God** does not reveal Himself through revelation but through scientific **laws.** This idea flourished during the seventeenth and eighteenth centuries when the **Age of Enlightenment** was at its peak, and when science and rationalism were the popular trend. The word "Deism" is evolved from the Latin word for God, *Deus.* The term originally referred to a belief in one God, as compared to the belief in no God (**atheism**) and the belief in many Gods (**polytheism**).

Deism involves the belief in the existence of God based solely on rational grounds, without any reliance on revelation or scripture or on any specific teachings of a **church.** Deists argued that after God's initial work of **creation,** He withdrew, leaving the world and all of its natural laws to operate independent of Him. In so doing, God left behind the laws of nature which could give humans some insight

into His being. However, a few Deists believe that God still intervenes in human affairs from time to time. According to Deist ideas, God has not selected a chosen people (e.g., **Jews** or Christians) to be the recipients of any special revelation or gifts.

Deists also deny the existence of the Christian **Trinity** (the belief that God exists as three persons—**Father,** Son, and **Holy Spirit**—who are united in one being). They view **Jesus** as a teacher, philosopher, and healer, but not as the **son of God.** They deny the existence of **miracles.** Instead they hold that the world operates by natural and self-sustaining laws of God. In addition, they believe that a practical morality can be derived from reason without the need of instruction from religious doctrines said to be from God. When Deists pray, they express their gratitude to God for His works only, but they refrain from asking for special privileges.

Demiurge, The

The creator of the universe in Gnostic beliefs. The same term can be found in ancient Judaic lore, where the Demiurge is also named as creator of the universe. **Plato** described the Demiurge as the deity who fashions the material world. According to lore, the Demiurge or maker-god created the world in the shape of a revolving sphere. This sphere, made of **soul**-matter, was fashioned from the harmonious fusion of the four elements, earth, water, fire, and air. After the **creation** of the world, the remnants of soul-matter were made into human souls.

Demon

A fallen **angel** who assists **Satan** in the opposition of **God.** The word demon originated from the Greek word *daimon,* a supernatural being who intercedes between God and **mankind.** When the Septuagint was translated, the "daimons" and "demons" were merged, and the daimons became the "**evil** demons." Demons, according to Judaic and Christian lore, are fallen angels that dwell in the lower realms near the vicinity of the Earth. Some of them fell from **grace** when they chose to come to the Earth and have sexual relations with women. The books of 1 **Enoch** and **Genesis** both tell stories of the angels who forsook their places in **Heaven** to come to Earth to take wives for themselves from among the **daughters of men,** an act considered unnatural and against God. In addition, the offspring of these fallen angels are also referred to as demons.

Other angels fell and became demons when they rebelled against God and followed Satan. Satan and one third of the angels were thrown out of Heaven down to the Earth by the Archangel **Michael,** leader of God's heavenly army. In **Islam,** Satan and his demons were thrown out of Heaven when they refused to bow down and worship **Adam** after God instructed them to do so. In Islam, demons are called shaitans, and are sometimes referred to as black angels.

Besides the demons that were thrown out of heaven, there are others of a different category. According to Judeo-Christian beliefs, demons wreak havoc on the lives of humans. They are also believed to be responsible for influencing the world in immorality, crime, natural disasters, wars, hunger, disease, and all maladies that cause human suffering on Earth, all done in an effort to turn humans against God. In the testament of **Solomon,** the demons go up to the heavens and fly among the stars, listening to the decisions that God makes regarding the lives of men. They are sometimes referred to as the "sons of darkness" and "unclean spirits" (Acts 5:16).

In ancient times it was believed that each angel had one or more demons

which he could render powerless. In order for humans to thwart the demons, one would have to know the names of these angels. King Solomon communicated with many of the most powerful demons when they were interfering with the building of his temple. He accomplished this through a magic ring that God had given him to render the demons powerless. In Zoroastrianism, **Angra Mainyu** is the demon which goes against God. See Fallen Angels.

Deng

Creator and **sky god** of the Dinka people in the Sudan. He is also a god of rain and fertility.

Descartes, René (1596–1650)

French philosopher, scientist, and mathematician. Descartes said: "Whatever is contained in a clear and distinct idea of a thing must be predicated of that thing; but a clear and distinct idea of an absolutely perfect Being contains the notion of actual existence; therefore since we have the idea of an absolutely perfect Being such a Being must really exist."

Design Argument

An argument to prove **God's** existence by looking at the order and apparent design in **creation** and the universe as a whole. See Teleological Argument.

Despotes

A word used in the original Greek translation of the **Bible** meaning "**Lord**" or "**God**." It was used five times in the Bible's **New Testament.**

Destruction

In the **Bible's Old Testament** we read of **God** in several instances engaging in destructive acts. The most memorable is the **Flood** in the days of **Noah** that wiped out Earth's entire population. That flood tale is so real that it can be found in legends from ancient cultures around the world. There were also accounts of **Hebrews** who were destroyed for disobedient acts. God destroyed Pharaoh's army who chased after the Hebrews once they fled from **Egypt**. There is also the account of the two cities of **Sodom** and **Gomorrah** that displeased God because of their immoral ways. We also read of a future time in which God will wage war and destruction against wicked humanity, which Christians believe is **Armageddon**. In Armageddon, God will destroy governments opposed to Him, unrighteous people, as well as everything else representing this period of time on Earth. It is believed that God brings forth destruction through the use of **angels**. Jewish lore says that there are 90,000 angels of destruction. Each carries a sword symbolizing punishment, destruction, and their service to God.

In the Book of **Ezekiel**, the angels of destruction are sent to the city of Jerusalem. The account says, "Then I heard God shout, 'Come here, you men who are going to punish the city. Bring your weapons with you.' At once six men came from the outer north gate of the Temple, each one carrying a weapon. With them was a man dressed in linen, carrying something to write with. They all came and stood by the bronze **altar**. The **Lord** called to the man in linen, 'Go through the city of Jerusalem and put a mark on the forehead of everyone who is distressed because of all the disgusting things being done in the city.' And I heard God say to the other men, 'Follow him through the city and spare no one; have **mercy** on no one. Kill the old men, young men, young women, mothers, and **children**. But don't touch anyone who has the mark on his forehead'" (Ezekiel 9:1–6).

Deuteronomy

A **Bible** book. The second record of God's laws, Deuteronomy stresses obedience to God.

Devi

In **Hinduism**, the manifestation of God in the female form.

Devil

God's **adversary**, also known as **Satan**. The word devil comes from the Greek word *diabolos* which means "slanderer." Some believe that the word devil arrived from the Indo-European **Devi** (goddess). It is also said to come from the **Persian** *daeva* which means evil spirit. It is believed that the Devil is behind all of the wickedness in the world. It was the Devil, according to Judeo-Christian lore, who caused the **Fall of Man**, severing his pure ties with God, and causing him to be thrown out of **Paradise**. He is said to have done this in an effort to win the worship of the newly created humans for himself, as he wanted to be like God. The Devil and his hordes forsook their place in **Heaven** to come down to Earth. He is the Chief of **Demons**.

Dhikr

Dhikr is mainly an **Islam**ic term, meaning remembrance of **God**. Dhikr is an act of faithfulness during and after the time that **prayers** are said.

Didymus of Alexandria (313–398)

Greek grammarian and theologian, also referred to as Didymus the Blind (he lost his eyesight at the age of four). He was a celebrated head of the catechetical school at Alexandria. Even though Didymus was a layman and blind, he is hailed as one of the most learned men of his period, memorizing large portions of the **Bible** at a time. By using secretaries, he dictated several exegetical works. His writing entitled *On the Holy Ghost* was translated by St. Jerome, who studied briefly with him. Didymus was later condemned for **Origen**ism by the Third Council of Constantinople and the Second Council of Nicaea. About **God,** Didymus writes: "God is simple and of an incomposite and spiritual nature, having neither ears nor organs of speech. A solitary essence and unlimitable, he is composed of no numbers and parts."

Dimnet, Ernest (1866–1954)

French cleric and writer. He wrote *The Art of Thinking,* 1930. Says Dimnet, "You can believe in **God** without believing in immortality, but it is hard to see how anyone can believe in immortality and not believe in God."

Dionysius the Pseudo-Areopagite

A noted Syrian writer who conceived the most widely accepted hierarchy of **God's angels** ever written. During the first century, he wrote four books on mysticism, *Celestial Hierarchies, On the Ecclesiastical Hierarchy, The Divine Names,* and *Ten Letters.* These writings earned him the respect of several popes. His book entitled *Celestial Hierarchies* was about the makeup and characteristics of angels. Although he is believed to have been an Armenian monk, in this writing, he pretended to be Dionysius the Areopagite. (Dionysius the Areopagite was a judge of the court of the Areopagus.) He was also a convert of the Apostle Paul, and he later became the first Bishop of Athens. In 1450 it was discovered that he was a sham, which is why he later became known as the Pseudo-Areopagite (or the Pseudo-Dionysius).

Although others wrote and published angelic hierarchies, his was later adopted by the Catholic **Church.** Today it is the most widely recognized ranking of angels. In conceiving the hierarchy, Dionysius took the names of the orders of angels from the **Bible.** From the **Old Testament** he listed the **Seraphim, Cherubim,** and **Thrones** as the three highest orders of angels, and the ones closest to God. He took the other orders from the **New Testament,** from the apostle Paul's letters to the Colossians and the Ephesians (Colossians 1:16; Ephesians 1:21). He ranked the angels in the following order: The first choir consisted of the Seraphim, Cherubim, and Thrones. The second choir included the **Dominations, Virtues,** and **Powers.** The third choir held the **Principalities, Archangels,** and Angels. The seven archangels according to Dionysius are: **Michael, Gabriel, Raphael, Uriel,** Chamuel, Jophiel, and Zadkiel.

Dispensationalism

A Christian belief teaching that **God** employs various methods of governing His **divine** will while corresponding with various periods of time. There are believed to be seven dispensations: 1) Innocence, 2) Conscience, 3) Civil government, 4) Promise, 5) **Law,** 6) **Grace,** and 7) the Kingdom. Dispensationalists interpret the scriptures in light of these (or other) dispensations.

Disputa (Dispute Over the Sacrament)

Fresco by the great Renaissance painter Raphael, painted in 1509 for the Vatican. The fresco is divided into two levels: **Heaven** is portrayed in the upper level and Earth in the lower level. The scene portrays a debate on the lower level between men including philosophers, poets, and popes. Among them are Saint **Augustine** and Dante **Alighieri.** Above the debate scene is Heaven, symbolized by gold. Here **Jesus** sits upon a throne; the **Holy Spirit** is symbolized by a **dove**; the apostles, saints, and **patriarchs** are in the process of worshiping. At the top of this scene is **God** with **angels** surrounding Him, placed above the throne of Jesus **Christ**. Here God is portrayed as the highest authority in the universe. From the picture, one senses that God has all of the answers to life's mysteries and is above the debate going on below Him. Raphael portrays Him as an older and wiser person wearing a beard, a symbol of His being ancient and **eternal**.

Divination

The act of foretelling future events or discovering secret things through the use of spiritual or mystical tools. Divination in one form or another has been practiced by most civilizations and various forms of religions throughout history. In ancient times, it was primarily used as a means of communicating with **God** or the gods, just as praying is today. It was a means to determine the will of God in predicting one's future.

Divination practices have been traced as far back as the Cro-Magnon people, who, fifty thousand years ago, determined the seasons from the movements of the stars and planets, believing that God was communicating with them through the celestial bodies. As civilizations began to develop, belief in divination grew stronger. Humans began to look for messages from God through signs. By the time humans began communicating in writing, the practice of foretelling events by means of signs was firmly established.

Divination was used in nearly all ancient civilizations, each having its own specialties. In most societies, divination was considered an official institution, part of both the religious and the political systems, both of which were hesitant to make any sure decision without consulting God first. It was

so important that the fate of entire **nations** sometimes depended upon answers received from diviners. Most ancient rulers such as those of **Greece**, **Rome**, and **Egypt** employed a personal reader, who acted in an official capacity and was consulted on all major decisions. In addition, almost every army had a seer who traveled with them to predict the success or failure of battles. Divination practices were not restricted to governments. The commoners were also concerned about their futures, and sought out answers to questions regarding their love lives, careers, families, businesses, and more. For them, divination was profoundly serious, and was found in all aspects of their lives, personal, political, and religious.

JUDEO-CHRISTIAN BELIEFS. In Judeo-Christian beliefs there are instances of divination mentioned in the Scriptures by which God made his will known.

Examples of these include divination by lot, by which God intimated his will (**Joshua** 7:13). The land of Canaan was divided by lots (Numbers 26:55,56); Achan's guilt was detected (Joshua 7:16–19); Saul was elected king (1 Samuel 10:20, 21); and Matthias was chosen to the apostleship by lots (Acts 1:26). It was thus also that the scapegoat was determined (Leviticus 16:8–10).

There was divination by dreams (**Genesis** 20:6; **Deuteronomy** 13:1,3; Judges 7:13,15; Matthew 1:20; 2:12,13,19,22). This is illustrated in the history of **Joseph** (Genesis 41:25–32) and of **Daniel** (2:27; 4:19–28). By **divine** appointment there was also divination by the **Urim and Thummim** (Numbers 27:21), and by the ephod.

There are also a number of instances in the **Old Testament** where respected leaders were involved with magical, divination and occult activities apparently without any condemnations from God. In Genesis 44:5, Joseph's household manager refers to a silver drinking cup ". . . in which my **lord** drinketh and whereby indeed he divineth." Later, Joseph accuses his brothers of stealing the cup, saying "that such a **man** as I can certainly divine [the identity of the thieves]." These passages show that Joseph engaged in scrying. This is an ancient method of divination in which a cup or other vessel is filled with water and gazed into. The Urim and Thummim were two objects mentioned in Numbers 27:21 and 1 Samuel 28:6 of the **Hebrew** Scriptures. They were apparently devices that the high priest consulted to determine God's will. It is believed that they worked something like a pair of dice.

The **prophet** Daniel was employed for many years in **Babylon** as the chief occultist to the king. He was supervisor "of the magicians, astrologers, Chaldeans, and soothsayers" (Daniel 5:11). However, in Deuteronomy 18:10, God forbade the **Israel**ites from engaging in divination. "There shall not be found among you anyone that useth divination." The original Hebrew word for divination is *qosem q'samim,* foretelling the future by using lots or a similar system.

Divine

State of being of or like **God** or a god.

Divine Attributes

Attributes traditionally associated with **God** include: **omnibenevolence, omnipotence, omnipresence,** and **omniscience.** Omnibenevolence is defined as perfect moral goodness, the complete desire for good. Traditionally it has been thought that God does not merely happen to be good but that He must be so and that He is unable to do what is wrong. Omnipotence means that God is all-powerful. Revelation

19:6 states: "And I heard as it were the voice of a great multitude, and as the voice of many waters, and as the voice of mighty thunderings, saying, Alleluia: for the **Lord** God omnipotent reigneth." Omnipresence is God's ability to be many places or everywhere at the same time. He is said to be in **Heaven** and on Earth at the same time. As the Psalmist once exclaimed: "Whither shall I go from your **spirit?** or whither shall I flee from your presence?" "I am a God at hand as well as afar off," says God. "Do not I fill heaven and earth?" Omniscience means unlimited knowledge, that "God knows all things." The monotheistic God of **Judaism, Christianity,** and **Islam** is an all-knowing God believed to be conscious of, and conversant with, the thought of all His **creation.** This is shown in 2 Chronicles 16:9: "For the eyes of the Lord run to and fro throughout the whole earth." The knowledge of God's **divine** attributes affect His relationship with His earthly **children.** This can be seen in our human behaviors, our understanding of good and **evil,** and what we expect in the afterlife.

Divine Comedy, The

See Alighieri, Dante.

Divine Decrees

Messages from **God** that are given to humans. Both the **Hebrew** scriptures and the Christian scriptures are well known for their **divine** decrees from God. One of the most famous accounts comes from **Genesis** 3:17–19. There God gave a decree that would affect humankind forever. As legend has it, **Adam and Eve** sinned when they ate from the **Tree of Life.** Because of this God gave this decree, "Cursed is the ground because of you; in toil you shall eat of it all the days of your life; thorns and thistles it shall bring forth for you; and you shall eat the plants of the field.

By the sweat of your face you shall eat bread until you return to the ground, for out of it you were taken; you are **dust,** and to dust you shall return."

In another account in Genesis 18:1–2, the **prophet Abraham** was visited by three **angels** as he sat at the entrance of his tent. There he received two decrees from God. The account states, "The Lord appeared to Abraham by the oaks of **Mamre,** as he sat at the entrance of his tent in the heat of the day. He looked up and saw three men standing near him." The angels had come to tell Abraham that his elderly wife **Sarah** would give birth to a son. The angels also informed him of the impending **destruction** of two nearby cities, **Sodom** and **Gomorrah.**

Hagar, the maidservant of Abraham's wife Sarah received two pronouncements from God. Each time an angel appeared to her while she was in the wilderness. The first came after she had fled into the wilderness to escape the wrath of Sarah. The angel told her at that time that she was going to give birth to a son, and that she should call him **Ishmael** (Genesis 16:1–14). The second visitation occurred when she wandered into the wilderness after Abraham sent her away at Sarah's request. Exhausted and dehydrated, Hagar put her son Ishmael under a bush and walked away, asking God not to let her see it when the child died. From **Heaven** God heard the child crying and sent an angel to speak to her. The angel called out to her, telling her not to be afraid, that God would one day turn Ishmael's seed into a great **nation** (Genesis 21:17–19).

In the Book of Judges (13:1–5), **Manoah** (the father of **Samson**) and his wife received two visitations from an **angel of the Lord** sent to them by God. The angel informed them that they would have a son who was to be "dedicated to God as a Nazirite." The angel

told them that their son would deliver the **Israelites** from the Philistines, a pronouncement that later came true.

Moses, the deliverer of the Hebrews, received a message from God that changed his life. His first encounter with God occurred on **Mount Sinai,** where God spoke to Moses through a **burning bush** (Exodus 3:2). God, using an angel as his **spokesman,** informed Moses that he was to deliver the Hebrews from bondage to the **Egyptians.** In fact, God told him directly, "Come and let me send you to Pharaoh and you bring my people the sons of Israel out of Egypt." God went on to say, "After you have brought the people out of Egypt, you people will serve the true God on this mountain" (Exodus 3:10–11).

In the **New Testament** two people received divine decrees from God. **Zechariah,** the father of **John the Baptist,** was informed by God through an angel that he would become a father. This was to be a **miracle** since he and his wife were both old and his wife **Elizabeth** was barren. Zechariah said to the angel, "How shall I know if this is so. See also I am an old man, and my wife is old also." The angel replied, "I am **Gabriel.** I stand in the presence of God, who sent me to speak to you and tell you this good news."

Perhaps the most well known pronouncement went to the **Virgin Mary,** who received a message from God that she was to become pregnant and have a child, even though she was a virgin. In this announcement the angel said, ". . . and, look! You will conceive in your womb and give birth to a son, and you are to call his name **Jesus.** This one will be great and will be called son of the **Most High**" (Luke 1:31–32).

Divine Right

The right of authority to govern as granted by **God. Divine** right is usually claimed by monarchs.

Divinity

The quality or condition of being **God** or Godlike.

Djanna (Al-Janna)

In **Islam,** Djanna is the **paradise** garden of **Allah (God)**. In Djanna, rivers of wine and honey flow and there are magnificent orchards. The fortunate blessed recline on couches, eat fruit, and have wine served to them. There they experience peace and the satisfaction of the **soul** in God. It's a place of rest and refreshment in which the righteous live in the presence of God.

Djibril

See Jibril.

Dominations

The fourth order of **angels** in the angelic hierarchy. Taking their orders directly from **God,** the Dominations are the angels who integrate the material and spiritual worlds. According to **Dionysius**, it is through the Dominations that the majesty of God is manifested. It is also through the efforts of the Dominations that the order of the cosmos is maintained. With God's direction, they handle the details of cosmic life while regulating the tasks of the angels.

Dove

In Christendom, doves represent **God's Holy Spirit**. The Holy Spirit appeared as a dove over the head of **Jesus** at his **baptism**. Because of this, the dove has also become a symbol of peace on Earth.

Doxology

A hymn, usually in a set formula, that expresses praise to **God**. The words in the **Bible's** Luke 2:14 ("Glory to God in the highest **heaven**") have influenced later Christian doxologies.

Dreams

In ancient times, the interpretation of dreams was an important means of discerning the **divine** will of **God**. Every ancient king retained diviners to interpret dreams. The **Old Testament's Joseph** and **Daniel** are the best-known dream interpreters in the **Bible**. Today, there are many interpretations for dreaming about God. Some of the most common are as follows: 1) Dreaming of God is said to be a sign of universal love, harmony, and oneness. It means complete self-acceptance in that moment in time. 2) If the dreamer was brought up in a strict religious environment, dreaming of God could be a sign of scolding from God, especially if the person is involved in something about which they feel guilty. 3) If one dreams of worshipping God, they may have cause to repent of an error of their own making. It is said that God speaks more often to those who do wrong than those who do right.

Duns Scotus, John (1265–1308)

Scottish theologian and philosopher. He was the founder of a school of Scholasticism known as Scotism. He was sometimes referred to as "the subtle doctor" because of his thorough analysis into the nature of reality and **God**. In his view, the most important concern in **theology** is God. He believed that the existence of things depends on a free decision made by God. He taught that God's will is free and not based upon any particular motivation. In his work entitled *De Primo Principio,* he gives an impressive multi-layered argument for God's existence in which he combines parts of the **ontological**, cosmological, and **teleological arguments**.

Dürer, Albrecht (1471–1528)

See *Adoration of the Trinity.*

Dust

Fine, dry, powdery earth. According to Jewish, Christian, and **Islamic** beliefs, **God** formed **Man** from the dust (the words soil and mud have also been used). **Genesis** 2:7 explains: "then God formed man from the dust of the ground, and breathed into his nostrils the breath of life; and the man became a living being." After the fall of **Adam and Eve,** God in his anger said to them: "By the sweat of your face you shall eat bread until you return to the ground, for out of it you were taken; you are dust, and to dust you shall return" (Genesis 3:19). "Ashes to ashes, dust to dust" are words often spoken at gravesites during funerals. The phrase is taken from God's words to **Adam** in Genesis 3:19, reminding him that he was created from the ground and would return there.

Dxui

Creator god of the Bushmen of South Central **Africa.**

Dyeus

The **God** of the **Aryans**. Around four or five thousand years ago (about 2500 B.C.) the Aryans (also referred to as the Indo-Europeans) settled in **Iran** and **India.** Their supreme god was Dyeus. Dyeus was the shining god of the **sky** who provided the rain and who was the defeater of enemies with storms and bolts of lightning. His consort was the Earth **Goddess** (or Mother Earth) who caused the vegetation to grow. Around them revolved other celestial beings and gods, as well as the heavenly bodies.

E

I know that He exists.
Somewhere—in Silence—
He has hid his rare life
From our gross eyes.

—*Emily Dickinson*

Eadie, Betty J. (1942–)

Author of the phenomenal book *Embraced by the Light.* In November of 1973, at the age of thirty-one, Betty J. Eadie "died" following surgery. Next, Eadie journeyed to the Other Side where she met **Jesus**. There, she was given a message to share with others when she returned to the physical world. In her world-renowned book, Eadie shares this message and chronicles her near-**death** experience. The book was hailed as "the most profound and detailed near-death experience ever recorded." Eadie has shared her experience with thousands. By sharing her message of **God's** love, Eadie helps people to overcome their fear of dying.

Eadie writes in *Embraced by the Light:* "God has a vantage point we can never perceive. He sees into our **eternal** pasts and futures and knows our eternal needs. In his great love he answers **prayers** according to this eternal and omniscient perspective. He answers all prayers perfectly." In her book *The Ripple Effect,* Eadie states, "One of the grandest mysteries of God is his fore-knowledge. Truth is knowledge of things as they were, as they are, and as they are to come. God, possessing all truth, has the ability to know all things in advance."

Earth Mother

Considered to be the feminine aspect of **God.** In ancient beliefs she was partnered with **Father Sky.**

Eckhart, Meister (1260–1328)

German Christian mystical theologian. Meister Eckhart is considered to be one of the great Christian mystics. He was born at Hochheim in Thringen, Germany, in 1260 of a family of knights; he entered the Dominican order (**Roman Catholic** religious order) when he was 15. In his distinguished career he became a Professor of **Theology** in Paris and took a leading pastoral and organizational role in the Dominican Order.

It has been said that Eckhart was a **man** of a single intent, and that intent was **God.** In his doctrines about God, Eckhart went beyond the tolerance of his time (eventually to the point of being charged with heresy), and some say beyond the capacity of our time as well. Eckhart made claims that appeared as if he thought God was nothing more than nature itself and that this God/nature created itself. These views worried the German bishops, and Eckhart was punished.

Yet what Eckhart discovered about God and His relationship with humankind was a gift he wished to give to others, a gift that he gave in great abundance, through sermons and writings that have been passed down to today. Eckhart had the ability to communicate his feelings of God's presence and nearness to humans. So great was this sense of God that he began a movement centering on mysticism in Germany. The depth and universality of Eckhart's teaching draws seekers of God and truth, Christian and non-Christian alike, to his spiritual works and ideas and thoughts on God.

About God Eckhart comments: "Whoever possesses God in their being, has him in a **divine** manner, and he shines out to them in all things; for them all things taste of God and in all things it is God's image that they see." He also states, "God is infinite in his simplicity and simple in his **infinity.** Therefore he is everywhere and is everywhere complete. God is in the innermost part of each and every thing."

Eddy, Mary Baker (1821–1910)

The founder of **Christian Science.** A deeply religious woman who was reared in traditional **Christianity,** Eddy was born in New England on a farm in Bow, New Hampshire. She spent her childhood and much of her adult life in poor health. As a result she spent years trying out various remedies to help, but to no avail. Then in 1866 she was healed of a serious injury after experiencing a spiritual revelation she claimed to have had while reading an account of one of **Jesus'** healings (Matthew 9:1–8). This led to her discovery of what she came to understand as the science of Christianity, which she named Christian Science.

Christian Science is a **faith** that believes in **God's** power to miraculously cure the sick, and that discourages the use of modern medicine, favoring instead the use of spiritual healing. Eddy also wrote a book entitled *Science and Health with a Key to the Scriptures,* which she claims was dictated to her by God. Christian Scientists accept her book, as well as the **Bible,** as inspired. In addition, Eddy founded one of the country's major newspapers, the *Christian Science Monitor.* Christian Science continues to thrive today, with followers from around the world. Said Eddy: "If Christianity is not scientific, and science is not God, then there is no invariable **law,** and truth becomes an accident."

Edwards, Jonathan (1703–1758)

Congregational preacher and theologian in the American colonies whose sermons stirred the religious revival called the Great Awakening (a revival movement that swept the Colonies with religious fervor and sought to convert all it passed). Edwards has been called "a great **man** of **God**" and is considered to be one of the greatest American theologians and the most famous of colonial figures. Born in East Windsor, Connecticut, he was the product of a family of famous clergymen. As a child, Edwards felt drawn to God, praying to God five times a day, and spending time with other boys talking about God and praying together. As a man, Edwards delivered stirring sermons, energetically taking to the pulpit and delivering bristling hellfire and brimstone sermons such as "Sinners in the Hands of an Angry God."

Said Edwards: "I felt God, so to speak, at the first appearance of a thunder storm; and used to take the opportunity, at such times, to fix myself in order to view the clouds, and see the lightnings play, and hear the majestic and awful voice of God's thunder, which oftentimes was exceedingly entertaining, leading me to sweet contemplations of my great and glorious God." He also wrote, "Truth is the consistency and agreement of our ideas with the ideas of God. . . . God is truth itself."

Egypt

A country in northeastern **Africa.** Few places on Earth possess as rich and well-preserved a past as Egypt. Egypt's monuments, such as the Sphinx and the pyramids, are icons of antiquity. Ancient Egyptian religion was polytheistic, with a pantheon of gods and **goddess**es, the supreme god being **Osiris.** These gods and goddesses were worshipped at local shrines and great temples. The Egyptians had as many as two thousand gods and goddesses. Some, such as Amun, were worshipped throughout the whole country, while others had only a local following. The gods differed in nature and abilities and were neither all-knowing nor all-powerful. According to the **Bible,** it was the Egyptians who held the **Hebrews** in bondage. It was Egypt's Pharaoh who ignored the pleas of the Hebrews until God intervened with **Moses** as his representative to convince Pharaoh to release the Hebrews. Egypt also played other roles in Biblical and Jewish history. **Abraham** and **Sarah** lived there temporarily (**Genesis** 12:10–20); **Joseph** was taken there (Genesis 37:28) and eventually made governor (Genesis 41:37–47:26); and **Jesus** was taken there as an infant (Matthew 2:13–15). Today, modern Egypt is considered the cultural center of the **Islam**ic world, serving as a crossroads between East and West, old and new.

Ein Sof (The Infinite)

In the Cabala, the Ein Sof represents the true hidden **essence of God,** which is entirely unknown to humans. It is believed that all human knowledge of **God** is really of the ten emanated Sefirot.

Einstein, Albert (1879–1955)

German-born American theoretical physicist, recognized as the most well-known scientist of the twentieth century. He is said to have shaped the concept of the world as we know it. Born on March 14, 1879, in Ulm, Germany, Einstein spent his youth in Munich, where his family owned a small store that manufactured electric machinery. Even as a child, he displayed a great curiosity about nature and a huge capacity to grasp difficult mathematical concepts. As an adult he rose to fame in 1905 when his theory of relativity was made public. In the same year, Einstein published findings that led to the foundation of modern-day quantum mechanics, and he published a paper that proved the atomic theory of matter. Einstein studied the idea of **God** with the same thoroughness with which he studied the physical world, stating: "I want to know how God created this world. I am not interested in this or that phenomenon, in the spectrum of this or that element. I want to know His thoughts; the rest are details." Einstein's beliefs in God have been the subject of much speculation. However, he made himself clear in the matter saying, "I believe in **Spinoza's** God who reveals Himself in the orderly harmony of what exists, not in a God who concerns Himself with fates and actions of human beings."

El

The word El has two meanings. 1) An ancient **Hebrew** word meaning **God.** It is used 250 times in the **Old Testament.** El is linguistically equivalent to the Arabic **Allah.** 2) Supreme god of the ancient Canaanite pantheon. He was the primary creator god and presided over the fate of humans.

El Elyon

An ancient **Hebrew** term sometimes used in the original translation of the **Old Testament** when referring to **God**. It means **Most High** God.

El Olam

A **Hebrew** term meaning **Everlasting God**, or God of Eternity.

El Roi

A **Hebrew** term meaning **God** Sees.

El Shaddai

One of **God's** names in the Jewish tradition which means God **Almighty** (also **Lord** God the Almighty) or "God is All Sufficient." The name is usually translated as God Almighty. The derivation of the word *Shaddai* is not known although it is believed by some to be derived from the root meaning "to heap benefits." The word *El* stands for God, while the origin of *Shaddai* is not known. According to some opinions, it is taken from the word breast and means nurturer or provider. It is also said to mean "the One who said dai," where the word *dai* means enough. It is said that when God created the universe, it expanded until He said "DAI!"

The name El Shaddai speaks of a God who is powerful enough to provide for all of the needs of humankind. In **Genesis** 17:1 the name is used for the first time. There, **Abraham** is given a promise from Almighty God. In **Exodus** (6:3), God told **Moses** that he had appeared to Abraham, **Isaac**, and **Jacob** as El Shaddai. He went on to state that He did not make Himself known to them by His **Holy** Name which is **Yahweh.**

Elah

An ancient Aramaic word meaning god. In **Daniel** (the Aramaic sections), Elah is used both for pagan gods and the true **God**. Elah is equivalent to the Hebrew "Eloah."

Elders

Revelation 4:11 tells of twenty-four spirits referred to as Elders. These Elders stand before the **throne of God**, praising **God** by singing: "You are worthy, our **Lord** and God, to receive glory and honor and power, for you created all things, and by your will they existed and were created."

Elect, Election

A term used by some religions to denote those who are chosen by **God** or the gods to dwell in the afterlife, in **Heaven**, or **paradise**. In ancient times, the Greeks believed that the earthly **children** fathered by the gods were destined to have wonderful lives and after **death** to dwell with the gods in paradise. To the **Egypt**ians, all Pharaohs were gods whose fate was sealed upon their birth. That fate being that they, upon their death, would dwell forever with **Osiris** in a marvelous afterlife. The term elect is also a Christian term which refers to God's choice of people who will go to Heaven, or in some Christian terminology, who will be saved. In other words, the elect are those called by God to **salvation.** These elect are selected not by their actions (i.e., morality, charity, kindness, etc.), but simply because God chooses them. This selection is believed to have occurred before the foundation of the world, making the elect predestined to go to Heaven.

This view of election was especially held by Calvinists who believed that the elect could be identified by their wealth, indicating God's favor and blessings toward them. According to **Mormon** doctrine, the elect of God are those men and women who have demonstrated great **faith**fulness to the teachings of **Jesus Christ.** Mormons believe that they will be elevated to godhood in the afterlife. For **Latter-Day Saints,** the term "godhood" denotes the attainment of such a state—one of having all **divine** attributes and doing as God does and being as God is. **Jehovah's Witnesses** teach that there are 144,000 individuals chosen (or elected) by God who will go to Heaven.

El-Elohe-Israel

A **Hebrew** term meaning, "**God** of Israel."

Elijah (My God Is Yahweh)

Hebrew **prophet**. Elijah was a prophet during the reign of King Ahab, and He had a very special relationship with **God**. Elijah's mission was to destroy the worship of foreign gods and to restore exclusive loyalty to God. God rewarded Elijah's earthly deeds in his departure from Earth. Elijah was taken from Earth in a chariot of fire enveloped in a whirlwind (2 Kings 2:11). According to ancient Jewish lore, Elijah became a great **angel** in **Heaven**.

Elizabeth (One Who Worships God)

Wife of the priest **Zechariah** and the mother of **John the Baptist** (the cousin of **Jesus** who led the way for Jesus' ministry). She was a descendent of the daughters of **Aaron** and a relative of Jesus' mother **Mary** (Luke 1:5; 36). Like Mary, **God** favored her. According to Luke 1:6, Elizabeth and her husband Zechariah pleased God by living good lives and obeying God's laws and commands. Elizabeth was therefore chosen by God to become pregnant and give birth to John the Baptist even though she and her husband were both elderly.

The account at Luke 1:8–13 states: "One day Zechariah was doing his work as a priest in the Temple, taking his turn in the daily service. According to the custom followed by the priests, he was chosen by lot to burn **incense** on the **altar**. So he went into the Temple of the **Lord**, while the crowd of people

outside prayed during the hour when the incense was burned. An **angel of the Lord** appeared to him, standing at the right side of the altar where the incense was burned. When Zechariah saw him, he was alarmed and felt afraid. But the angel said to him, 'Don't be afraid, Zechariah! God has heard your prayer, and your wife Elizabeth will bear you a son. You are to name him John.'"

El-Karubiyan (Those Brought Near to God)

The **Islamic** word for **Cherubim**. In Islamic beliefs the El-Karubiyan glorify **God** night and day continuously.

Elliott, Elisabeth

Christian Missionary. "To experience the glory of **God's** will for us means absolute trust. It means the will to do his will, and it means joy."

Elliott, Jim (1927–1956)

Christian Missionary. "Wherever you are, be all there. Live to the hilt every situation you believe to be the will of **God**."

Eloah

A **Hebrew** word for God. It is the singular form of **Elohim**. It also means "The Adorable One."

Elohim

The first name used for **God** in scripture. It is an ancient **Hebrew** word meaning "God." It is the plural form (three or more) of the singular noun *Eloah*. In the **Old Testament**, it is used 2,570 times as compared to 57 times for its singular form. The name is used in scripture when emphasizing God's might, His creative power, and His **attributes** of justice and rulership. It was also frequently used interchangeably with **Yahweh**, the proper name for **Israel's** God. Ancient Israelites also used Elohim as a proper plural form to refer to gods of **nations** other than Israel. For example, Elohim was used in reference first to pagan gods such as Baal-zebub and Ishtar, but it also was used to represent entire pantheons of pagan gods. However, the majority of appearances of this term came from the Hebrews in their reference to God. In addition, the term Elohim was sometimes used to refer to the **Sons of God (angels)**. Variations of Elohim include, **El**, Eloha, Elohai (my God), and Elohaynu (our God).

Emeli-hi
The Tuareg's (tribal people of the Sahara) name for **God.**

Emerson, Ralph Waldo (1803–1882)
One of America's most influential authors, philosophers, and thinkers. Born on May 25, 1803, in Boston, Massachusetts, Emerson began his career as a minister. He later helped to create the principles of **Transcendentalism,** a movement that flourished in New England during his time. Transcendentalists believed in **God's immanence** in **Man** and nature. They also believed in individualism, thinking that an individual's **intuition** is the highest source of knowledge. They stressed self-reliance and rejection of traditional authority, and Emerson eloquently articulated these views in many of his papers. About God, Emerson writes, "Standing on the bare ground—my head bathed by the blithe air and uplifted into infinite space—all mean egotism vanishes. I become a transparent eyeball; I am nothing; I see all; the currents of the Universal Being circulate through me; I am part and parcel of God."

Emmanouel
An ancient **Hebrew** name used when referring to **God.** In the **Bible's** Testament of **Solomon** it is a name used

to thwart **demons** that are so strong that only God can render them powerless.

Emmanuel (God Is with Us)
See Immanuel.

Empires
See Nations.

Endless and Eternal
Another name for **God** in the manner of **"Alpha and Omega,"** or "the Beginning and the End."

Enlightenment
A higher state of consciousness in which the person becomes aware of his connection with **God** and realizes he is a part of the **divine,** a part of God.

Enlil
See Assyria.

Enoch
A great **Hebrew prophet** who, according to the **Bible,** had a close relationship with **God.** He was the seventh descendent of **Adam and Eve;** the son of Jared, and father of Methuselah. In **Islamic** beliefs he is called Idris, and was also a prophet. He is characterized in the Bible as a righteous **man** devoted to God. Some translations refer to him as a "man who walked with God." Because of this devotion and unique relationship with God, tradition holds that Enoch never saw **death.** In fact, at the age of 365, God "took him," the Bible states. The account in **Genesis** reads: "Enoch lived in fellowship with God for 300 years. He lived to be 365 years old. He spent his life in fellowship with God, and then he disappeared, because God took him away" (Genesis 5:22-24). During the time of Enoch, 365 years was considered a short lifespan. His son Methuselah lived to be 969. However, because he was a man

dedicated to God, a righteous man, it is thought that Enoch was too good of a person to continue to dwell on the Earth, and that is why God "took him."

Legend has it that upon his arrival in **Heaven,** God transformed him into a mighty **angel.** Enoch's unique and mysterious death, plus the fact that he died at a mere 365, started an Enoch **mythology** which can be found in the Book of Enoch, the lengthiest work in the **Pseudepigrapha.** The book, ascribed pseudonymously to Enoch, consists of seven sections. However, the underlying theme of the book is God's coming Judgment.

Epictetus (c. 55–c. 135 A.D.)

Greek Stoic philosopher. According to his works, Epictetus was concerned primarily with the issue of morality in his attempt to define the good. He emphasized separating one's self from the concerns of the world and practicing detachment *(apatheia)* which means "the mastering of passions." He stressed that because humankind can neither know nor control their destiny, they must accept **God's** unchanging will. He felt that humans are mainly limited, irrational creatures, but that the world, as ruled by God through His pure and limitless logic, is forever perfect.

Eschatology

The study of the end of the world or **God's Judgment Day.** The word is derived from the Greek word *eschatos* which means last, and *logos* which means study.

Essence of God

A phrase used to convey **God's** personal **attributes.** The attributes traditionally include: **omnibenevolence, omnipotence, omnipresence, omniscience.** They also include spirituality, **grace, mercy,** and **love.** Love is believed to be the strongest of all God's qualities

and is at the very core of God's essence. Ancient Jewish tradition holds that God's love is so strong that it radiates from Him down through the heavens and is filtered to the Earth through the **angels.** God's attributes are believed to be present in God at all times, but not all are manifest at the same time. God's attributes are revealed to humans through the various religions of the Earth and through human beings themselves, who are made in the **image of God.** See Divine Attributes.

Essenes

A Jewish community in Palestine at the time of **Jesus;** its members practiced strict adherence to Jewish **law.** The sect flourished from the first century B.C. through the first century A.D. They were also the writers of the Dead Sea Scrolls. The **love** of **God** was a fundamental teaching of the Essenes, but they also taught love of virtue, and love of one's fellow humans.

Eternal

A **divine attribute** of God meaning that He is timeless, **everlasting,** and enduring forever. It means that God is without beginning or end.

Eternal Being

One of **God's** titles.

Eternal Death

The circumstance of a **sinner** being forever separated from **God.**

Eternal Life

A term used for those who will reside forever with **God** in **Heaven/Paradise.**

Eternal Secrets

Another name for **God's Mysteries of Heaven.**

Eternal, The

One of **God's** titles.

Euphrates

The largest river in western Asia. In **Hebrew** it is called Perath; in Assyria it was called Purat; in the **Persian** cuneiform it was Ufratush; and in Greek it was Euphrates, which means "sweet water." The Euphrates played an important role in **God's covenant** with **Abraham** and his descendants. The Euphrates River marks the northern boundary of the territory promised by God to **Israel.**

In the **Bible,** there are several references to the Euphrates. It is first mentioned in **Genesis** 2:10,14 as one of the rivers of **Paradise.** There it says: "A stream flowed in Eden and watered the garden; beyond Eden it divided into four rivers. The fourth river is the Euphrates." It is next referred to in connection with the covenant which God made with Abraham at Genesis 15:18. There God promised to Abraham's descendants the land from the river of **Egypt** to the river Euphrates. The passage reads: "On that day the **Lord** made a covenant with Abram, saying, to your descendants I give this land, from the river of Egypt to the great river, the river Euphrates." This covenant was afterwards fulfilled in the extended conquests of **David** (see accounts at 2 Samuel 8:2–14, 1 Chronicles 18:3, and 1 Kings 4:24).

God also speaks of the Euphrates at **Deuteronomy** 1:6–7 where it says, "The Lord our God spoke to us at Horeb, saying, 'You have stayed long enough at this mountain. Resume your journey, and go into the hill country of the Amorites as well as into the neighboring regions—the Arabah, the hill country, the Shephelah, the Negeb, and the seacoast—the land of the Canaanites and the Lebanon, as far as the great river, the river Euphrates.'" Deuteronomy 11:24 says, "Every place on which you set foot shall be yours; your territory shall extend from the wilderness to the Lebanon and from the River, the river Euphrates, to the Western Sea." **Joshua** 1:4 states, "From the wilderness and the Lebanon as far as the great river, the river Euphrates, all the land of the Hittites, to the Great Sea in the west shall be your territory."

Revelation (9:13–15) mentions four **angels** who are bound in the great Euphrates River. They are let loose to kill **sinful** men during the last days of God's great war. The account states, "And the sixth angel sounded, and I heard a voice from the four horns of the **golden altar** which is before God, saying to the sixth angel which had the **trumpet,** loose the four angels which are bound in the great river Euphrates."

Eve (Life Giver)

The first created woman and the wife of **Adam** according to Judeo-Christian beliefs. She is considered to be the mother of all humankind, all **nations,** tribes and tongues. The **Bible** states that Eve was created by **God** to provide companionship to Adam. In God's revelation of **creation** to **Moses,** God made it clear that Eve had been created in God's image, just as Adam had. **Genesis** 1:27 states, "So God created **man** in His own image; in the image of God He created him; male and female He created them." According to Genesis, Eve was tricked by a serpent (said to be a disguised **Satan**) into tasting the fruit from the **tree of knowledge** of good and **evil,** which had been forbidden to them by God. It was the one and only thing that God had denied them and clearly instructed them to avoid. When the serpent spoke to her, he accused God of lying and of holding back knowledge from her and Adam (Genesis 3:1-7). "The serpent said to her, 'Did God really tell you not to eat fruit from any tree in the garden?' Eve replied, 'We may eat the fruit of any tree in the garden. Except the tree in the middle of it. God told us not to eat the fruit of that tree or even touch it; if we do, we will die.' The serpent next said, 'That's not true; you will not die. God said that because he knows that when you eat it, you will be like God and know what is good and what is bad.'" Because of what the serpent had said to her a seed of doubt was planted in her heart and Eve ate from the tree. Later her husband Adam ate from it as well. The two were immediately cast out of **paradise** with God declaring that because of her disobedience, Eve's pain in childbearing would increase and she would be subject to her husband. After leaving paradise, Eve gave birth to many children, **Cain** being the first son and **Abel** being the second. However, **Adam and Eve's** life was hard, and the two who apparently lost their immortal status once they **sin**ned, eventually died. The children of Eve have since been in constant turmoil deciding between good and evil.

Everlasting

The word used when referring to the life span or life of **God.** God has no beginning and no ending. God is **eternal.** His **eternal life** is properly called "everlasting life."

Evil

There are two kinds of evil: moral and physical. Moral evil (i.e., theft, murder, etc.) is willful **sin,** while physical evil (i.e., famine, illness, natural disasters, etc.) is natural harm. Why is there evil? Throughout the centuries there has been much cruelty, bloodshed, and outright evil that has caused suffering to millions people, causing many to ask, "If there is a **God,** why does He permit evil?" There are many theories on the subject. One noted idea was that of Saint **Augustine.** He wrote, "For the **almighty** God would never permit the existence of anything evil among His works, if He were not so omnipotent and good that He can bring good even out of evil. For what is that which we call evil but the

absence of good?" This means that evil has not been created by God, whose **creation** is entirely good. Evil is the privation, or absence, of good, as darkness is the absence of **light. Jews** and Christians believe the answer to this question is found in the opening chapters of **Genesis,** in which the creation of the world and all in it are described as perfect, happy, and without suffering or anything remotely evil. The first **man** and woman were put in a beautiful **paradise** setting, a garden home called Eden. God told them to cultivate the Earth and take care of it. He also told them to be fruitful and become many and fill the Earth (Genesis 1:28; 2:15).

God, like any parent, took care of their needs. He gave them one order, and that was not to eat from the **tree of knowledge** of good and evil. It was the one thing that God denied them. However, a time came when **Adam and Eve,** as the first humans, chose to disobey God, and at the suggestion of the famous serpent, ate the **forbidden fruit** introducing evil into the world. Afterward the two were cast out of their paradise home. The belief is that when the first couple chose to sin they fell from perfection, therefore alienating themselves from God. Afterward, when they had **children,** the children reflected their parents and were also born imperfect and into sin. In addition, the absence of God leaves a void. Because of God's absence in their life, because of this void, there was more of a chance of wrongdoing. This departure from God's protection then opened a floodgate of sin, wrongdoing, and what have come to be known as evil acts.

Another point of view taken from some of the metaphysical thought popular today (also found in Judaic belief) is that evil is a necessary evil, meaning that the purpose of evil is to teach humans the meaning of good. The belief is that we are all **souls** in a physical body that existed first in **Heaven.** It was our choice to come to the Earth to experience, grow, and learn lessons. The fact that there is evil actually benefits our souls as we grow and learn from these experiences. Ultimately, the purpose of evil is to teach us the meaning of good. This is accomplished by living and surviving life in this world.

In many of the world's religions, evil is attributed to the existence of an evil deity, usually an **adversary** of God. Some of the most notorious include the **Devil** in Judeo-Christian and **Islamic** beliefs and **Angra Mainyu** in Zoroastrianism, both of which have been attributed similar personality traits.

In Judeo-Christian and Islamic beliefs the Devil is God's adversary, also known as **Satan** or in Islam as **Iblis.** Satan and his followers are credited with causing all of the evil in the world.

The **spirit** of darkness in Zoroastrianism is Angra Mainyu. He is **Ahura Mazda's** (God) adversary. He is also called "the destructive Spirit." Zoroastrians believe him to be the creator of **death,** disease, and evil, and hold him responsible for all of mankind's sorrows.

Excellent One, The

In 1 **Enoch, God** is described as "the Excellent One."

Exemplarism

The doctrine that all **creation** is patterned after exemplar causes or ideas in the mind of **God.**

Exodus

In the biblical Book of Exodus, under **Moses'** direction, **God** rescues the **Israelites** from bondage in **Egypt** and introduces them to a new beginning and a new life. The Exodus included God's deliverance of the **Hebrews** from slavery, their wandering in the wilderness, the **covenant** with God at **Mount Sinai,**

and the provision of the **tabernacle** and the **ark of the covenant.** The book is set in the Nile Delta in Egypt and the Sinai peninsula around 1325–1225 B.C.

Extradimensional Nature of God

The belief that **God** exists in several dimensions at once. The idea is that God could not have created the universe if He were in it, He therefore must have existed in another dimension during the **creation.** In fact, the Judeo-Christian **Bible** states that the physical universe cannot hold Him. According to particle physics and relativity, at least ten dimensions of space existed at the creation of the universe. It is believed that God must be able to operate in all of those ten dimensions, plus more, in order to have created the universe.

Ezekiel (God Strengthens)

A major **prophet** of the **Old Testament.** During the exile of the **Jews, God** used Ezekiel to bring comfort and hope to the people. Much of Ezekiel's message regards **sin** and judgment. His book includes a vision of God, the parable of the two eagles and the vine, prophecies against foreign **nations,** and the vision of the valley of dry bones, which God brings to life. In his message to the **Israelites,** Ezekiel proclaimed that God in His magnificence and holiness could not accept impurity and the worship of **false gods** from his people. He foresaw the fall of Jerusalem, but spoke of the hope of repentance, restoration, and renewed worship. In his vision of God, Ezekiel tells of seeing the actual dwelling place of God: "The **Lord's** spirit lifted me up and took me into the inner courtyard, where I saw that the Temple was filled with the **glory of the Lord.** I heard the Lord speak to me out of the Temple. 'Mortal **man,** here is my throne. I will live here among the people of Israel and rule them forever.'"

F

> God must not be thought of as a physical being, or as having any kind of body. He is pure mind. He moves and acts without needing any corporeal space, or size, or form, or color, or any other property of matter.
>
> —*Origen*

Face of God

A term used in biblical times. During this period, to seek the Face of **God** meant attending public worship. Over the centuries there have been various references to the Face of God, which some call the **Beatific Vision.** In the **Bible,** there are scriptures that refer to the Face of God. Psalms 27:8 says: "'Come,' my heart says, 'seek his face!' Your face, **Lord,** do I seek." Also at Psalms 34:16 we find, "The face of the Lord is against **evil**doers." **Exodus** 33:11 says, "Thus the Lord used to speak to **Moses** face to face, as one speaks to a friend." At the very end of his famous poem, *The Divine Comedy,* Dante asks to see God's Face. American hymn writer and poetess Fanny **Crosby,** who was blind, hoped that God would be the first face she saw in the afterlife. **Gandhi,** in a heartfelt and dramatic statement declared, "What I have been striving and pining to achieve these thirty years is to see God face to face."

Faith

A word that refers to **Man's spiritual** trust in **God.**

Fall of Man

According to Judeo-Christian beliefs, the **Fall** of **Man** can be traced back to the beginning of humankind's history, to the newly created man and woman in the **Garden of Eden. God** created the Garden of Eden for **Adam, Eve,** and their offspring as a place in which they could reside peacefully and happily forever. There they lived a life of ease, free from pain and the everyday struggles we face today. Their lifestyle and that of their future **children** depended upon their obedience to one simple command given to them by God: to not eat from the **tree of knowledge** of good and **evil.**

The account states, "Now the snake (also serpent) was the most cunning animal that the **Lord** God had made. The snake asked the woman, 'Did God really tell you not to eat from any tree in the garden?' 'We may eat the fruit of any tree in the garden,' the woman answered, 'except the tree in the middle of it. God told us not to eat the fruit of that tree or even touch it; if we do, we will die.' The snake replied, 'That's not true; you will not die. God said that because he knows that when you eat it, you will be like God and know what is good and what is bad'" (**Genesis** 2:15–17).

Adam and Eve disobeyed God's command and the "Fall of Man" began. In Genesis 3:1–7 it says, "The woman saw how beautiful the tree was and how good its fruit would be to eat, and she thought how wonderful it would be to become wise. So she took some of the fruit and ate it. Then she gave some to her husband, and he also ate it. As soon as they had eaten it, they were given understanding and realized that they were naked; so they sewed fig leaves together and covered themselves." This act of rebellion shattered their close relationship with God. God banished the couple from their **paradise** home and sent them into an uncultivated world where they had to learn to fend for themselves. God addressed Eve this way, "I will increase your trouble in pregnancy and your pain in giving birth. In spite of this, you will still have desire for your husband, yet you will be subject to him" (Genesis 3:16). God said to Adam, "You listened to your wife and ate the fruit which I told you not to eat. Because of what you have done, the ground will be under a **curse.** You will have to work hard all your life to make it produce enough food for you. You were made from soil, and you will become soil again" (Genesis 3:17-19). "So God sent him out of the Garden of Eden and made him cultivate the soil from which he had been formed. Then at the east side of the garden he put living creatures and a flaming sword which turned in all directions. This was to keep anyone from coming near the tree that gives life" (Genesis 3:23–24).

As a result of their disobedience, wrongdoing and **sin** were introduced into the world. Their children that followed and all humans since have been affected by this one act. They all suffered the consequences of the first parents. John **Milton** wrote about the Fall in his poem *Paradise Lost,* in which he retold the story of Man's first rebellious act to God and Man's consequential loss of paradise. In *Paradise Lost,* Milton shows his readers that "to obey is best" and that if we do then we will ultimately regain access to a different paradise in **Heaven.** The entire account of the Fall of Man can be read in Genesis, chapters 2 and 3.

Fall, The

See Fall of Man.

Fallen Angels

Angels who have fallen from **God's grace.** The idea of "fallen angels" is found mainly in **Judaism, Christianity,** and **Islam.** One story tells of a **great rebellion** that occurred in **Heaven.** This rebellion is believed to have happened before the **creation** of **Man.** There was a **war in Heaven. Satan** (a former angel said to be of great beauty and in some legends loyal to God) rebelled against God and in the process found some followers among the angels who warred against God's army led by the Archangel **Michael.** Michael and God's heavenly army were victorious and cast Satan and his hordes toward the vicinity of the Earth.

The **Bible** states, "And war broke out in heaven: Michael and his angels battled with the dragon and the dragon and its angels battled but did not prevail, neither was a place found for them any longer in heaven. So down the great dragon was hurled, the original serpent, the one called **Devil** and Satan, who is misleading the entire inhabited earth; he was hurled down to the earth, and his angels were hurled down with him" (Revelation 12:7–9).

Another account is that of the **"Watchers"** referred to in the Bible as "the **sons of God."** These angels noticed the **"daughters of men"** and found them to be beautiful and came to the Earth and took them as wives, forsaking their positions in Heaven.

Genesis 6:2 states: "Then the sons of the true God began to notice the daughters of men, that they were good-looking; and they went taking wives for themselves, namely, all whom they chose." The Watchers, because of this act, were forbidden from reentering Heaven.

False God

A god that is invented by **Man.** It is a controversial term since each individual, each culture, no matter what they are calling god, considers their god to be real. In the **Bible** any god of another culture was considered a false god.

Farabi, Al- (870–950)

Notable **Iranian Islamic** philosopher. Al-Farabi studied in Baghdad and later flourished in Aleppo as a Sufi mystic. He was the first **Muslim** to bring the philosophies of **Plato** and **Aristotle** to the Arab world. He strove to reconcile Aristotelian ideas with Islamic principles. He wrote in the tradition of Aristotle about metaphysics, politics, and music, and was regarded by Arabs as the greatest philosophical authority after Aristotle. He often spoke about his ideas on who and what **God** is. He believed that the universe emanates continuously from God and taught that people should work toward becoming one with God. He also held that God created the world through the use of rational intelligence.

About God, he wrote, "It is very difficult to know what God is because of the limitation of our intellect and its union with matter. Just as **light** is the principle by which colours become visible, in like manner it would seem logical to say that a perfect light should produce a perfect vision. Instead, the very opposite occurs. A perfect light dazzles the vision. The same is true of God. The imperfect knowledge we have of God is due to the fact that He is infinitely perfect. That explains why His infinitely perfect being bewilders our mind. But if we could strip our nature of all that we call 'matter', then certainly our knowledge of His being would be quite perfect."

Fasting

The abstinence from food for the purposes of showing devotion to **God.**

Father

Only in the **Bible's New Testament** does the word "father" become a proper name for **God.** This was consistent with **Christ's** message to the world of a loving God, not the God of wrath as depicted in the **Old Testament.** See also Abba.

Father Sky

The name of the male aspect of **God** in **Native American** religion.

Female Aspect of God

See Shekinah.

Fenelon, François (1651–1715)

Roman Catholic theologian. Fenelon was born in France in 1651, heir to seven centuries of noble ancestry. At a young age he zealously embraced the teachings of **Christianity,** and, desiring to be like **Jesus,** entered the seminary of Saint-Sulpice. He was ordained in 1675 and became Archbishop of Cambrai in 1695. He wrote several works, notably *The Adventures of Telemachus* (which received the French king's censure for its political undertones) and *Explanation of the Sayings of the Saints on the Interior Life.* This book was condemned by the Pope, after which Fénelon retired to Cambrai.

About **God,** Fenelon wrote: "The smallest things become great when God requires them of us; they are small only in themselves; they are always great when they are done for God, and when they serve to unite us with Him **eternally**. . . ." "Tell God all that is in your heart, as one unloads one's heart to a dear friend. . . . People who have no secrets from each other never want for subjects of conversation; they do not . . . weigh their words, because there is nothing to be kept back. . . . Blessed are they who attain to such familiar, unreserved intercourse with God."

Fidi Mukullu

Creator god of the Bena Lulua people of Zaire.

Finuweigh

A Philippine creator god.

Fire and Brimstone

Brimstone, an old name for sulfur, is generally found in volcanic areas. **Genesis** says that **God** destroyed the cities of **Sodom** and **Gomorrah** with fire and brimstone. It is believed by some that the **Bible** may have been referring to a volcano (Genesis 19:24).

First and the Last

A title used for **God.** It implies God's sovereignty. See Alpha and Omega.

Five Pillars, The

See Islam.

Five Ways

A standard term used in describing the five **arguments for the existence of God** as given by Thomas **Aquinas** in his *Summa Theologica.* See Causality Argument.

Flood

Many versions of an ancient flood story exist around the world in various cultures and religions. Most involve **God** or a god bringing about a flood that covers the Earth, often sent to purify the Earth of humans. Most versions involve a hero and possibly his family surviving it. The survivors of such floods often became the progenitors of a new race of human beings.

MESOPOTAMIA. In the eleventh tablet of the Semitic **Babylonian** epic of the legendary King Gilgamesh, there is a flood story which some believe is the source of the biblical flood story. The story involves a legendary king named Gilgamesh who was on a quest for **eternal life.** Along the way he meets Utnapishtim, who has been given the gift of immortality by the gods. Ut napishtim was a hero of old who had survived a flood by building a boat.

SUMERIANS. The Sumerian flood myth is the oldest (about 2000 B.C.). In the Sumerian story, the gods decide to destroy humankind with a flood. The god Enki, who is opposed to this decision, instructs a worthy man named Ziusudra to build a large boat in which to save himself, his family, and a few other people, along with **animals.** In the later second-millennium B.C. Babylonian version, the god Ziusudra has become Utnapishtim, and Enki has become Ea.

HINDUISM. The Hindu god **Vishnu's** first **incarnation** was as Matsya, a fish. Vishnu took this form to warn the first **man,** Manu, of a flood. He sent Manu a ship and ordered him to load it with the Vedas and two animals of every species, thereby saving all life from **destruction.**

GREECE. In Greek **mythology, Zeus** sent a flood to destroy the humans of the Bronze Age. According to lore, only a few survived that flood including a man and woman who were inside a chest.

ROME. In Roman lore, Jupiter, angered at the **evil** ways of humanity, resolved to destroy it. He was about to set the Earth to burning, but considered that that might set **Heaven** itself on fire, so he decided to flood the Earth instead. With Neptune's help, he caused a storm and an earthquake to flood everything but the summit of Parnassus, where Deucalion and his wife Pyrrha came by boat and found refuge.

LITHUANIA. From Heaven the supreme god Pramzimas saw nothing but war and strife among humans. In his wrath, he sent a flood to destroy the Earth and all its inhabitants. As Pramzimas looked down on the Earth to observe the progress of the rains, he mistakenly dropped shells from the nuts he was eating. One shell landed on the top of a tall mountain. There, people who were fleeing the flood along with some animals climbed into the shell to escape the waters. Later, Pramzimas ordered the rains to subside. The people in the shell dispersed, except for one elderly couple who stayed where they landed. To reassure them, God sent the **rainbow** and told them to jump over the bones of the Earth nine times. They did so, and up sprang nine couples, from which the nine Lithuanian tribes descended.

EGYPT. In Egypt, people had become rebellious. Because of this, Atum (God) decided to destroy all he had made and return the Earth to the Primordial Water, its original state.

JUDAISM. Perhaps the most popular flood story is that of **Noah** found at **Genesis** 6:1–9:17. Biblical scholars date the writing of Genesis, from which the story of Noah is taken, at sometime between 2,900 and 2,400 years ago. In that account God sends a great flood to punish **sinful** humanity. The **Hebrew** story emphasizes the idea of humanity's sinfulness. The Flood is a punishment, and Noah is saved so that humankind can be reborn in a cleansed state. Noah, one of the early Hebrew **patriarchs,** was a decent and kindly man who found favor in God's eyes. He lived during a period when man had become evil and sinful, doing nothing

but bad in God's eyes. It was so bad that God came to regret having created humankind, and in His anger, decided to destroy all living things by a flood. God said to Noah, "I have decided to put an end to all mankind. I will destroy them completely, because the world is full of their violent deeds."

The **Bible** tells us that God "gave Noah instructions for building an **ark.** The Ark would be large enough to hold his entire family as well as two of every animal on the earth. When the ark was completed, God sent the rains. Noah and all inside of the ark were saved. The rest of humanity was destroyed. Afterward, God promised that he would never destroy the world by water again. He sent a rainbow as a sign of his promise." Scientists today say they have found evidence of a catastrophic flood thousands of years ago.

Forbidden Fruit

See Adam; Eve; Fall of Man.

Fountain

The source or the spring from which water flows. In the **Bible, God** is called "the fountain of living water." He says, "For my people have committed two **evils**: they have forsaken me, the fountain of living water, and dug out cisterns for themselves, cracked cisterns that can hold no water" (**Jeremiah** 2:13). Psalms 36:9, in speaking about God, says, "For with you is the fountain of life; in your **light** we see light."

Four Horsemen of the Apocalypse

Four allegorical figures found in Revelation. According to Revelation (6:1–8), **God** sends each of the horsemen out with different missions. They appear at the onset of the cataclysmic events, destined to destroy the world as we know it. The rider on the white horse has had several interpretations.

However, he is believed by most to represent **Jesus.** The rider on the red horse is war; the rider on the black horse is famine; and the rider on the pale horse is **death.**

Francis of Assisi, Saint (1181–1226)

Founder of the Franciscans. The son of a rich Italian merchant named Pietro di Bernardone, he underwent a conversion at age twenty-two after **God** spoke to him in a ruined **church.** From that day forward he put God at the center of his life. Having renounced his wealth, he became known for his generosity to the sick and needy and for his devoutness to God. Francis called for simplicity of life and humility before God. As a result of his piousness, Saint Francis has been revered for centuries for his message of **love,** joy, and peace. He is perhaps most known for his **prayer** to God entitled: "**Lord,** make me an instrument of thy peace!" The prayer emphasizes Francis' love of God and desire to serve. It is as follows:

> Lord, make me an instrument of thy peace! That where there is hatred, I may bring love. That where there is wrong, I may bring the spirit of forgiveness. That where there is discord, I may bring harmony. That where there is error, I may bring truth. That where there is doubt, I may bring **faith.** That where there is despair, I may bring hope. That where there are shadows, I may bring light. That where there is sadness, I may bring joy. Lord, grant that I may seek rather to comfort, than to be comforted. To understand, than to be understood. To love, than to be loved. For it is by self-forgetting that one finds. It is by forgiving that one is forgiven. It is by dying that one awakens to **Eternal Life.**

Free Will

The ability to choose a course of action or make a decision without being subject to restraints. It is said that the greatest gift of **God** to humans is free will, allowing humans to move through their spiritual evolution at their own pace. Humans, however, are not the only people in God's **creation** who are believed to have free will. The **angels** are also thought to have this free choice of action.

Origen of Alexandria maintained that God created a number of **spiritual** beings who were equal and free. Some, through their free will, chose to leave the their positions in **Heaven** and slowly drifted away from God, some drifting so far away that they became dark spirits (or **demons**). In the metaphysical arena it is believed among some that as spirits living in Heaven with God, we choose through our free will to come to Earth (with God's blessing) to perfect our **souls.** It is believed that we choose our parents and life circumstances according to this free will, and that our lives on Earth have a plan. Once we are born into this lifetime however, we must stick with that **divine** plan, and our free will then becomes limited as we live out the paths that we charted for ourselves.

Italian humanist philosopher Pico Della Mirandola spoke on the subject of free will, "God placed **man** in the middle of the world without a secure place, without a distinctive identity, without a special function, while all these things were granted to the rest of his creatures. Man is created neither earthly nor heavenly; he can degenerate into a beast, he can ascend to heaven; everything depends solely and entirely on his will. It is granted to man to possess what he wished, to be what he wants." In **Christianity** the belief in free will is a means of explaining the existence of **evil** by claiming that God gave His human creations free will, defined as the ability to make a choice outside of any previous programming.

Fruits of the Spirit

According to the **New Testament**, an approved person in the eyes of **God** would exemplify the fruits of the spirit. These desirable qualities were laid out in Galatians 5:22–23: **love**, joy, peace, longsuffering, kindness, goodness, faithfulness, gentleness, and self-control.

Fuller, Richard Buckminster (1895–1983)

A renowned American scientist and philosopher. He is considered to be one of the key innovators in the twentieth century and one of the first futurists and global thinkers. It was Fuller who coined the term "Spaceship Earth." He is noted for his innovative use of technology to deal with global problems facing humanity in the second half of the twentieth century. Says Fuller on life's success and **God:** "I am quite confident there is nothing that I have undertaken to do that others couldn't do equally well or better under the same economic circumstances. I was supported only by my **faith** in God and my vigorously pursued working assumption that it is God's intent to make humans an economic success so that they can and may in due course fulfill an essential—and only mind-renderable—functioning in the Universe."

G

There is no other God, nor has there been heretofore, nor will there be hereafter, except God the Father unbegotten, without beginning, from whom is all beginning.
—*Saint Patrick*

Gabriel (God Is My Strength)

One of the two highest-ranking **archangels** in **Judaism, Christianity,** and **Islam.** He is thought to be one of the closest **angels** to **God.** He holds the titles of Angel of Revelation, Hero of God, and **Voice of God**, because of the work he performs for God. He is symbolized by the **trumpet** which represents God's voice. According to scripture, his work predominately consists of delivering important announcements to humans on God's behalf. Therefore, he is also referred to as God's personal **spokesman.**

Gabriel is first encountered in the **Old Testament** when he appears to **Daniel** (8:16) to explain a vision. He later appears to Daniel a second time to announce the coming of the **Messiah.** In the **New Testament** he announces the birth of **John the Baptist** to **Zechariah** (Luke 1:11–22), and the birth of Jesus to **Mary** (Luke 1:26–33). During the Middle Ages, Christians believed Gabriel to be the Angel of **Light.** In the beliefs of the Essenes, he was the Angel of Life.

Additional titles held by Gabriel include: Chief Ambassador to Humanity, Chief Ambassador to God, Ruling Prince of the **Cherubim**, Divine Herald, Angel of Revelation, Angel of Truth, Prince of Justice, Trumpeter of the **Last Judgment**, Angel of Vengeance, Angel of Death, Angel of the Annunciation, Angel of the Resurrection, Angel of Revelation, Angel of **Mercy**, and Angel of Judgment.

ISLAM. In Islam, Gabriel is called **Jibril.** It was Jibril who revealed the **Koran** to **Muhammad.** For this reason he is also called the Faithful **Spirit**, Faithful Servant, and the Bringer of Good News. He first appeared to Muhammad when he was meditating on a mountain near **Mecca.** Stunned, Muhammad turned away. However, everywhere he turned Jibril's face appeared. On another occasion, Jibril appeared and ordered Muhammad to call men to God. One night, angels appeared to Muhammad to prepare him for a journey through **Heaven.** Jibril awakened Muhammad and removed his heart. After washing and purifying the heart, Jibril put it back into Muhammad's body. Muhammad was then filled with wisdom and **faith.** On the Night of Glory, when Jibril dictated the Koran to Muhammad, his wings were outstretched, his face illuminated, and between his eyes was written, "There is no God, but God, and Muhammad is the **prophet** of God."

Galilei, Galileo
(1564–1642)

Italian physicist and astronomer. He is credited with inventing the microscope, and building a telescope with which he studied and discovered sunspots and lunar **mountains** and valleys. His most spectacular discovery was that of the four major satellites of **Jupiter.** In the world of physics, he uncovered the **laws** of falling bodies and the motions of projectiles. He also discovered the phases of the planet Venus. Regarding **God** and the idea of religion, Galileo made the following comments:

"I do not feel obliged to believe that same God who endowed us with sense, reason, and intellect had intended for us to forgo their use."

"I think that in the discussion of natural problems we ought to begin not with the Scriptures, but with experiments, and demonstrations."

"It vexes me when they would constrain science by the authority of the Scriptures, and yet do not consider themselves bound to answer reason and experiment."

"It is surely harmful to souls to make it a heresy to believe what is proved."

Gallup, George
(1901–1984)

American public opinion analyst and statistician. About **God,** Gallup once stated, "I could prove God statistically. Take the human body alone—the chance that all its functions would just happen is a statistical monstrosity."

Gandhi, Mahatma
(1869–1948)

Indian nationalist leader, who, appalled by the treatment of Indians, established his country's freedom through a nonviolent revolution. Even though Gandhi grew up Hindu, and lived his life according to those beliefs,

he remained open-minded about other religions, believing that they all lead to the truth of **God.** Said Gandhi, "I consider myself a Hindu, Christian, **Muslim,** Jew, Buddhist, and Confucian." He believed that Truth is God and so in seeking to know Truth, we seek to know God. He felt that all people were brothers and sisters because all came from the same God, and each individual carries God within him.

On the subject of non-violence and God, Gandhi stated: "The **spirit** of non-violence necessarily leads to humility. Non-violence means reliance on God, the **rock** of ages. If we would seek his aid, we must approach Him with a humble and contrite heart." About God, Gandhi said: "God is **Light,** not darkness. God is **Love,** not hate. God is truth, not untruth. God alone is great." And finally, "What I have been striving and pining to achieve these thirty years is to see God face to face."

Garden of Eden

The place created by **God** as the home for the first human beings. It was a beautiful, lush garden **paradise,** full of exquisite fruit-bearing plants. **Genesis** says this about the **creation** of the Garden after the first **man** was created: "Then the **Lord** God planted a garden in Eden, in the East, and there he put the man he had formed. He made all kinds of beautiful trees grow there and produce good fruit. In the middle of the garden stood the tree that gives life and the tree that gives knowledge of what is good and what is bad. Then the Lord God placed the man in the Garden of Eden to cultivate it and guard it. He told him, 'You may eat the fruit of any tree in the garden, except the tree that gives knowledge of what is good and what is bad. You must not eat the fruit of that tree; if you do, you will die the same day'" (Genesis 2:8–17). However, **Adam** and his wife **Eve** were later expelled from the Garden for disobeying God's command and eating the **forbidden fruit.** After the expulsion of the first couple, God placed two **angels** and a turning, flaming sword east of Eden to guard the **Tree of Life.**

Garden of Gethsemane

A garden near the Mount of Olives, East of Jerusalem beyond the Kidron valley. The Garden was a place where **Jesus** would go in private to approach God in **prayer.** On the eve of his **death,** Jesus went to the Garden of Gethsemane to pray for comfort and strength from God, saying: "**Father,** if you are willing, remove this cup from me; yet, not my will but yours be done." God immediately sent an **angel** to the garden to strengthen him. The account states, "Then an angel from **heaven** appeared to him and gave him strength" (Luke 22:42–43). The Garden of Gethsemane was also the place where Jesus was betrayed by Judas.

Gathas (Songs)

The seventeen hymns of **Zoroaster,** written around 1200 B.C. They are ranked among the most precious gems of the world's religious literature. They were written by Zoroaster to praise and glorify **Ahura Mazda,** the name of God in Zoroastrianism. The following is a line taken from a song in the Gathas in honor of God. "When I held Thee in my very eyes, then I realized Thee in my mind, O Mazda, as the First and also the Last for all eternity" (Yasna, 31:8).

Gauguin, Paul (1848–1903)

French painter and woodcut artist. Gauguin included **angels** in many of his works. One of his most famous works, *Vision After the Sermon, Jacob Wrestling with the Angel,* portrays the account of Jacob wrestling with an **angel of God** or as some say, **God** himself.

Gautama, Siddhartha

See Buddhism.

Gematria

See Numbers.

Genesis

The first Book of the **Old Testament.** The events in Genesis take place around 2000–1650 B.C., and its authorship, is attributed to **Moses** under **divine** inspiration. The name Genesis means "birth." The basic aim of Genesis is to relate all of **creation** and history to **God,** and to give an account of what God has done. It begins with the pronouncement that God created the universe, and ends with an assurance that God will continue showing concern for His people. Throughout Genesis, the main character is God, who judges and reprimands wrongdoers, guides and assists His people, and helps shape their lives.

Genesis can be divided into two parts. Chapters 1–11 tell of the creation of the world, humankind, and also the **fall** of humankind from a state of perfection, introducing the beginning of **sin** and suffering in the world. It gives the accounts of **Adam and Eve, Cain** and **Abel,** the great **Flood,** and the tower of **Babylon.** Chapters 12–50 give the history of the early ancestors of the **Israel**ites. It covers the stories of **Abraham, Isaac, Jacob,** Jacob's twelve sons, his son **Joseph,** and the events that brought Jacob, his sons, and their families to live in **Egypt.**

OUTLINE OF CONTENTS. Creation of the universe and of humankind (Genesis 1:1–2:25); The beginning of sin and suffering (Genesis 3:1–24); From Adam to **Noah** (Genesis 4:1–5:32); Noah and the flood (Genesis 6:1–10:32); The tower of Babylon

(Genesis 11:1–9); From Shem to Abram (Genesis 11:10–32); The **patriarchs:** Abraham, Isaac, Jacob (Genesis 12:1–35:29); The descendants of Esau (Genesis 36:1–43); Joseph and his brothers (Genesis 37:1–45:28); and the Israelites in Egypt (Genesis 46:1–50:26).

Ghanian Proverb

"There is no need to point out **God** to a child."

Gideon

One of the **Bible's** heroes. Gideon, the fifth judge of **Israel**, was the youngest son of Joash, from the Abierzite line of Manasseh. Although his father was a worshiper of **Baal**, Gideon believed in **God**. Gideon was called to be a judge during the seven years that the **Hebrews** came under the rule of Midian. The Midianites would attack the Hebrews and destroy their crops, leaving them with nothing. Out of fear for their lives, and as a means of shielding themselves, they made their homes in dens and caves in the **mountains.** They begged God to deliver them. God, who had heard their **prayers** from **Heaven**, chose Gideon to deliver them. He sent an **angel** to inform Gideon of his **divine** appointment, and to assure him that God would be with him during the war with the Midianites.

The account in the Book of Judges (6:11–14) says: "The **Lord's** angel came to the village of Ophrah and sat under the oak tree that belonged to Joash, a **man** of the clan of Abiezer. His son Gideon was threshing some wheat secretly in a wine press, so that the Midianites would not see him. The Lord's angel appeared to him there and said, 'The Lord is with you brave and mighty man!' Gideon said to him, 'If I may ask, sir, why has all this happened to us if God is with us? What happened to all the wonderful things that our fathers told us God used to do—how he brought them out of **Egypt?** God has abandoned us and left us to the **mercy** of the Midianites.' Then God ordered him, 'Go with all your great strength and rescue **Israel** from the Midianites. I myself am sending you.'"

Afterward, Gideon gathered an army together. To make certain that God was going to use him, Gideon asked God for a sign. He placed some wool on the ground and told God, "If in the morning there is dew only on the wool but not on the ground, then I will know that you are going to use me to rescue Israel." The next morning Gideon was able to wring enough dew out of the wool to fill a bowl with water. Then, however, Gideon asked God to reverse the **miracle.** He said to God, "Don't be angry with me. Please let me make one more test with the wool. This time let the wool be dry, and the ground be wet." That night God did that very thing. God next told Gideon that his army was too large. Following God's directions, Gideon reduced the number from many thousands to three hundred. Then with this tiny army, God gave the Israelites victory over the Midianites (Judges 7). After the victory, the Israelites asked Gideon to be their ruler; Gideon declined the offer because of his belief that God was the king of Israel.

Gloria in Excelsis Deo

A Latin phrase that means "Glory to **God** in the highest." It was part of the song the **angels** sang to the shepherds after announcing the birth of **Jesus** (Luke 2:14). The entire scripture reads, "Glory to God in the highest, and on earth peace, and good will toward men!"

Glorious One, The

In 1 **Enoch, God** is described as "the Glorious One."

Glory of the Lord

The word glory can be found in the **Bible's Old Testament** to refer to **God's** brilliance. For example, it was used to refer to God's fiery presence at Sinai in **Exodus** 24:16, "The glory of the **Lord** settled on **Mount Sinai,** and the cloud covered it for six days." It was also used to describe God's radiance that filled the **Tabernacle** at Exodus 40:34, "The cloud covered the **tent of meeting,** and the glory of the Lord filled the tabernacle." Most Bible translations use the word "Glory" or the phrase "Glory of the Lord," while others such as the *Good News Bible* use the term "dazzling **light.**"

Gnosticism (Knowledge)

A movement in Greek philosophy that stressed the secret knowledge of **God** as an escape from the material world. Gnosticism thrived during the second and third centuries A.D. The term Gnosticism stems from the Greek word *gnosis* which means "revealed knowledge." Its beliefs held a mixture of **astrology, reincarnation,** and Greek philosophy. Gnostics placed special emphasis upon a contrast between the material and **spiritual** realms. They believed in a spiritual world which was good, and a material world which was **evil.** Gnostics believed that there was a mysterious knowledge of the **divine** realm and God. They believed that flickers of God fell from the spiritual world into the material world and were captured in the bodies of humans. The flickers from God that dwell within humans were said to have been sent there by God to save humankind. By being reawakened by knowledge, this godly aspect of humankind could go back to its rightful position within the spiritual realm.

According to Gnostic lore, from the original mysterious God, lesser gods were produced. The last of these was Sophia. Sophia longed for the forbidden, to be knowledgeable about God, who remained mysterious and unknowable. From her longing, the **demiurge,** an evil entity, was formed and is said to have fashioned the cosmos and the world within.

God

There are three meanings to the word God. 1) The one Supreme and Infinite Personal Being, the Creator and Ruler of the universe, to whom **Man** owes obedience and worship; 2) the common or generic name for the gods of the polytheistic religions; 3) an **idol.** In general terms, God is a being envisioned as the perfect, omnipotent, omniscient creator of the universe and the primary object of worship in religious practices, particularly, the monotheistic beliefs. Some religions believe God is one, others that God is dual, and still others that God is a **trinity.** God, the great **faiths** assure us, is everywhere. With a lower case "g," the word denotes lesser deities.

About God, the **Koran** states:

"God! There is no god but he, the Living, the Selfsubsistent! Slumber seizes him not, neither sleep. To him belongs whatever is in the **Heavens** and whatsoever is in the Earth. Who is there that shall intercede with Him except by His will? He knows what is present with men and what shall befall them, nothing of His knowledge do they comprehend, save what He wills. His throne is as high as the Heavens and the Earth, and the keeping of them wearies Him not. And He is High, the **Mighty One**" (Sura 2:256).

God Almighty

One of **God's** names in the Jewish tradition.

God of Heaven

According to Emmanuael Swedenborg, who claimed to speak to **angels, Jesus** is the **God of Heaven**. In his book *Heaven and Hell,* Swedenborg spoke of this, saying, "People from the **church** should have no uncertainty about the **Lord's** being the God of heaven, since He Himself has taught that everything of the **Father's** is His (Matthew 11:27, John 16:25, 17:2) and that He owns all power in heaven and on earth (Matthew 28:18). He said, 'in heaven and on earth' because heaven's ruler also rules earth, the one being dependent on the other. Ruling heaven and earth means receiving from Him everything good, which is the property of **love,** and everything true, which is the property of **faith.** This means all intelligence and wisdom, and therefore all happiness; in a word, it is receiving **eternal life.**"

God of Light

In Persian lore, the **God of Light** was **Mithra**. Legend has it that he was once one of the twenty-eight **angels** that surrounded **Ahura Mazda.** He later became the God of Light.

God of Love

In Roman **mythology,** Cupid was the winged god of **love.** In Greek mythology, it was Eros. Both gods served as archetypal **angels** for **Judaism** and **Christianity.**

God of the Dead

In Etruscan lore, Charon was the god of the dead. He carried the **souls** of the dead to Hades. The **angel** of **death** was later patterned after him.

God of the Underworld

A title held by **Satan.**

Goddess

A term used to affirm the feminine aspect of **God.**

God's Children

See Bene ha-Elohim.

God's Destroyer

The meaning of the name **Abaddon;** an **angel** found in Revelation.

God's Friend

Abraham of the **Bible** was known as God's friend because of his special relationship with God.

God's Mountain

See Mount Sinai.

God's Servants

A title held by the **angels.** It was taken from the Book of **Hebrews** (1:14) where it says, "What are the angels, then? They are **spirits** who serve **God** and are sent by him to help those who are to receive **salvation.**"

Gog and Magog

Two powers in **Christianity's** apocalyptic beliefs that are opposed to **God.** They will be the last world powers to be crushed before the **Kingdom of God** is ushered in.

Golden Altar

The magnificent **altar** that stands before the **throne of God.** According to the **Bible,** it is where the **prayers** of the saints are offered up to **God.** Around the altar, the **angels** gather to listen to these prayers.

Golden Censer

The censer carried by an **angel** to the **golden altar** which stands before **God's** throne. According to the **Bible,** the **incense** inside is to be offered with the **prayers** of the saints to God. Revelation (8:3) states, "Another angel with a golden censer came and stood at the **altar;** he was given a great quantity of incense to offer with the prayers of all the saints on the golden altar that is before the throne."

Goldsmith, Joel S. (1892–1964)

Founder of the Infinite Way. A teacher of practical mysticism. Goldsmith devoted most of his life to the discovery and teaching of **spiritual** principles which he founded and called the Infinite Way. He is the first Western metaphysical master to lecture and travel the world, and to have his own words recorded. More than thirty books have been compiled from his tape-recorded lectures and class work including *The Infinite Way, Practicing the Presence,* and *The Art of Meditation.* Covering all aspects of spirituality, Goldsmith's straightforward, non-denominational teachings have helped countless thousands to look inside themselves and find "the infinite way." Says Goldsmith in *The Infinite Way:* "To know that we are the fulfillment of **God,** that we are that place in consciousness where God shines through, is to be spiritually minded. The realization that every individual is the presence of God, that all that is, is God appearing, is spiritual consciousness."

Gomorrah

One of two cities described in the **Old Testament** that was destroyed by **God** because of the wickedness of its people (**Genesis** 19:24–28). The other city was **Sodom.**

Gott

The German word for **God.**

Grace

A purely Christian term. It refers to the undeserved **love** and favor of **God** toward humans. It is believed that God is good to humans because He loves them and for no other reason. This in essence is the "grace of God." In the **Bible,** God demonstrated His grace to the **Hebrews** on numerous occasions. In the **New Testament,** the grace of God is seen in the ministry and **sacrifice** of **Jesus Christ,** through which God freely gives **salvation** to undeserving humans.

Graham, Billy (1918–)

Renowned American evangelist. He has reached millions of people around the world with his dynamic preaching and eloquent sermons. Born in Charlotte, North Carolina, Graham was educated at Bob Jones University, the Florida **Bible** Institute, and Wheaton College. He was ordained in the Southern Baptist Convention in 1939 and became pastor of the First Baptist **Church** of Western Springs, Illinois, in 1943. In 1949, Graham began preaching on a larger scale, embarking on a series of tours of the United States and Europe. Today, Graham is known worldwide via television, motion pictures, and *Decision* (the magazine of the Billy Graham Evangelistic Association); he is also known through the radio program *The Hour of Decision,* and through a syndicated newspaper column. Graham has written numerous books including his autobiography, *Just As I Am,* which was published in 1997. In this, Graham comments: "**God** created us in His image. He created us and **loves** us so that we may live in harmony and fellowship with Him. We are not here by chance. God put us here for a purpose, and our lives are never fulfilled and complete until His purpose becomes the foundation and center of our lives."

Great Glory, The

In 1 **Enoch, God** is described as "the Great Glory."

Great Spirit

Creator Being in most Native American beliefs. The name refers to the great force which controls all of nature. See Native Americans.

Greece

See Zeus.

Grigori

Another name for the **Watchers** (**angels** who forsook their **God**-given positions to come to Earth).

Guardian Angels

Angels that are assigned by **God** for protection. Guardian angels often appear at a moment's notice to rescue their charges from harm. They appear sometimes in human form, sometimes in the form of an animal, and sometimes as a voice or a vision. Many people have relayed experiences of being rescued by invisible hands, or through a dream which they had before a danger occurred.

RELIGIONS AND CULTURES. The concept of guardian angels can be found in both the ancient and modern worlds. Ancient Romans believed that guardian **spirits** called *Lares* protected each family. Romans also believed in *Genius* spirits who protected men and boys; and *Juno* spirits who guarded women and girls. Pakistani and Burmese people believe in guardian spirits called *Nats* who were thought to dwell next to the people they were guarding. In **Islam** there are the *Malaika,* known as the guardians of mankind, and the *Hafazah* who protect humans against the *Jinn* (**demons**). Guardian spirits called *Genii* are found throughout the Near East. In Zoroastrianism there are the *Fravashi,* ancestral spirits who are also guardian angels. **Native Americans** believe in guardian spirits whom they see as much like the guardian angels of other religious systems. Each clan or tribe has a guardian which is believed to remain with them forever. Personal guardian spirits are sought after by individual members of a tribe. In **Catholicism** it is taught that every child has two guardian angels, one good and one bad, each sitting upon a shoulder.

CHILDREN. It has been suggested that children have several guardian angels. This is because children are more vulnerable and in need of more protection when they are young. As they grow, they are thought to need less angelic protection as they become aware of the dangers around them. Some, but not all, of the angels leave a child as he matures. The famous Austrian clairvoyant Rudolf Steiner believed that the guardian angels are with a person through each **incarnation** and carry the complete history of the **soul.** Once the individual has finished the last incarnation, the guardian angel's role is completed and he leaves that individual.

PERSONAL ANGELS. The guardian angels of individuals come from the angelic order called Angels. They rank last in the angelic hierarchy and are the closest angels to mankind. They are assigned to individuals at birth to protect and guide them. They are sometimes referred to as personal angels and companion angels. Guardian angels use a variety of ways to reach individuals including their intuition, thoughts, and dreams. Sometimes, they work through people and manipulate circumstances in order to relay messages. Although guardian angels do appear from time to time, most of their work is done invisibly. When they do appear, however, they may take on a variety of forms including people, **animals, lights,** etc. When appearing as humans, they appear in forms that are in accord with the beliefs of the individual, disguising themselves in the appropriate cultural clothing. There are many reports of angels appearing in full angelic regalia, including halos and wings.

GUARDIAN ANGEL **PRAYER.** In Catholicism, the Guardian Angel Prayer is a prayer taught to children. It speaks of God sending angels to children for protection and guidance. It says: "Angel of God, my guardian dear, To whom His love commits me here; Ever this day [or night] be at my side, To light and guard, to rule and guide."

Guru

Spiritual counselor or teacher. In Tibet and **India**, the guru is considered to be the highest manifestation of **God** in the world. The word *guru* is a Sanskrit word meaning teacher, honored person, religious person, or saint.

Guru Nanak (1469–1539)

Founder of the Sikh **faith.** The first of ten Sikh gurus, Nanak was born into a family of Hindu merchants in the village of Talvandi, near the city of Lahore, Pakistan. It is said that from an early age Nanak was endowed with extraordinary **spiritual** powers. Tales of strange episodes and miraculous occur-rences were reported throughout his life. During his late twenties or early thirties, Nanak set off on a series of **pilgrimages** in search of **enlightenment.** Around 1520, he returned to the northern Indian region of the Punjab. In the years that followed, his reputation as a spiritual master spread, and he attracted a steadily increasing number of followers whom he called Sikhs, which means "learners."

Nanak advocated belief in one invisible **God.** To Nanak, God was simultaneously transcendent and immediately immanent, or existing within humanity. Nanak sought to see beyond the illusions of everyday existence in order to achieve *sahaj,* which is a union with God. About God Nanak says: "The **lord** can never be established nor created; the formless one is limitlessly complete in Himself" "Even Kings and emperors with heaps of wealth and vast dominion cannot compare with an ant filled with the **love** of God."

H

If God be for us, who can be against us?
—*Archbishop Desmond Tutu*

Habakkuk

Minor **prophet** of the **Bible's Old Testament.** Habakkuk's book of **prophecy** is a kind of dialogue between himself and **God.** There is little known about the prophet Habakkuk. Both the authorship and the date in which the book was written is undetermined (although it is thought to date from the end of the seventh century B.C.). Chapter 1 starts with Habakkuk asking God why He fails to punish the wicked and the unjust. God's answer is that His justice will always triumph, even if it takes time. God informs the prophet that He is raising up the Chaldeans to overtake the land. However, Habakkuk is against this idea, protesting that the Chaldeans are harsh and idolatrous, and should not be used by God. In chapter 2, God answers Habakkuk, telling him that the Chaldeans will be judged for their arrogance and brutality, and that the faithful and righteous would be rewarded. Chapter 3 is a beautiful **prayer** that speaks joyfully of an encounter with God. An excerpt from Habakkuk (3–4, 19) follows:

His splendor covers the heavens, and the earth is full of praise. He comes with the brightness of lightning; **light** flashes from his hand, there where his power is hidden.

The Sovereign **Lord** gives me strength. He makes me sure-footed as a deer and keeps me safe on the **mountains**.

Hagar

The maidservant to **Abraham's** wife **Sarah.** She was visited twice by an **angel** from **God.** The first time came after she had fled into the wilderness to escape the wrath of Sarah. God told her at that time that she was going to give birth to a son, and that she should call him **Ishmael** (**Genesis** 16:1–14). The second visitation occurred when she wandered into the wilderness after Abraham sent her away at Sarah's request. Exhausted and dehydrated, Hagar put her son Ishmael under a bush and walked away, asking God not to let her see it when the child died. From **Heaven,** God heard the child crying and sent an angel to speak to her. The angel called out to her, telling her not to be afraid, that God would one day turn Ishmael's seed into a great nation (Genesis 21:17–19).

Hajj

See Islam.

Hallelujah(s)

Songs of praise to **God.** The word hallelujah is **Hebrew** meaning "praise the **Lord**." It contains an abbreviated version of God's name: "JAH." The word "Jah" is short for **Jehovah**, which is a version of God's name in Judeo-Christian beliefs. Jah is found many times in the Book of Psalms, most often in the phrase "praise the Lord" instead of hallelujah. It appears in Revelation 19:6 where it says, "Hallelujah! For our Lord God **Almighty** reigns."

Hand of God

A metaphorical term referring to the care of **God** over humanity.

Hari

In Hindu **theology**, the supreme personality of the **God**head.

Harmagedon

See Armageddon.

Hartley, David (1705–1757)

British philosopher and physician. Born in Armley, Yorkshire, in England, and educated at **Jesus** College, University of Cambridge; Hartley became founder of associational psychology. His major works included *Observations on Man, His Frame, His Duty, and His Expectations* (2 volumes, 1749). This book was the first attempt to explain all the phenomena of the mind by a theory of association. Although Hartley was a physician, he started out in life with the idea of becoming a minister. He changed his mind after realizing that his **faith** was not strong enough. Even so, his scientific concepts had **spiritual** undertones. The loftiest goal of human behavior was, he said, "the perception of **God**." Hartley comments ". . . the idea of God, and the Ways by which his Goodness and Happiness are made manifest, must, at last, take place of, and absorb other Ideas, and He himself become, according to the Language of the Scriptures, All in All."

Hartshorne, Charles (1897–2000)

American theologian, philosopher, and educator. Hartshorne was one of the leading proponents of "process thought" which considers **God** a participant in cosmic evolution. Hartshorne envisioned God as being twofold: limited and limitless, conscious and unconscious, **everlasting** and temporal. In Hartshorne's philosophy God's perfection is seen in the evolution as well as the creativity of all living beings. Hartshorne argued for God's existence using what is called a global argument which integrates versions of the ontological, cosmological, design, epistemic, moral, and aesthetic arguments.

Hasidim

Jewish religious movement that began in the mid-eighteenth century in Eastern Europe and persists to this day in Europe, the United States, and **Israel**. The word Hasidim is **Hebrew** and means "the pious ones." In the books of Maccabees and the Talmud, the term refers to those who distinguish themselves by devotion to Jewish **law** and by charitable deeds. Hasidic beliefs are based mostly on Talmudic and medieval Jewish mysticism. Its main focus is establishing a close and loving relationship with **God**, teaching that all could know God equally well. In Hasidic beliefs God is everywhere, even in **evil**. Believers must strive to turn evil into good. It is through **meditation**, **prayer**, study, and charitable works that one is led to an understanding of God. It is the Hasid's desire to act out of **love** for God and humankind, praying for all God's **creation**.

Hayyoth

Also called "**heaven**ly beasts," the Hayyoth are **Angels** of Fire who reside in the **Seventh Heaven** with **God**, supporting God's throne. According to apocryphal lore, Raziel spreads his wings over the Hayyoth so that their fiery breath does not incinerate the attending angels around God's throne. They are also credited with holding up the universe. Each time their wings spread they break out in **hallelujahs** to God. The **prophet Ezekiel** saw them in a vision (Ezekiel 1:23,24). Ezekiel wrote, "There under the dome stood the creatures, each stretching out two wings toward the ones next to it and covering its body with the other two wings. I heard the noise their wings made in flight; it sounded like the roar of the sea, like the noise of a huge army, like the voice of **Almighty** God. When they stopped flying, they folded their wings, but there was still a sound coming from above the dome over their heads." They are the equivalent of the order of angels called the **Cherubim,** and are also called **Divine** Beasts.

Heaven

The dwelling place of **God** and His **spiritual** family. It is also referred to as **Paradise.** Heaven is generally believed to be a place of great beauty and pleasure where there is no sickness, old age, or **death,** a place where happiness lasts forever and a hundred years is as one day. It is thought to be a place of peace, beauty, and wisdom, where there are no pain or tears, a place to which the **soul** returns after death, when the pain and suffering of this life becomes a faded memory. It is believed to be ultimately a place of continuous joy where God cares for us and where we are always with Him.

BELIEFS IN HEAVEN. In Judeo-Christian beliefs, Heaven is a place where good people go to be with God. Christians in general believe that the souls of the righteous are admitted immediately into Heaven after death. There they experience **eternal** joy and have a clear vision of God sometimes called the **"beatific vision."** In **Islam,** Heaven is referred to as Paradise; a place of unspeakable happiness and unrestricted and inexhaustible delight. There **Allah** (God) sits on his throne surrounded by **angels** who minister to Him. The **Celts** believed in an Other World (variously called "the Land of the Living," "Delightful Plain," and "Land of the Young") where there was no old age, sickness, or dying.

SCRIPTURE. The **prophet Enoch** visited Heaven where he witnessed angels in school and working. There were some who were responsible for studying the fauna and the flora of Heaven and Earth. There were angels who recorded the seasons of the years, others who studied the rivers and the seas, and others who study the fruits of the Earth and the plants and herbs which give nourishment to earthly creatures. In John **Milton's** *Paradise Lost,* the walls of Heaven are made of "crystal." According to Revelation, the streets of Heaven are paved with gold, with gates of pearl, where God sits on a throne and believers see Him face to face. There are also said to be seven realms of Heaven, sometimes referred to as the Seven Heavens.

In the **Old Testament** there is no clear distinction between "heaven" and "the heavens." Heaven was both the sky from which the rain fell and it was also the dwelling place of God. The **New Testament** suggests a physical location above the Earth. For example, when praying, **Jesus** raised his eyes to Heaven, and later during the **Ascension** he was taken up to Heaven. According to testimonials from near-death experiences, there is much to do and learn in Heaven. There one can find libraries, music, arts, literature, research centers, gardens, and more. In Heaven one is constantly growing in the knowledge of God, the ultimate goal being the perfecting of one's soul. The most wonderful aspect of

Heaven is that humans are forever in God's presence.

Heavenly Archives

Scripture tells us that there are heavenly archives in which records are kept containing the history and deeds of humankind. There are specific books and scrolls that are read by God and that are protected and kept by ministering spirits. These have become known as the Heavenly Archives. It is here that the Book of Records is kept. This is the same book in which the deeds of humans are recorded, and from which God will read on Judgment Day. According to one account, the Heavenly Archives are housed in what is called the Hall of Records, described as a very large spiritual library, a repository of knowledge, where information is received psychically. It has been described as a library of the mind.

Heavenly Books

The sacred books of God. According to scriptures, prophets, and new age thinkers, there are heavenly books that are stored in great buildings and in what is called the Heavenly Archives. The sacred books are for God's eyes only. We know little about these books, only what the scriptures tell us.

SCRIPTURAL SOURCES. At Exodus 32:32, Moses begs God for the sake of Israel's forgiveness, to "blot me out of the book which you have written." Daniel 7:10 speaks of books being opened, saying, "The court sat in judgment, and the books were opened." Revelation 20:12 also speaks of books being opened, "And I saw the dead, great and small, standing before the throne, and books were opened. Also another book was opened, the Book of Life. And the dead were judged according to their works, as recorded in the books."

In Daniel 10:21, he refers to the Book of Truth, "But I am to tell you what is inscribed in the Book of Truth." The Book of Malachi speaks of a Book of Remembrance that was written about those who feared God. "Then those who revered the Lord spoke with one another. The Lord took note and listened, and a Book of Remembrance was written before him of those who revered the Lord and thought on his name." Enoch spoke of the Book of Records saying, "He takes out the scroll box in which the book of records is kept, and brings it into the presence of the Holy One (God)" (3 Enoch 27:1).

In addition to the scriptures, new age philosophers speak of a spiritual library known as the Akashic Records, also said to be a complete record of God's memory. The records are housed in a great library and all of God's spiritual family have access to them.

Heavenly Hierarchy

According to Jewish tradition, there is a hierarchy to the universe. In that hierarchy, God is located both at the center of the universe and at the highest point of the hierarchy. The angels radiate outward from His Presence, some being close to the center while others move further and further away from God. In his book entitled *Angels, an Endangered Species,* Malcolm Godwin talks about this heavenly hierarchy giving this description. "It is a dynamic and ever-changing scenario. Angels are arranged on three descending levels. Each level has three orders of angels. The highest level is made up of the Seraphim, Cherubim, and the Thrones. These are in direct communion with God and receive his full Illumination. The next level orbiting God is composed of the Dominations, Virtues, and Powers who receive the Divine Illumination from the first Triad and then in turn, transmit it to the lowest triad, where the Principalities, Archangels, and Angels dwell. These then convey that illumination to humankind."

Heavenly Hosts

A term referring to **God's** many thousands of **angels**. The word "host" means an assembly of angels. In **Heaven**, the host of angels stand near God's throne. The Book of 1 Kings (22:19) states, "I saw the **Lord** sitting on his throne, and all the host of heaven standing beside him on his right hand and his left."

Hebrew(s)

Another name for **Israel**, God's chosen people in the **Bible**.

Hell

In Christian beliefs hell is the perpetual home of those damned by **God**. It is believed that the **souls** in hell are in **Satan's** possession and are forever deprived of seeing God. A person separated from God is considered to be in agony, this in itself is a form of hell and the worst possible circumstance. In legend, hell is a place of **fire and brimstone** where those who go there are physically tormented forever. Some people believe the fire to be literal, some metaphorical. **Islam** believes in a similar hell. In ancient Jewish beliefs, Sheol or Tophet was a kind of hell in which souls roamed about sorrowfully. Later, Sheol became very much like the Christian hell. Ancient Greeks believed that upon dying, spirits of the dead went to an underworld called Hades.

Henotheism

The word henotheism is taken from the Greek word *henos* which means "one" and *theos* which means "**God**." Its meaning is that there are many gods, but devotion is owed to only one.

Henry, Patrick (1736–1799)

American orator and statesman. Henry embodied the spirit of American courage and patriotism. His fiery patriotic speeches earned him the title of "Orator of Liberty" among his contemporaries; he was instrumental in leading the Colonies toward a revolution. During the Second Virginia Convention, he delivered his most famous speech, "Give Me Liberty or Give Me **Death**," on March 23, 1775, at St. John's **Church** in Richmond. The speech's final words became the clarion call that prompted the Colonies into action and revolution.

The following is an excerpt from the speech, in which his **faith** in **God** was clearly demonstrated. ". . . Sir, we are not weak, if we make a proper use of the means which the God of nature hath placed in our power. Three millions of people, armed in the **Holy** cause of Liberty, and in such a country as that which we posses, are invincible by any force which our enemy can send against us. Besides, sir, we shall not fight our battle alone. There is a just God who presides over the destinies of **nations**; and who will raise up friends to fight our battle for us. The battle, sir, is not to the strong alone; it is to the vigilant, the active, the brave. . . . Is life so dear, or peace so sweet, as to be purchased at the price of chains and slavery? Forbid it, **Almighty** God! I know not what course others may take; but as for me, give me liberty or give me death!"

Heralds

Individuals who proclaim **God's** message. The **prophets** were considered heralds because they brought messages from God that included both doom and good news. **Angels** are sometimes called heralds because they bring announcements and proclamations for God to humankind.

Hesed

A **Hebrew** word found in the **Old Testament**. It was said to be difficult to translate, but is understood to refer to God's love. It was eventually translated as "loving-kindness," a term coined by Miles Coverdale (translator of the first printed English Bible). It was later put into the King James version of the Bible.

Hezekiah (God Is My Strength)

Character from the Bible. In the Book of 2 Kings (19:35), Hezekiah prays to God for protection from King Sennacherib of Assyria. God hears his prayers and sends an Angel of Death to slay Sennacherib's army. The account states: "That night an Angel of the Lord went to the Assyrian camp and killed 185,000 soldiers."

High God

Another name for the Supreme Being, or Supreme God. The High God is found among the beliefs of the illiterate peoples of North and South America, Africa, northern Asia, and Australian Aboriginal beliefs. The origin of the High God is thought to be very old, even before the conception of many of the pantheons of polytheism. It is said to have become very popular after the onset of Christianity and the belief in a monotheistic God, and the High God is even referred to as Father in some beliefs. Known to some as the Sky God, the High God is believed to be both all-powerful and all-knowing. He is thought to be either male or genderless; He is the creator of the universe, yet far removed from humanity and His creation. In certain societies He is portrayed as a weak god and was replaced by other more favored deities.

Hilary of Poitiers, Saint (315–367)

Bishop of Poitiers and Doctor of the Church. He was born in Poitiers, France, to pagan parents. Hilary later converted to Christianity. He lived during the period of the great controversy between Athanasius, who taught that Jesus is fully God, equal with the Father, and Arius, who opposed this idea. When Hilary said no to condemning Athanasius, the Arian emperor Constantius banished him to Phrygia. He was in exile for three years, and during this period he wrote several essays. In his "Commentary on the Psalms," he states: "First it must be remembered that God is incorporeal. He does not consist of certain parts and distinct members, making up one body. For we read in the gospel that God is a spirit: invisible, therefore, and an eternal nature, immeasurable and self-sufficient. It is also written that a spirit does not have flesh and bones. For of these the members of a body consist, and of these the substance of God has no need. God, however, who is everywhere and in all things, is all-hearing, all-seeing, all-doing, and all-assisting."

Hildegard of Bingen (1098–1179)

German composer, abbess, mystic, and writer. She has been called one of the most important figures in the history of the Middle Ages, and the greatest woman of her time. Born in Böckelheim, Germany, Hildegard knew at a very young age that she wanted to spend her life serving God. At the age of eight she was placed by her aristocratic parents in the care of nuns at Disibodenberg, near Bingen, Germany. She later became head of the convent. There she became known as a powerful mystic, spending much of her time meditating on the mysteries of God, having visions in which she saw Heaven and Hell, and giving prophecies about the future. She recorded these visions in a book entitled *Scivias,* which took her ten years to complete, and which brought her much fame throughout Europe.

She wrote of her vision of God, in which she described Heaven as a royal court where the saints are dressed in silk, standing about the **throne of God.** She envisioned the throne of God as being surrounded by nine concentric circles of **angels.** The most wonderful part of Heaven, according to Hildegard, is beholding the **Beatific Vision** (the **Face of God**). Of her relationship with God, Hildegard wrote these beautiful lines: "Listen: there was once a king sitting on his throne. Around Him stood great and wonderfully beautiful columns ornamented with ivory, bearing the banners of the king with great honor. Then it pleased the king to raise a small feather from the ground, and he commanded it to fly. The feather flew, not because of anything in itself but because the air bore it along. Thus am I, a feather on the breath of God."

Hinduism

Major world religion that originated from the ancient religions of **India.** In Hinduism, **God** can be understood in several ways. Philosophically, God is understood as **Brahma,** the one **eternal,** embracing all that is. In popular religion, many gods are worshipped having his or her own function; however, these too are understood to be manifestations of Brahma. In this way Hinduism stresses God's **immanence** as seen in the abundance of gods that illustrate the many faces of God the Unknown as He interacts with mankind.

The three principal gods, charged with creating, preserving, and destroying, are joined as the Trimurti, also known as the three powers, similar to the Christian **Trinity.** The creator in Hinduism, however, does not create in the Judeo-Christian sense. In Hinduism the world is eternal and He is simply the God who has been from the beginning. In bhakti Hinduism, the god Isvara is conceived as an individual and

is not unlike the Judeo-Christian God. There is also the idea of mediation expressed through the belief in the **incarnation** of God as **man** in avatars such as **Krishna,** a popular Hindu god.

Holy

The word holy means pure. Holiness is a quality of **God** in most religions. It is a word most commonly used in Judeo-Christian worship, in reference to God or things related or close to God. The God of Judeo-Christian beliefs is described in the **Bible** as holy, devoid of **sin,** and without the capability of sinning. The holiness of God is depicted as being so lofty, that sinful human beings would never be able to attain it. He is so Holy in fact that humans can never come before God as holy. In Biblical times God and His chosen people (the **Jews**) stood out from the surrounding peoples because of the high standards of the true God. These standards set God apart and contributed to his holiness. A scripture in **Isaiah** speaks of this, in which God says, "My thoughts are not your thoughts, nor are your ways My ways. . . . For as the heavens are higher than the earth, so are My ways higher than your ways."

Holy Ghost

In Christian doctrine, the **Holy** Ghost is the third person of the **Trinity.** The Holy Ghost is sometimes referred to as the **Holy Spirit.**

Holy, Holy, Holy

A phrase that is found in the **Bible,** in the Book of **Isaiah** and in Revelation. In a vision, Isaiah (6:3) sees **angels** saying the words, "Holy, holy, holy, is the **Lord Almighty;** the whole earth is full of his glory!" In another vision found in Revelation 4:8 the four living creatures are saying, "Holy, holy, holy, is the Lord **God** Almighty, who was, and is, and is to come."

Holy of Holies

See Most Holy Place.

Holy Spirit

In some religious beliefs the **Holy Spirit** is **God's** power (also referred to as the "Force of God"). In others the Holy **Spirit** is God Himself. In still others, the Holy Spirit is thought to be a separate entity: a higher angelic being that is part of God, but separate from God. The Holy Spirit is also a part of the **Trinity**, which consists of God, **Jesus**, and the Holy Spirit. In the **New Testament**, the **Angel of the Lord** is personalized as the Holy Spirit. When Jesus was baptized, the Holy Spirit appeared in the form of a **dove** above his head. In Matthew 3:16 it states, "And when Jesus had been baptized, just as he came up from the water, suddenly the heavens were opened to him and he saw the **Spirit of God** descending like a dove and alighting on him." In Zoroastrianism the Holy Spirit is the **Supreme Being, Ahura Mazda.** Names for the Holy Spirit include: **Holy Ghost;** Counselor; Comforter; **Spirit of the Lord;** Baptiser; **Spirit of God;** Advocate; Strengthener; Sanctifier; Spirit of **Christ;** Spirit of Truth; Spirit of **Grace;** Spirit of **Mercy;** Spirit of God; Spirit of Holiness; Spirit of Life. In the Old and New Testaments the Holy Spirit is symbolized by breath or wind, fire, water, oil, light, and a dove.

Holy Spirits

A phrase used in Zoroastrianism when referring to the **Amesha Spentas**. In the Zoroastrian beliefs, these are **archangels** who work closely with **God**.

Holy Trinity

See Trinity.

Homousian

One who holds the theory that **God** the **Father** and God the Son are identical in substance. The word is a Greek term, taken from the words *homos* (same) and *ousia* (essense), making it mean "of the same substance." The phrase came to be used extensively during the fourth century to specify the mainstream Christological idea that **Jesus** was of the same substance as God. It was believed by some that Jesus, being the **mediator** between God and humankind, was not **eternal,** and therefore not of the "**Divine** substance," but a creature brought forth by the **free will** of God. The term was directed against the Arian view that **Christ** was "of similar substance" to God.

Horeb, Mount

The sacred mountain on which **God** gave **Moses** the **Ten Commandments.** It is also called **Mount Sinai.**

Hornets

According to the **Bible, God** sent swarming hornets three times ahead of the **Israelites** into the land of Canaan to drive out their enemies. The hornets have been a source of debate among scholars. Some view the reference to hornets literally, while others see them as a symbol of **Egypt,** just as Isaiah 7:18 refers to the fly as such and just as the bee is a symbol for Assyria in the same verse. Most view the hornets as a symbol of God's direct intervention, which paralyzed the enemy.

Horus the Elder

An ancient creator god in **Egypt**ian **mythology.** He was especially venerated in pre-Dynastic Upper Egypt. Horus was the **sky god,** and his eyes were believed to be the sun and moon. He represented light and goodness. According to lore, he once battled Set, the god of darkness and **evil.** In art, he is portrayed as a falcon. In a passage from the Coffin Texts (passage 148) Horus speaks: "I am Horus, the great Falcon upon the ramparts of the house of him of the hidden name. My flight has reached the horizon. I have passed by the gods of Nut. I have gone further than the gods of old. Even the most ancient bird could not equal my very first flight. I have removed my place beyond the powers of Seth, the foe of my father **Osiris.** No other god could do what I have done. I have brought the ways of eternity to the twilight of the morning. I am unique in my flight."

Hosanna of Mantua

See Andreasi, Osanna.

Hosea (God Has Saved)

A **prophet** of **Israel** in the eighth century B.C. His book is the first of the twelve Minor **Prophets.** Hosea had a home life that illustrated the relationship of **God** and Israel. The first three books of Hosea deal with his marriage to a prostitute. God tells Hosea to marry a prostitute, father **children** with her, and give his children names symbolizing Israel's religious unfaithfulness. Hosea does as God instructs him and marries a woman named Gomer. Gomer repeatedly betrayed Hosea by taking lovers and Hosea had to suffer the embarrassment and shame of her unfaithfulness. God used her unfaithfulness as a metaphor to illustrate how Israel prostituted itself by worshipping other gods. In addition, Gomer eventually leaves him for another man; however, God tells Hosea to take her back. By doing so, Hosea demonstrates God's **long-suffering love** for His people, no matter what their **sins.** The rest of the book is concerned with noting the sin of God's people, impending judgment, exhortations to repentance, and God's **love.**

Hosts, Lord of

A title held by **God.** It is used in the **Old Testament** at 1 Samuel 17:45, where God is referred to as the **Lord** of Hosts by the young **David** who was talking to a giant Philistine with whom he was about to do battle. The title represents God's authority as leader of the **heavenly hosts** and the heavenly army.

Howe, Julia Ward (1819–1910)

Author of "The Battle Hymn of the Republic," the anthem of the Union troops during the **Civil War** and a classic of our nation's musical repertoire. She was also the first woman to be elected to the American Academy of Arts and Letters and was the founder of Mother's Day. Howe's works include the *Life of Margaret Fuller* (1883), *From Sunset Ridge: Poems Old and New* (1898), and *Reminiscences 1819-1899* (1899). Julia Ward Howe spoke at the Parliament of the World's Religions at the 1893 Columbian Exposition, Chicago World's Fair. Her topic, "What is Religion?" outlined Howe's understanding of general religion and what religions have to teach each other.

The following is an excerpt from that speech in which she spoke with passion about **God.** "I think nothing is religion which puts one individual absolutely above others, and surely nothing is religion which puts one sex above another. Religion is primarily our relation to the Supreme, to God himself. It is for him to judge; it is for him to say where we belong, who is highest and who is not; of that we know nothing. And any religion which will **sacrifice** a certain set of human beings for the enjoyment or aggrandizement or advantage of another is no religion. It is a thing which may be allowed, but it is against true religion. Any religion which sacrifices women to the brutality of men is no religion."

The following is Howe's famous "Battle Hymn of the Republic," written as an inspiration to Union soldiers fighting against slavery, a poem in which her **faith** in God is clearly seen.

THE BATTLE HYMN OF THE REPUBLIC
Mine eyes have seen the glory of the
coming of the **Lord;**
He is trampling out the vintage
where grapes of wrath are stored;
He hath loosed the fateful lightning
of His terrible swift sword,
His truth is marching on.

Glory, glory, **hallelujah!** Glory, glory,
hallelujah!
Glory, glory, hallelujah! His truth is
marching on.

I have seen Him in the watch-fires
of a hundred circling camps;
They have builded Him an **altar** in
the evening dews and damps;
I can read His righteous sentence by
the dim and flaring lamps,
His day is marching on.

I have read a fiery gospel writ in
burnish'd rows of steel,
"As ye deal with my contemners, so
with you my **grace** shall deal";
Let the Hero, born of woman, crush
the serpent with his heel
Since God is marching on.

He has sounded forth the **trumpet**
that shall never call retreat;
He is sifting out the hearts of men
before His Judgment Seat.
Oh! Be swift, my **soul,** to answer
Him, be jubilant, my feet!
Our God is marching on.

In the beauty of the lilies **Christ** was
born across the sea,
With a glory in his bosom that
transfigures you and me;
As he died to make men **holy,** let us
die to make men free,
While God is marching on.

Hurakan

Creator god of the Quiche **Mayans.**
When the gods became angry with the
first humans, Hurakan sent a **flood** to
annihilate them. A variation of the
name Hurakan is Hurukan.

Huveane

Creator god of the Basuto people of
Lesotho.

Hypostatic Union

A theological term used in describing the union of the two natures (**divine**
and human) in the person of **Jesus.**
Hypostasis means, literally, that which
lies beneath as basis or foundation. The
belief is that **God** "fused" the human
nature of **Christ** with his divine nature
in the hypostatic union. According to
this teaching Jesus is completely God
and also completely **Man,** so he therefore has two natures, those of God and
Man.

I

If God did not exist, it would be necessary to invent him.

—Voltaire

I AM

A title used by **God** when referring to Himself, while addressing **Moses** for the first time. The account at **Exodus** 3:14 states, "Moses said to God, 'If I come to the **Israel**ites and say to them, "The God of your ancestors has sent me to you," and they ask me, "What is his name?" What shall I say to them?' God said to Moses, 'I AM WHO I AM.' He said further, 'thus you shall say to the Israelites, "I AM has sent me to you."'" It has been theorized that in the words "I AM" God was stating the following: I am **eternal**, I am **holy**, I am self-existent, I am self-sufficient, I am omnipotent, I am omnipresent, and I am the creator and sustainer of all that exists.

Iblis

The spirit of darkness **(Satan)** in **Islam.** The name Iblis is Arabic and is thought to have derived from the Greek word *diabolos,* which means **devil.** He is understood to be a fallen **angel,** the tempter of **Eve,** and the head of the legions of **demons.** Iblis is said, of all the angels, to have loved **God** the most. When God created **Adam,** He told the angels to bow down and worship him. Iblis refused. Because of this disobedient act, God ordered him from His presence. The **Koran** states that when Adam was created, God told the angels to prostrate themselves saying, "Fall ye prostrate before Adam! And they fell prostrate, all save Iblis, who was not of those who make prostration. He said: What hindered thee that thou did not fall prostrate when I bid thee? [Iblis] said: I am better than he. Thou createdst me of fire, while him Thou didst create of mud. He said: Then go down hence! It is not for Thee to show pride here, so go forth! Lo! Thou art of those degraded" (Koran, VII). Until **Judgment Day,** Iblis will lead the demons in corrupting humankind by tempting them to **sin** and to commit **evil.** A variation of the name Iblis is Eblis.

Ibn Gabirol, Solomon ben Yehuda (1021–1058)

Spanish Jewish philosopher and poet. Born in Malaga, he is one of the greatest Spanish medieval poets. He was also one of the earliest philosophers of Moorish Spain and a leading Neoplatonist. More than 400 poems appear in the published editions of his work, and new ones are still being discovered. His outstanding philosophical work, *The Fountain of Life,* influenced generations of Western medieval thinkers. His most famous poem is "The Kingly Crown," a hymn of glory to the greatness of God.

Ibn Rushd

See Averroes.

Ibn Sina

See Avicenna.

Ibrahim

See Abraham.

Iconoclasm

See Idol/Idolatry.

Idol/Idolatry

An image of a god (or an image or person that is held to be a god) used as an object of worship. The word idol comes from the Greek word *eidolon,* which means "image." An idol can be any image or figure (such as a statue, sculpture, painting, mosaic, or mural) representing a god or **goddess.** Most of the worlds religions, old and new, view the use of idols as normal and encourage the use of images of religious figures in worship. However, in **Hebrew,** Christian, and **Muslim** beliefs all forms or representations of **God** used in worship are forbidden. Idolatry was first brought to the attention of the ancient Hebrews through their association with neighbors who worshipped several gods through the use of idols. It was made clear to the Hebrews that such practices were forbidden to them.

In **Exodus** 20:3–5, God forbids the worship of foreign gods and the images that were made to represent Him, saying, "you shall have no other gods before me. You shall not make for yourself an idol, whether in the form of anything that is in **heaven** above, or that is on the earth beneath, or that is in the water under the earth. You shall not bow down to them or worship them." In addition, a number of Hebrew **prophets,** including **Elijah** and Elisha (I Kings 18:22-40), **Amos** (Amos 2:4), **Hosea** (Hosea 4:12-13), and **Isaiah** (Isaiah 17:7-8), condemned idolatry.

Christians continued to heed the warning of Exodus and did not participate in worshipping idols or creating forms of God of any kind. However, they ran into problems in Greco-Roman society. There, images of the gods and goddesses were ever-present, and Christians could be charged with treason for refusing to offer **sacrifices** before the emperor's image.

Islam's resistance to idolatry is the legacy of Judeo-Christian beliefs. The Arab tribes of the pre-Islamic era worshipped many gods in the forms of figurines and some were even nature subjects such as stones and trees. After the seizure of **Mecca** in 630, **Muhammad** had all the idols of the Kaaba (the central shrine of Islam) destroyed. In fact, Islam forbids the making of a representation of any living thing, whether or not it is intended to be worshipped. The **Koran** contains many prohibitions against idols and idolatry. For example, Muslims may neither marry a woman idolater nor give their daughters to idolaters in marriage (2:220–221). The Koran itself reminds us of the falsity of all alleged gods. To the worshippers of man-made objects, it asks: "Do you worship what you have carved yourself?" (37:95) "Or have you taken unto you others beside Him to be your protectors, even such as have no power either for good or for harm to themselves?" (13:16)

To the worshippers of heavenly bodies it cites the story of **Abraham:** "When night outspread over him he saw a star and said, 'This is my **Lord.**' But when it set he said, 'I **love** not the setters.' When he saw the moon rising, he said, 'This is my Lord.' But when it set he said, 'If my Lord does not guide me I shall surely be of the people gone astray.' When he saw the sun rising, he said, 'This is my Lord; this is greater.' But when it set he said, 'O my people, surely I quit that which you associate, I have turned my face to Him Who originated the heavens and the earth; a man of pure faith, I am not of the idolaters'" (6:76–79).

Ikenga

God of the Ibo peoples of Nigeria.

Illumination

See Light.

Image of God

A term found in the **creation** story of **Genesis** (1:26). The account in Genesis says: "Then **God** said, 'Let us make **man** in our image, in our likeness.'" The idea of whether or not God meant this literally has been a source of debate for centuries. Although it is generally believed that God meant this in a spiritual sense, there are still some who take this scripture literally.

Imago Dei

A Latin term meaning **"image of God."** The phrase is taken from **Genesis** (1:27) where it says, "So **God** created humankind in his image, in the image of God he created them; male and female he created them." The doctrine of Imago Dei is not speaking of a physical image of God but of His **divine** nature. Humans being created in God's image therefore mirror His characteristics and have inherited His divine nature, reflecting such qualities as morality, spirituality, as well as His intellectual nature. In addition, they have total centeredness, creative freedom, and the abilities of self-determination and self-transcendence.

Imana

Creator god of the Rwandans.

Immaculate Conception

A Roman Catholic teaching regarding **Mary,** the mother of **Jesus'** sinlessness. The Immaculate Conception was declared a **divine**ly revealed dogma by Pope Pius IX (1854). The belief is that Mary, although conceived by natural means, was from the moment of conception, by the **grace** of **God,** free from any stain of **original sin.** The term is sometimes confused with the Virgin Birth.

Immanence

An attribute of **God,** meaning that God is everywhere and in all things.

Immanuel

A **Hebrew** name meaning **"God is with us,"** used by the **prophet Isaiah** (7:14) in prophesying the birth of the **Messiah.** The verse is a well-known **prophecy** which speaks about a young woman who will bear a son and will name him Immanuel. The prophecy is again mentioned in Matthew 1:20–23 when God, through an **angel,** gives **Joseph** a message in a dream. In the dream, an angel says, "Joseph, do not be afraid to take **Mary** as your wife, for the child conceived in her is from the **Holy Spirit.** She will bear a son, and you are to name him **Jesus,** for he will save his people from their **sins."** All this took place to fulfill what had been spoken by the **Lord** through the prophet: "Look, the virgin shall conceive and bear a son, and they shall name him **Emmanuel."**

Immutability

A term that speaks to **God's** permanence and unchanging nature. God is believed in many religions to be immutable, meaning that God does not change in any way.

In God We Trust

The motto of the United States of America. The phrase can be found on U.S. currency. The motto is taken from the **Genesis creation** account of the **Bible.** According to the United States

107

Department of Treasury, the motto "In God We Trust" came about due to religious sentiment during the **Civil War.** During that period, devout citizens petitioned the Secretary of the Treasury (Salmon P. Chase) to recognize God on coins. On April 22, 1864, Congress passed an Amendment authorizing the motto to be placed on the two-cent coin. It has appeared on a variety of coins through the years, and appeared on paper money in 1957. The phrase was eventually printed on all paper bills.

Incarnation

In Christian **theology, God's** presence on Earth in the person of **Jesus Christ.** Early Christians believed that Jesus was God in the flesh. They believed him to be the embodiment of the prophesied **"Immanuel,"** meaning, "God is with us" (**Isaiah** 7:14; Matthew 1:23). Many Christians embrace the idea of God incarnate and believe that God became **Man** to die for our **sins** and that this is the **atonement.** Many others have found it hard to believe that a **holy** and powerful God would come and walk among sinful humankind, and have therefore rejected the doctrine.

Incense

The smoke of incense symbolizes worship to **God** in the monotheistic religions and worship of the gods in the polytheistic religions. In the **Bible, David** speaks to God, saying: "Let my **prayer** be counted as incense before you, and the lifting up of my hands as an evening sacrifice" (Psalms 141:2). Since ancient times, incense has always been used in prayer and rituals. It is believed that the incense carries prayers to God.

Among the ancient **Hebrews,** incense played an important role in their worship and **sacrifices** offered to God. It was offered with prayer, supplication, and in praise. In the **Old Testament,** the **altar** of incense, also referred to as the **Golden Altar,** was located in the ancient **Israel**ite **tabernacle** (or **Tent of Meeting**). The tabernacle was the Israelites' central **place of worship.** The High Priest **Aaron** burned fragrant incense on the altar in the morning when he dressed the lamps, and in the evening when he set up the lamps. The offering of the incense was to be performed by the Hebrews throughout their generations. Priests regularly burned incense before God (**Exodus** 30:7–8).

To the Israelites, incense was **holy.** They were disallowed by God to make it with anything other than the Sanctuary formula and were not allowed to use it for personal pleasure. If they did so, they would be set apart from the people (Exodus 30:37-38). In addition to being used for worship, incense also appeased God's wrath against wrongful acts (Numbers 16:44-48). The Bible speaks of a **Golden Censer** carried by an **angel.** The Golden Censer was carried to the **golden altar** which stands before God's throne. The incense inside is to be offered with the prayers of the saints to God. Revelation (8:3) states, "Another angel with a golden censer came and stood at the altar; he was given a great quantity of incense to offer with the prayers of all the saints on the golden altar that is before the throne."

Independence
See Aseity.

India
See Hinduism.

Indra (Virile Power)

Lord of **Heaven** and king of the gods in Vedism and **Hinduism.** In Vedic **mythology** he is the god of controlling the storms and rain. He is also the god of battle and is the most famous Vedic god, with more than 250 hymns of the Veda addressed to him. In Hinduism, Indra is portrayed with a beard of lightning, representing his role as the god of thunder, lightning, and storms. He is credited with creating fire inside the clouds of heaven. In later Hinduism, he endures in mythology but is no longer worshipped.

Infinity

In most religions, **God** is believed to be **eternal,** not bound by space and time. Revelation supports the idea that God is infinite as it says: "'I am the Alpha and the Omega, who is, and who was, and who is to come, the **Almighty'**" (Revelation 1:8). Psalms 90:2 says, "Before the **mountains** themselves were born, Or you proceeded to bring forth as with labor pains the earth and the productive land, Even from time indefinite to time indefinite you are God."

Infralapsarianism (After the Fall)

The view that **God's** selection of some people for **salvation** followed, and was a consequence of, humanity's **fall** from **grace.**

Inner Circle

The Talmud states that before the **Creation, God** held a consultation with His inner circle of **angels** for their advice on His intended plan to create **Man.** That inner circle consisted of the angels of truth, justice, peace, and charity.

Intermediaries

Angels appear in numerous religious traditions in the role of intermediaries between humans and **God.** In ancient times there were gods and **goddess**es such as the winged god Hermes, and the goddess Iris of Greek **mythology,** who carried messages for the gods.

Later, with the development of the monotheistic religions, angels stood in place of God as intermediaries carrying out God's **divine** will. In the **Bible,** the Archangel **Gabriel** served as an announcer of births and interpreter of visions and prophecies. Other angels, such as the **Angel of the Lord,** served in other intermediary roles, such as ushering **Lot** and his family out of **Sodom** before its destruction, and rescuing three **Hebrew** men from a fiery furnace.

God is believed to need such intermediary help because He is too powerful a force for humankind to come face to face with. The Bible explains that no **man** can see God's face and live (**Exodus** 33:20). Therefore, the angels are needed to stand in place of God. In some religious traditions, angels are believed to carry the **prayers** of humans to God and to deliver messages from God to humans. The angels who act as intermediaries generally come from the orders of the **archangels** and angels.

Interrogation of the Dead

See Questioning of the Dead.

Intuition

According to *Merriam-Webster's New World Dictionary,* the intuition is "the direct knowing or learning of something without the conscious use of reasoning." It is believed by some that intuition is a direct channel from **God** and that this direct knowing comes straight from Him. It is believed to be God's way of speaking to people, warning them and keeping them safe. It is also thought that **angels** and **spirit guides** act on God's behalf when using this means of communication.

Io

Supreme god of the Maori of New Zealand and other Polynesian peoples.

Iran

See Persia.

Irenaeus, Saint (c. 125–c. 202)

Greek theologian, bishop of Lyons, and Father of the **Church.** He was the first Father of the Church to systematize Christian principles and is quoted frequently by later theologians. Only two of his works survive, *Against Heresies* and *Epideixix.* Irenaeus of Lyons wrote, "Far removed is the **Father** of all from those things which operate among men, the affections and passions. He is simple, not composed of parts, without structure, altogether like and equal to himself alone. He is all mind, all **spirit,** all thought, all intelligent, all reason . . . all **light,** all **fountain** of every good, and this is the manner in which the religious and the pious are accustomed to speak of **God."**

Irish

See Celts.

Isaac (2066 B.C.–1886 B.C.)

The son of the **prophet Abraham** and his wife **Sarah.** He was a **miracle** from **God,** a promised son given to them in their old age. His birth was announced to Abraham by one of three **angels** who visited him. Abraham was 100 years old when Isaac was born (**Genesis** 21:5), and Sarah, at age 90, had been unable to have children (Genesis 16:1, 17:17). However, because God had found favor with Abraham, He blessed him by saying: "Your wife Sarah will bear you a son, and you will call him Isaac. I will establish My **Covenant** with him as an **everlasting** covenant for his descendants after him" (Genesis 17:19). Isaac's older half-brother was **Ishmael,** son of Abraham and **Hagar.** Isaac was also the father of Esau and **Jacob,** whom God renamed **Israel.**

When speaking to **Moses,** God spoke of Isaac when mentioning his forefathers, noting his position of importance in God's eyes. God said, "I Am The God of your father, The God of Abraham, The God of Isaac, and The God of Jacob" (**Exodus** 3:6). When Isaac was a young man, God tested Abraham's **faith** and obedience by commanding him to offer Isaac as a **sacrifice.** God said to Abraham, "Take your son, your only son Isaac, whom you love, and go to the region of Moriah. Sacrifice him there as a burnt offering on one of the **mountains** I will tell you about" (Genesis 22:2). However, just as he was about to kill Isaac, God sent an angel to stop him saying, "Do not do anything to him. Now I know that you fear God, because you have not withheld from Me your son, your only son" (Genesis 22:12). God then provided a ram to sacrifice in Isaac's place.

Later, Abraham sent a servant to Haran, the place that he had left many years before, to find a wife for Isaac. The servant met Rebekah beside a well and brought her to Canaan to be Isaac's wife. At the age of 40, Isaac married Rebekah (Genesis 25:20). After they had been married for 20 years, Rebekah became pregnant. God told her that she carried "two **nations**" in her womb. He revealed that the two nations would be divided and the firstborn would serve the younger. Isaac named his sons Esau and Jacob; Esau the elder son, and Jacob the younger son. Isaac favored Esau and Rebekah favored Jacob. In Isaac's old age, Rebekah and Jacob tricked him into blessing Jacob. Isaac lived a very long life before dying at Hebron. There, he was buried by Jacob and Esau in what is today known as the Tomb of the Patriarchs, the burial place of Abraham, Sarah, Isaac, Rebekah, Jacob/Israel, and Leah (Genesis 35:28-29, 49:31).

Isaiah (God Saves)

A **prophet** in **Israel** during the eighth century B.C. The Book of Isaiah is the first book of the **Old Testament's** major prophets. The son of Amoz and the first of the greater prophets, Isaiah has been called the greatest of the Old Testament prophets. When he was twenty-five he had a profound vision of **God,** and from that day forward devoted himself to prophesizing. Isaiah was called by God to warn of judgment on all who turn away from Him. His book, the twenty-third of the Old Testament, covers sixty years of **prophecy** in Jerusalem. It reproves the **sins** of the **Jews** and other **nations,** and foreshadows the coming of **Christ.** He is also called "prince of prophets." In a vision Isaiah saw flaming **angels** above the Throne of God. Each had six wings. Two wings covered the angels' faces, two covered the feet and two were used for flying. These angels are generally thought to be the **Seraphim.** In addition, Isaiah was touched on the lips by a Seraph who was carrying a live coal. The coal was to cleanse him in order that he might speak to God without sin. Says Isaiah, "Then one of the Seraphs flew to me, holding a live coal that had been taken from the **altar** with a pair of tongs. The Seraph touched my mouth with it and said: 'Now that this has touched your lips, your guilt has departed and your sin is blotted out'" (Isaiah 6:6–7).

Ishmael (God Heard)

The son of the **prophet Abraham,** born to his wife **Sarah's** handmaid, **Hagar,** and the half-brother of **Isaac.** In **Islamic** tradition, Ishmael is an ancestor of the Arab peoples. Abraham's wife Sarah was old and barren. Because of this, she convinced Abraham to have a child with her maidservant Hagar. Hagar gave Abraham a son whom she named Ishmael. Later, **God** blessed Abraham and Sarah with a child in their old age, and they named him Isaac. After Isaac was born, Sarah did not want Ishmael to inherit anything, so she had Abraham send Hagar and Ishmael away into the desert. God, however, was watching and preserved and blessed Ishmael. Hagar and Ishmael fled to the south. Ishmael settled in the wilderness, married an **Egyptian** woman, and became the progenitor of 12 tribes in North **Arabia.** The region occupied by these Ishmaelites included most of central and northern Arabia.

In Islam, Ishmael is considered a prophet. The **Koran** states that "Abraham and Ishmael built the Kaaba [the House of God in **Mecca**] as the house of God." The spring is traditionally identified with a Meccan well near the Kaaba, which **Muslims** believe was built by Ishmael and Abraham. In addition, Muslims also recognize Arabs as Ishmael's descendants, thus distinguishing them from the **Israel**ites, the descendants of Isaac.

Islam (To Surrender to the Will of God)

One of the three major world religions that profess belief in a single **God.** Islam was founded in **Arabia** in the seventh century A.D. and is based on the teachings of **Muhammad.** One who practices Islam is called a **Muslim.** Muslims believe in one, unique, incomparable God. He is the one true God and only He alone has the right to be worshipped. Muslims follow the revelation (the **Koran**) which was given to Muhammad by God (referred to as **Allah** in Islam). Islam recognizes **Judaism** and **Christianity** as being religions of the same God, but they do not believe the revelations of these religions have been faithfully kept. In Islam obedience to God is the primary doctrine. In fact, the word Islam means "to surrender to the will of God." No other activity in a person's life takes priority over serving God. God in Islam is merciful and compassionate—a loving God and kind **father.** Many Muslims say, "In the name of God, the Merciful, the Compassionate" each time they begin to speak, read, write, or do just about anything.

Muslims view God as having seven basic characteristics: life, knowledge, power, will, hearing, seeing, and speech. They see Him as being personal, transcendent, and unique. However, none of these characteristics are to be taken in any anthropomorphic sense. His will is absolute, and everything that happens depends on it. In addition, Muslims are forbidden to depict God in any form. The primary creed is that "There is no god but God, and Muhammad is the **prophet** of God."

At one point, Muhammad was asked by his contemporaries about God. The answer came directly from God Himself in the form of a short chapter (112) of the Koran which reads: "In the name of God, the Merciful, the Compassionate. Say (O Muhammad) He is God the One God, the **Everlasting** Refuge, who has not begotten, nor has been begotten, and equal to Him is not anyone." With the exception of one, each of the 114 chapters of the Koran starts with the verse: "In the name of God, the Merciful, the Compassionate." In one of the sayings of Muhammad we are told that "God is more loving and kinder than a mother to her dear child."

FIVE PILLARS OF ISLAM. In Islam, the most important way of expressing one's loyalty and **faith** in God is through what is termed the "Five Pillars of Islam" or the *Arkan al-din.* 1) The First Pillar is the most important. It is the open profession of belief in Allah as the one God. This profession is done in front of two people who act as witnesses to this declaration of faith. The words are spoken

as follows, "I witness that there is no God but Allah and that Muhammad is His servant and Prophet." This is known as the *shahadah.* It must be spoken aloud and accurately with full understanding of the meaning and with commitment and devotion in one's heart. 2) The Second Pillar is **prayer** five times daily, or *salat.* Praying several times a day reminds the Muslim of the need to praise God and to surrender to His will. 3) The Third Pillar is the giving of alms, or *zakat.* The Koran states that Muslims should give part of their wealth to those in need. 4) The Fourth Pillar is fasting, or *sawm,* during the month of Ramadan. During the fast it is forbidden to eat, drink, or smoke between the hours of sunrise and sunset. 5) The Fifth Pillar is the pilgrimage to **Mecca** called the *Hajj.* Allah, the **Most High** says, "And proclaim unto mankind the pilgrimage. . . . They will come unto thee on foot and on every lean camel; they will come from every deep ravine" (Sura 22). The pilgrimage to Mecca is one which every Muslim must attempt once in his or her life. However, it is to be tried only if it does not involve hardship for the traveler and his or her family. This is the only Pillar that is not compulsory.

THE FIVE ARTICLES OF FAITH. The Five Articles of Faith are contained within the Muslim creed. They are: 1) Belief in one God, 2) Belief in God's **angels,** 3) Belief in the revealed books, 4) Belief in God's prophets, and 5) Belief in the day of God's judgment. Muslims, believing in only the **divinity** of the true God, reject the divinity of **Jesus.** However, they honor him as an important prophet of God. In addition, they recognize the **Archangels Jibril** and Mikhail, known to **Judaism** and **Christianity** as **Gabriel** and **Michael,** respectively. See Adhan; Bismillah; Kalima.

Israel (Struggles with God)

Originally, he was the Biblical patriarch **Jacob**. His name was later changed to Israel after wrestling with **God** or an **Angel of God**. The name Israel means "struggles with God." According to the **Bible**, Jacob, who was the son of **Isaac**, wrestled with this spiritual "person" all night. The person asked Jacob to let him go, but Jacob refused saying that he would let him go only after he received a blessing from him.

According to the account in **Genesis**, "Jacob got up and took his two wives, his two concubines, and his eleven children, and crossed the Jabbok River. After he had sent them across, he also sent across all that he owned, but he stayed behind alone. Then a **man** came and wrestled with him just before daybreak. When the man saw that he was not winning the struggle, he hit Jacob on the hip, and it was thrown out of joint. The man said, 'Let me go; daylight is coming.' 'I won't, unless you bless me,' Jacob answered. 'What is your name?' The man asked. 'Jacob,' he answered. The man said, 'Your name will no longer be Jacob. You have struggled with God and with men, and you have won; so your name will be Israel'" (Genesis 32:22–28).

The nation of Israel descended from Jacob, now called Israel and his twelve sons (the ancestors of the twelve tribes of Israel). The nation of Israel is also referred to as "all Israel," **"children of Israel,"** and as Israelites. The kingdom formed when the nation of Israel separated in two after King **Solomon** died (1 Kings 11). Ten of the twelve tribes of Israel produced the northern kingdom of Israel; the two other tribes formed the southern kingdom of Judah (Genesis 32:28).

Israfel

The **Islamic angel** of music. According to Islamic lore, Israfel glorifies **God** with many tongues in a thousand languages. Israfel looks daily to **Hell** and cries so hard that his tears would **flood** the Earth if God did not intercede and stop their flow. The **Koran** speaks of Israfel thus: ". . . the angel Israfel, whose heart-strings are a lute, and who has the sweetest voice of all God's creatures." Edgar Allan Poe wrote about this angel in a poem entitled "Israfel." In the poem Poe wrote, "None sing so wildly well, as the angel Israfel. And the giddy stars (so legends tell), Ceasing their hymns, attend the spell, Of his voice, all mute."

Isten

Hungarian supreme god.

Izanagi and Izanami

Japanese creator god and **goddess**. According to lore, Izanagi and Izanami came down from **Heaven** to construct the Earth. The other gods and goddesses are their descendants. Izanagi (creator god) along with Izanami (creator goddess) created part of the semidivine original human couple in Japanese legend. Their **children** became the first gods and the ancestors of the human race.

J

Of all the crowns JEHOVAH bears,
Salvation is his dearest claim;
That gracious sound well-pleas'd he hears,
And owns EMMANUEL for his name.
—*William Cowper*

Jacob (2006 B.C.–1859 B.C.)

In the **Old Testament,** he is the son of **Isaac** and Rebekah, renamed **Israel** by **God.** God chose Jacob to inherit the promises he had given to Isaac. Jacob was the brother of Esau, and the grandson of **Abraham** and **Sarah.** Jacob was known for trickery. He came out of the womb grasping his brother Esau's heel. Later he persuaded Esau to sell him his birthright and tricked Isaac into blessing him instead of Esau. Fearing his brother's anger, he fled to live with his uncle Laban. On the way he had a dream in which he saw a ladder (now referred to as Jacob's Ladder) extending to **Heaven** with **angels** of God on it.

It was then that God vowed to keep his promise to Abraham through Jacob and his descendants. He came to Jacob in a dream. The **Bible** says (**Genesis** 28:12), "And he dreamed that there was a ladder set up on the earth, the top of it reaching to heaven; and the angels of God were ascending and descending on it. And the **Lord** stood beside him and said, 'I am the Lord, the God of Abraham your father and the God of Isaac; the land on which you lie I will give to you and to your offspring; and your offspring shall be like the dust of the earth, and you shall spread abroad to the west and to the east and to the north and to the south; and all the families of the earth shall be blessed in you and your offspring. Know that I am with you and will keep you wherever you go, and will bring you back to this land; for I will not leave you until I have done what I have promised you.' Then Jacob woke from his sleep and said, 'Surely the Lord is in this place—and I did not know it!' And he was afraid, and said, 'How awesome is this place! This is none other than the house of God, and this is the gate of heaven.'"

Jacob later married two sisters, Rachel and Leah, and also had two concubines, Bilhah and Zilpah. Between the four women Jacob fathered twelve sons. Jacob became rich while working for his uncle Laban. Eventually jealousy among Laban's sons forced Jacob to flee back to Canaan in spite of his fear of Esau. On the way he wrestled an angel all night. In the morning the angel changed Jacob's name to Israel and he became the father of the nation that bears his name. His sons gave their names to the twelve tribes of Israel. Jacob eventually moved to **Egypt** to be with his son **Joseph,** who had been sold there as a slave, but later rose to prominence in Pharaoh's court.

Jacob's Ladder

See Jacob.

Japan

Shinto and **Buddhism** are the main religions of Japan. A small minority of Japanese are Christians. Shinto, meaning "the way of the gods," is a native Japanese religion. Its followers worship the forces of nature, and its gods often personify the forces of nature. Buddhism was founded by Siddhartha **Gautama,** an Indian prince born in Kapilavastu, **India.** Unlike most religions, Buddhists do not believe in **God,** a **Supreme Being,** or a **Divine** Entity that created the world or that rules the world. The emphasis in Buddhism is not in having **faith** in an unknowable God or afterlife, but lies in the knowledge that focuses on transcending the self. Buddhists don't concern themselves about God or god(s). They concern themselves with the Dharma, which is neither a god or gods. It is "truth" or "reality." See Shintoism.

Javeh

A variation of the **Hebrew** name of **God,** Yahweh.

Jealous

In the **Bible's Old Testament, God** is sometimes described as a "jealous god." The idea of a jealous God can be traced back to comments made by God to the **Israel**ites in the Old Testament. When used to describe God, the word "jealous" is used to refer to God's anger against the unfaithful people of Israel. **Exodus** 20:5 says, "You shall not bow down to them or worship them; for I the **Lord** your God am a jealous God." **Deuteronomy** 4:24 says, "For the Lord your God is a devouring fire, a jealous God."

Jefferson, Thomas (1743–1826)

America's third president (1801–1809) and author of the Declaration of Independence. He has been hailed as one of the most brilliant individuals in history. His interests were never-ending, and his successes were great and wide-ranging. Some of his diverse interests and professions included: philosopher, educator, naturalist, politician, scientist, architect, inventor, musician, writer, and pioneer in scientific farming. In addition, Jefferson was the leading spokesman for democracy during that period. Like many educated men of his day, Jefferson practiced **Deism** (the philosophical idea that **God** does not reveal Himself through revelation, but through scientific **laws**). Deists believed that God leaves **Man** to his own affairs. Even though Jefferson was popular with the people, he was often criticized for his spiritual and religious beliefs. The following are experts taken from Jefferson's writings on God.

The God who gave us life gave us liberty at the same time.
—Rights of British America,1774.

God has formed us moral agents . . . that we may promote the happiness of those with whom He has placed us in society, by acting honestly towards all, benevolently to those who fall within our way, respecting sacredly their rights, bodily and mental, and cherishing especially their freedom of conscience, as we value our own.

—Thomas Jefferson to Miles King, 1814.

Fix reason firmly in her seat, and call to her tribunal every fact, every opinion. Question with boldness even the existence of a God;

because, if there is one, he must more approve of the homage of reason, than that of blindfolded fear.

—Thomas Jefferson to Peter Carr, 1787.

Jehovah (The Eternal Ever-Loving One)

A version of the personal name of God in Judaism and Christianity. The name Jehovah was originally listed in the Bible more than seven thousand times. For example, the King James Version, Psalm 83:18, reads: "That men may know that thou, whose name is alone is JEHOVAH, art the most high over all the earth." In the English Bibles it is replaced with LORD or GOD in all capital letters, because of the Hebrew belief that God's name is too sacred to pronounce.

The word Jehovah arose from the consonants YHWH, JHVH, or JHWH with the vowels of a separate word, *Adonai* (Lord) inserted. What its original vowels were is a matter of speculation because the name came to be regarded as too sacred to be spoken. Therefore today, the original pronunciation of the name is believed lost. Shortened forms include *Jah* (see Psalms 68:4, for example) and *Jahu* (in proper names). It indicates that the name was originally spoken *Jaweh* or *Yahwe* (often spelled Yahweh in modern usage). In addition, God's name is found in most Bibles at Revelation 19:1–6 as part of the expression "Alleluia" or "Hallelujah." This means "praise Jah," a shortened form of Jehovah. Jehovah is also a covenant name. That means it is a name God uses with people with whom He is committed. Jehovah can be used in the singular or plural, and as masculine or feminine.

Jehovah Elohim

Ancient Hebrew name for God. It means "the Lord God."

Jehovah's Witnesses

Official name of the religion that believes it is important to know and use God's personal name.

Jehovah-Jireh

Ancient Hebrew name for God. It means "The Lord will Provide."

Jehovah-M'kaddesh

Ancient Hebrew name for God. It means "The Lord Who Sanctifies."

Jehovah-Nissi

Ancient Hebrew name for God. It means "The Lord is Our Banner."

Jehovah-Rohi

Ancient Hebrew name for God. It means "The Lord is Our Shepherd."

Jehovah-Rophe

Ancient Hebrew name for God. It means "The Lord Who Heals."

Jehovah-Sabaoth

Ancient Hebrew name for God. It means "The Lord of Hosts."

Jehovah-Shalom

Ancient Hebrew name for God. It means "The Lord is Our Peace."

Jehovah-Shammah

Ancient Hebrew name for God. It means "The Lord is There."

Jehovah-Tsidkenu

Ancient Hebrew name for God. It means "The Lord is Our Righteousness."

Jeremiah (Yahweh Establishes)

A prophet chosen by God to speak in His name. A Hebrew priest and the son of Hilkiah, Jeremiah preached in Jerusalem under King Josiah and his successors. Jeremiah's prophecies, visions, and life story are narrated in the **Bible** book that bears his name; he was the second of the three major prophets. His message indicts his contemporaries for social injustice and religious apostasy. He lived in the priestly town of Anathoth, about three miles north of Jerusalem (1 Chronicles 6:60) from about 627 to 580 B.C., a crucial period in the history of Judah, the Southern Kingdom. Except for a brief period of independence under Josiah, Judah existed as a vassal under Assyria, **Egypt,** and **Babylon.**

Jeremiah began writing during the thirteenth year of Josiah's reign (Jeremiah 1:2, 25:3). Jeremiah was a man consumed by his commitment to God. He was scarcely out of childhood, around the age of thirteen, when God called him to be a prophet. Jeremiah heard the words, "Before I formed you in the womb I knew you, and before you were born I consecrated you." When Jeremiah protested that he was only a boy, God said, "Now I have put my words in your mouth" (Jeremiah 1:5,9). Jeremiah became a passionate prophet, pouring out his heart at great length and with great emotion to God. God told Jeremiah never to marry or have **children,** since conditions would soon become so awful in the land that children would die in great numbers and not even be mourned or buried. This was because of the **evil** that had infested the land. His visions included the almond rod and the boiling pot (Jeremiah 1:11–19); the potter's wheel (Jeremiah 18:1–11); and the good and the bad figs (Jeremiah 24:1–10). His scribe, **Baruch,** recorded his prophecies (Jeremiah 36:4–32).

Jerusalem Bible

A translation of the **Bible** that incorporated the name **Yahweh** (the **Hebrew** name of **God**) into the original places in the Bible where it had been omitted in other translations. Ancient Hebrews believed the name to be too sacred to be spoken or written. It was replaced instead with the word **LORD** in most places where the name of God or the letters **YHWH** were once written. First published in 1966, it was revised in 1985 and includes the **Apocrypha.**

Jesus of Nazareth (c. 6 B.C.–c. 30 A.D.)

Jewish **prophet,** teacher, and spiritual leader. He is the the key figure of **Christianity.** The life and teachings of Jesus are the inspiration for the Christian religion. Jesus preached and taught in Palestine almost 2,000 years ago. The name Jesus is the Greek version of a common **Hebrew** name, Joshua (Y'shua) or Je-Hoshua meaning savior or "**Jehovah** is **Salvation.**" The title **Christ** is derived from the Greek *christos,* a translation of the Hebrew *mashiakh* (**anointed one**), or **Messiah.**

In the **Old Testament, priests** and kings were anointed with oil upon taking office. This was a mark of great honor. A belief grew up that, one day, **God** would send an "anointed one," a Messiah to restore the fortunes of the Hebrews. Because Jesus' followers believed that he was this savior, they called him Messiah, or Christ. To Christians, Jesus is the **Son of God** and is **divine.** Christians believe that God sent him to Earth to save humanity. Only Christians have made this claim. Others, such as the **Muslims,** regard Jesus as an important prophet. In **Islam** he is called Isa. In the **Koran,** Isa stands with the host of **angels** nearest to God, and is considered to be a semi-angelic character. The **Jews** reject Jesus as the Messiah because of various reasons including their claim that Jesus did not fulfill Messianic prophecies given in the **Bible's** Old Testament.

Jews

See Israel.

Jibril

An **angel** sent from **God** to **Muhammad**. While Muhammad was meditating on a mountain near **Mecca**, the Archangel **Jibril** (**Gabriel** in Judeo-Christian belief) appeared to Muhammad and gave him a revelation from God. This revelation turned into **Islam's holy** book, the **Koran**. As Jibril dictated the Koran to Muhammad, his wings were outstretched, his face was illuminated, and between his eyes was written, "There is no God, but God, and Muhammad is the **prophet** of God." Jibril later appeared to Muhammad and told him to call men to God.

Job

A faithful servant of **God** whose life account is recorded in the **Bible**. The Book of Job deals with the problem of human suffering. It tells the story of Job, a good man, who loses everything yet still has deep **faith** in God. Job was a man who, according to the Bible, was "blameless and upright." A man "who feared God and turned away from **evil**" (Job 1:1). He was spiritual, very devoted to God, rich, the head of a large family, and led a comfortable, contented life. One day, the **angels** came to present themselves before God (Job 1:6), and **Satan** also came among them. God asked Satan what he thought of Job's piety and righteousness. Satan proposes that Job would curse God if he were to lose all his wealth; so God and Satan agree to test Job. Satan proceeds to take away Job's possessions, all his **children**, and finally inflicts extremely painful sores on him. In the end Job refuses to curse God and continues as a faithful servant of God. God in return blesses him with renewed health, giving twice as many riches and possessions as he had before. He also blessed him with seven sons and three daughters.

The story of Job has served for centuries as encouragement to people who have suffered and who feel that they are somehow being tested (Job 1:6–22; 2:1–10). Job states: "For I know that my redeemer liveth, and that he shall stand at the latter day upon the earth: And though . . . worms destroy this body, yet in my flesh shall I see God" (Job 19:25–26). In addition to Job's disasters and his deliverance by God, God also reveals His greatness to Job from a whirlwind. God's speech in the Book of Job has served as a powerful testimony to His greatness for centuries.

Joel (The Lord is God)

The author of the second book of the twelve minor **prophets**. The Book of Joel opens with a **destruction** brought by a plague of **locusts** and a prophesy of how **God** will bless and restore the land after the people repent. Joel then prophesizes about the gifts of the **Spirit** and the Last Days. The third and last chapter speaks of God's Judgment on the **nations**. God says in Joel 2:28–29, "And afterward, I will pour out my Spirit on all people. Your sons and daughters will prophesy, your old men will dream dreams, your young men will see visions."

John the Baptist

A biblical **prophet**. John the Baptist was a cousin of **Jesus**. In **Christianity**, he is believed to have been chosen by **God** to prepare the way for Jesus, and is called the forerunner of Jesus. His birth was foretold by the Archangel **Gabriel** who appeared to his father **Zechariah** on behalf of God to inform him that he and his wife **Elizabeth** would have a son. The **Bible** tells us, "An **angel of the Lord** appeared to him standing at the right side of the **altar**." The **angel** informed Zechariah that his wife Elizabeth, who was old and barren, would give birth to a son, and that they were to name him John. Zechariah said to the angel, "How shall I know if this is so? I am an old man, and my wife is old also." The angel replied, "I am Gabriel. I stand in the presence of God, who sent me to speak to you and tell you this good news. But you have not believed my message which will come true at the right time. Because you have not believed, you will be unable to speak; you will remain silent until the day my promise to you comes true" (Luke 1:5–19). Zechariah was mute until the day John was born.

Johnson, Samuel (1709–1784)

English writer and lexicographer. He was a major figure in eighteenth-century literature and an arbiter of taste, and he was renowned for the force and balance of his prose style. Next only to William Shakespeare, Samuel Johnson is perhaps the most quoted of English writers. The latter part of the eighteenth century is often referred to as "the Age of Johnson." As a child, Johnson stopped attending church and abandoned religion. A few years later, however, he began to think that it was wrong of him to do so without investigating the matter, and the pangs of guilt he had over not having read theology before rejecting it brought him to the conclusion that there must be a moral law and hence a Lawgiver. Johnson wrote a series of sermons for his friend John Taylor. One of them deals with trust in God. Johnson writes: "This constant and devout practice is both the effect, and cause, of confidence in God. Trust in God is to be obtained only by repentance, obedience, and supplication, not by nourishing in our hearts a confused idea of the goodness of God, or a firm persuasion that we are in a state of grace." Johnson died in London on December 13, 1784, and was buried in Westminster Abbey.

Jonah

A Hebrew prophet, the fifth of the twelve minor prophets. Jonah was called by God to go to the city of Nineveh to denounce the wickedness of its people and to warn them of God's anger. However, Jonah rebelled against God and took a ship going in the opposite direction. God sent a great storm, and the men feared for their lives. They blamed Jonah for bringing God's wrath upon them, and threw him overboard. God saved Jonah by sending a large fish to swallow him up. Jonah prayed to God from the fish's belly and was delivered onto dry land. Jonah responded with a psalm of thanks that God had delivered him (Jonah 1–2).

God again commanded him to go to Nineveh. This time Jonah obeyed and went to Nineveh to warn the people of the coming destruction. All the people promptly repented in the hope that God would spare them. A fast was proclaimed and even the king wore a sackcloth and ashes. Because of their repentance, God decided to spare the city from punishment. Jonah became angry that Nineveh escaped from judgment. He sheltered under a gourd which God then destroyed, showing Jonah that, as he regreted the loss of the gourd, God would pity the loss of so many people.

Jonah's Prayer to God:
(Jonah 2:1–10)
Then Jonah prayed to the Lord his God from the belly of the fish, saying, "I called to the Lord out of my distress, and he answered me; out of the belly of Sheol I cried, and you heard my voice.
You cast me into the deep,
Into the heart of the seas,
And the flood surrounded me;
All your waves and your billows
Passed over me."
Then I said, "I am driven away from your sight;

How shall I look again
Upon your **holy** temple?"
The waters closed in over me;
The deep surrounded me;
Weeds were wrapped around my head
At the roots of the **mountains.**
I went down to the land
Whose bars closed upon me forever;
Yet you brought up my life from the
  Pit,
O Lord my God.
As my life was ebbing away,
I remembered the Lord;
And my **prayer** came to you,
Into your holy temple.
Those who worship vain idols
Forsake their true loyalty.
But I with the voice of thanksgiving
Will **sacrifice** to you;
What I have vowed I will pay.
Deliverance belongs to the Lord!
Then God spoke to the fish and it
  spewed Jonah out upon the dry
  land.

Joseph (May God Add)

The son of **Jacob** and **Rachel**. **God** used Joseph in order to spare others. As a young man, Joseph was sold into slavery in **Egypt** but rose to the position of vizier there (**Genesis 37**). Joseph was Jacob's eleventh son and also his favorite. He incurred the hatred of his older brothers because of his father's favoritism and because of his own dreams, in which he appeared to be ruling over them. The brothers, after considering killing him, decided to sell him to some merchants. Next they placed **blood** on his coat and told their father that Joseph had been killed. Joseph was taken to Egypt and sold to Potiphar. Joseph found favor with Potiphar and was given the job of overseer. Later however, he was imprisoned on false charges of making advances toward Potiphar's wife.

In prison he successively interpreted dreams for other prisoners so Pharaoh, disturbed by one of his dreams, called on Joseph to interpret it. After interpreting Pharaoh's dream, which foretold seven plentiful years followed by seven years of famine, Joseph advised Pharaoh to store grain during the plentiful years. Pharaoh agreed and appointed Joseph as Governor, second in the land only to himself. In the process, Joseph became rich and powerful. When famine struck the land, Joseph's brothers traveled to Egypt seeking food. Failing to recognize him, Joseph held one of his brothers hostage and demanded that the rest of them bring their youngest brother Benjamin to Egypt. When they returned, Joseph revealed himself to them. He later brought his father Jacob to live in Egypt. After Jacob died, Joseph's brothers worried that he would hold a grudge against them, but Joseph replied, "Even though you intended to do harm to me, God intended it for good, in order to preserve a numerous people, as He is doing today" (Genesis 50:20).

Joshua (God Is Salvation)

The successor of **Moses**. Joshua was one of the spies who had first looked at Canaan (the land promised to the **Israel**ites), and led the people in conquering and settling the new land. Joshua was very nervous at the prospect of succeeding Moses. In order to increase his confidence, **God** sent an **angel** to appear to him. The angel appeared in the form of a **man,** and stood before Joshua with a sword drawn. Joshua asked the angel if he was one of his followers or one of the enemies. The angel replied "Neither; but as commander of the army of the **Lord** I have now come."

Joshua immediately prostrated himself and asked what the angel commanded of him. The angel asked only that he remove his sandals because the place where he was standing was **holy.**

After the appearance of the angel, Joshua had the courage needed to lead the **Hebrews**. Joshua's military feats were matched by his trust in God. He commanded several campaigns against the Canaanites. There were some dramatic events in which he was involved, such as the fall of the walls of Jericho, and the sun and moon standing still at his command. In all, Joshua and his troops conquered thirty-one kings in the new territory. He later divided the land among the Israelite tribes according to God's directions.

Judaeus, Philo (20–50 A.D.)

Alexandrian **Jewish** philosopher. The greatest Jewish philosopher of his age, his writings have had an enormous influence on both Jewish and Christian thought. Philo was born in Alexandria, **Egypt**, to a wealthy, aristocratic Jewish family and received a thorough education in the **Old Testament** and in Greek literature and philosophy. Philo was the first philosopher to attempt to reconcile the **Bible** with Greek philosophy. In so doing he developed an allegorical interpretation of Scripture that enabled him to find many of the doctrines of Greek philosophy in the **Torah**. Philo conceived of **God** as a being without **attributes**, emphasizing the total **transcendence** and perfection of God. He believed God to be a being so exalted above the world that an intermediate class of beings is needed to establish a point of contact between him and the world. Philo called this intermediate class of beings God's **Logos** (the creative force of God); he also called the Logos "the image of God." Philo believed the Logos to be beings with active powers, surrounding God as a number of attendant beings.

Along with the Logos, Philo posited a realm of beings or potencies that bridge the gap between the God and His **creation**. Philo believed that humans have an obligation to God to worship and revere Him as well as show **love** and righteousness to others. Philo once wrote: "God shows Himself to people as an angel—not that God changes, but that each **soul** receives the impression of His presence in a different and angelic form."

Judaism

The religious beliefs, practices, and way of life of the **Jews**, as founded in c. 2000 B.C. by **Abraham, Isaac**, and **Jacob**. Judaism espouses belief in a monotheistic **God**, who is creator of the universe and who leads His people, the Jews, by speaking through **prophets**. Judaism's stress on a single God represents an important turning point in the history of religion. Never before had **monotheism** been expressed or encouraged in worship. **Israel's** religion began when Abraham was called by God to leave his nomadic life, move to a new land, and become the founder of a great people. Abraham obeyed God, and the seed of the nation of Israel was born. The concepts of God that are most often emphasized in Judaism are of Creator, Judge, and Savior of **Man**. The fundamental beliefs of God in Judaism are that there is only one God, and that God is the ultimate authority.

Judgment Day

The day when all people who have ever lived will be stand before **God** to explain the actions of their lives. Judgment Day can be found among the beliefs of **Judaism, Christianity**, and **Islam**.

Julian of Norwich (1342–1429)

Medieval mystic and writer. She has the distinction of being the first woman to write a book in English. In May 1373, at age thirty, Julian of Norwich became gravely ill and at the point of **death**.

Then after seven days, the medical crisis passed and she had a series of fifteen visions, or "showings" as she referred to them. The visions brought her great joy and peace. She made a swift recovery, and wrote down her experiences in a short book. Soon afterward she became an anchoress (recluse) living in a small room attached to St. Julian's Church, prompting her to take the name of Julian. Her real name is now unknown. She dedicated the rest of her life to prayer, studying, and contemplation.

Julian eventually wrote the main book based on her experience, *The Revelations of Divine Love*, which has become a spiritual classic. People who knew her went to her for spiritual insight and guidance. After her death, she is still giving insight through her writings. Her book is a gentle meditation on God's eternal and all-encompassing love. In *The Revelations of Divine Love*, Julian writes: "God is kind in his Being. That is to say, the Goodness which is Kind, is God. He is the Ground: he is the Substance: he is the very thing called Kindness. And he is the very Father and the very Mother of kinds."

Jung, Carl (1875–1961)

Swiss psychiatrist, who founded the analytical school of depth psychology. According to the writings of Jung, very early in his life he had dreams and visions of a spiritual nature, which taught him that religion is a personal matter. He also claimed that God had a dark side, one that did not fit with the usual idea of an ever-loving God.

Juok

The creator god of the Shilluk peoples of East Africa.

Jupiter

The Lord of Heaven and Earth and chief of all the gods in ancient Roman beliefs. One of his most prominent forms was as Jupiter Optimus Maximus which means the all-good and all-powerful. Under this name he was the guardian of Rome and was worshipped in a temple on the Capitoline Hill. Under this title he ruled over the universe, functioned as the god of the state, controlled the realm, and made his will known through prophecy. As Jupiter Fidius he was known as guardian of law, protector of truth, and defender of justice and virtue. His sanctuary was of vital importance in Rome and the hub of its political life. As Jupiter Victor he was commander of the Roman army, leading them to victory. Other titles include: Caelestis (heavenly); Lucetius (of the light); Totans (thunderer); and Fulgurator (of the lightning). He is represented by the lightning bolt and the eagle. The Romans equated Jupiter with Zeus (the supreme god of the Greeks).

K

God's mercy hath no relation to time, no limitation in time. . . . Whom God loves He loves to the end; and not only to their end, to their death, but to His end; and His end is, that He might love them still.
—*John Donne*

Ka Tyeleo

Supreme god of the West **African** Senufo.

Kacoch

Mayan creator god. A variation of the name Kacoch is Cacoch.

Kadosh

Ancient **Hebrew** name for **God.** It means "**Holy** One." The **Old Testament** Book of **Isaiah** uses the expression "the Holy One of **Israel**" twenty-nine times.

Kalima

A term used in **Islam.** "Our Kalima" is the motto of **Muslims** representing their **faith** and feelings toward **God.** It reads in full: "There is no god but God, and **Muhammad** is the **Messenger** of God. I believe in God, the **angels,** the apostles, the revealed Books, **paradise** and **hell** and the Day of Resurrection. I accept the **Holy Koran** as the Book of God, and Muhammad, on whom be peace and the **blessings** of God, as the true **Prophet.**"

Kalumba

Creator god of the Luba peoples of Zaire.

Kanna

Ancient **Hebrew** name for **God.** It means **Jealous.**

Kant, Immanuel

See Age of Enlightenment.

Karei

Supreme Being of the Semang peoples of Malaya.

Katonda

Supreme Being in Bugandan beliefs.

Keating, Father Thomas (1923–)

Author, teacher, and monk. He is a member of the Cistercian order, founded by Saint Bernard in 1908. He is one of the founders of the **Centering Prayer** movement and of Contemplative Outreach. Keating has worked for many years to foster understanding among the world's religions. Keating says in his book *Awakenings,* "God is hidden in difficulties. If we can find him there, we will never lose him. Without difficulties, we do not know the power of God's **mercy** and the incredible destiny he has for each of us."

Keller, Helen (1880–1968)

American author and lecturer. She was blind and deaf from the age of two. In 1887, she was put in the care of Anne Sullivan, who became her teacher and lifelong companion. Keller made rapid progress, and in 1904 was graduated from Radcliffe College with honors. While still at Radcliffe, Helen Keller began her writing career which was to continue for fifty years. She wrote twelve books and numerous articles on blindness, deafness, social issues, and women's rights. She published and lectured widely to raise funds for the training of the blind and for other social causes. Regarding her belief in **God,** Keller writes, "I believe that God is in me, as the sun is in the colour and fragrance of a flower, the **Light** in my darkness, the Voice in my silence."

Kempis, Thomas A. (c. 1380–1471)

German monk. *The Imitation of Christ,* a devotional treatise that became immensely influential, has been traditionally ascribed to him. His original name was Thomas Hemerken. Born in Kempen, Prussia, he was educated at Deventer in the Netherlands. In the Netherlands, he became an Augustinian priest. The greater part of his life was passed in seclusion, counseling and writing. Thomas's writings are representative of the *devotio moderna,* a religious movement within Roman **Catholicism** from the end of the fourteenth to the sixteenth centuries stressing **meditation** and the inner life, attaching little importance to ritual and external works, and downgrading the highly speculative spirituality of the thirteenth and fourteenth centuries. Thomas also wrote sermons, religious biographies, and devotional books for the young. On **God,** Kempis wrote: "Oh, how great peace and quietness would he possess who should cut off all vain anxiety and place all his confidence in God." He also said, "**Man** proposes, but God disposes."

Kenosis

The teaching of the kenosis is an attempt to explain the relinquishing of the form of **God** by **Jesus** to become a **man.** It attempts to explain such paradoxes as how an all-knowing and all-powerful God could become a tiny human baby. Or how it is that the **Devil** could tempt him. The assertion is that God, upon becoming human, separated Himself from qualities of His deity to become a man, experience human feelings, and suffer **death.**

Kepler, Johannes (1571–1630)

German astronomer. He was professor of mathematics at Graz from 1593–1598 and the court mathematician to the **Holy** Roman Emperor Rudolf II. However, Kepler is chiefly remembered for Kepler's Laws, three mathematical statements that accurately describe the rotations of the planets around the sun. Kepler believed that **angels** move the planets, and act as coordinators of the enormous and complex actions of the entire universe. Kepler was a deeply pious man, and his writings contain numerous references to **God.** He views his work as a fulfillment of his Christian duty to understand the works of God. He believed that since **Man** was made in the image of God, it was possible to understand the universe that God had created. Furthermore, Kepler was convinced that God had made the universe according to a mathematical plan.

Kepler repeatedly thanked God for granting him insights, but the insights were presented as rational. Kepler said, "I give myself over to my rapture. I tremble; my **blood** leaps. God has waited 6000 years for a looker-on to His work." Also: "Since we astronomers are **priests** of the highest God in regard to the book of nature, it befits us to be thoughtful, not of the glory of our minds, but rather, above all else, of the glory of God."

Khoda

A general term denoting **God** in **Persia** and in **Hinduism.**

Khonvum

Chief god of the Pygmies.

King Jr., Martin Luther (1929–1968)

African-American clergyman and Nobel Prize winner. King was a major leader of the American civil rights movement and a leading promoter of nonviolent resistance to racial oppression. After his assassination in 1968, King became a symbol of protest in the fight for racial justice. King was bolstered by his **faith** in **God** and by the strength that such faith offered. A deeply religious man, King was ordained a Baptist minister in 1947. Indivisibly connected to his **love** of God was his determination to achieve civil rights for African Americans. In his speech at Clayborn Temple, Memphis, Tennessee, April 3, 1968, the evening before his assassination, King stated: "I just want to do God's will. And He's allowed me to go to the mountain. And I've looked over, and I've seen the **promised land!** So I'm happy tonight. I'm not worried about anything. I'm not fearing any **man.**"

King of Heaven and Earth

God in **Judaism, Christianity,** and **Islam** is known as the King of **Heaven** and Earth. In Assyrian beliefs, **Anu** was the "King of Heaven and Earth."

Kingdom of God

A term used in Judeo-Christian beliefs. There are three meanings to the term Kingdom of **God.** 1) The **Hebrew** kingdom as established by God. 2) A future **divine** kingdom to be ruled by **Christ.** 3) The **kingdom of Heaven.** The phrase "Kingdom of God" is used several times in the **New Testament** and it was the central theme of **Jesus'** teaching. In Mark 1:15, Jesus states, "The right time has come, and the Kingdom of God is near!" However, from Jesus' comments, it was apparent that the kingdom is not a specific place or an earthly government, as he said, "My kingdom does not belong to this world; if my kingdom belonged to this world, my followers would fight to keep me from being handed over to the Jewish authorities. No, my kingdom does not belong here!" (John 18:36). When Jesus spoke of "the Kingdom of God," he was describing God's rule over humanity. This is evident from Jesus' words at Luke 17:21 where he says, "the kingdom of god is within you." The New Revised Standard Version of the **Holy Bible** describes the Kingdom of God this way: "The **eternal** sovereignty or kingly rule of God, manifested in its acceptance by humanity on earth and the hope for the future."

Kingdom of Heaven

The word "kingdom" is used when referring to the place in **Heaven** in which **God** dwells. In **Judaism** and **Christianity,** the Kingdom of Heaven is the dwelling place of God and His **angels** as well as the righteous **souls** of individuals who once lived on the Earth.

Kitab-i-Iqan

See Book of Certitude.

Koran

The **Holy** Book of **Islam.** It is the Islamic counterpart of the Jewish **Torah** and the Christian **Bible. Muslims** regard the Koran as a revelation of **God** to **Muhammad**, mediated by **Jibril (Gabriel)** the Archangel of Revelation. They believe that God Himself, not Muhammad, is the author and therefore that the Koran is infallible. It was revealed to Muhammad in the **Arabian** Desert during the seventh century. The Koran was memorized by Muhammad and then dictated to his companions, and written down by scribes. Not one word of its 114 chapters (Suras) has been changed over the centuries, so that the Koran is in every detail the miraculous text which was given to Muhammad fourteen centuries ago. It was revealed to Muhammad over a period of 23 years and is regarded by Muslims as the **Word of God** and His final revelation to humankind. It is the prime source of every Muslim's **faith** and practice and deals with all the subjects which concern humanity, such as wisdom, doctrine, worship, and **law.** However, its basic theme is the relationship between God and His creatures. It also provides guidelines for a just society, proper human conduct, and an equitable economic system.

For Muslims, the Koran is the highest authority in all matters of faith, **theology,** and law. Muslims are careful in their handling of the Koran. They take special care not to lay the Koran on the ground or allow it to come into contact with anything unclean. One of the highest acts of devotion to God for Muslims is to memorize the entire Koran and then be able to recite it. One who has mastered the sacred text is called an *hafiz*. The opening statement of the Koran says:

In the Name of God, the Compassionate, the Merciful
Praise be to God, **Lord** of the worlds!
King on the Day of Reckoning!
Thee only do we worship, and to Thee do we cry for help.
Guide us on the straight path,

The path of those to whom Thou has been gracious;—with whom Thou art not angry, and who go not astray.

Krishna (Darkness)

One of the chief Hindu gods and the Supreme Personality of the Godhead. Krishna is said to be a historical person who appeared on Earth in **India** 5,000 years ago. According to some Hindu sects, he was the eighth or ninth **incarnation** of **Vishnu.** He is said to have stayed on Earth for 125 years and behaved like a human. His activities are said to have been unequaled.

Ku

Master god of the gods of Hawaii.

Kurios

Greek word for **"Lord"** found some 600 times in the original translation of the **New Testament.**

Kurkil

A raven creator god of a Mongol tribe in Siberia. He is believed to have created the universe and humankind.

Kurozumi-kyo

One of **Japan's** contemporary religions. The name is taken from its founder, Kurozumi Munetada (1780–1850), a Shinto priest. Followers worship the Shinto sun **goddess** Amaterasu as the **supreme god** and creator of the universe. They believe the other 8,000,000 Shinto gods to be manifestations of her.

Kyala

Creator god of the Nyakyusa peoples of South West Tanzania.

Kybalion, The

Ancient Hermetic teachings, explaining that there is only one mind, the **God** mind, and humans all share that mind.

L

God is like a vast ocean of love, and the Milky Way
galaxy is but a speck of foam floating in that ocean.

—Rumi

Lamb of God

A term used in **Christianity** to denote **Christ,** whose sacrificial **death** is believed to have removed the **sins** of the world. The idea of Christ as a lamb grew out of the **Old Testament** concept of the sacrificial lamb, particularly during **Passover.** In Latin, Lamb of God is *Agnus Dei.*

Land Flowing with Milk and Honey

A phrase taken from the **Old Testament.** It refers to a land that is rich and plentiful. In Biblical times this would have been considered a prime place to live. The **Bible** mentions "a land flowing with milk and honey" several times when referring to the place that **God** had promised the **Hebrews** to live once they left **Egypt.** For ancient peoples of the Middle East, the idea of a land flowing with milk and honey has long been associated with the **Islamic Heaven** or **paradise.** For example, the paradise portrayed by **God** in the **Koran** speaks of "rivers of fresh milk" and "rivers of pure honey." The milk and honey are considered special gifts of God.

Lao T'ien Yeh (Old Man Heaven)

Sung Chinese **high god.** See Yu Huang.

Last Judgment

The day when all people who have ever lived will be called before **God** to explain the actions of their lives. After the Last Judgment, virtuous **souls** will be conducted into **Heaven** where they will enjoy **eternal** life next to God.

Latin Proverb

"**God** will be present, whether asked or not."

Law, The

Rules of conduct given by **God** to **Moses** that regulated the lives and conduct of the **Hebrews.** The Law mirrors God's **holy,** righteous, and moral character. The Law is the very reflection of the nature of God because He desired His chosen people to emulate and reflect His character. Therefore, since God is pure, the Law is pure; since God is holy, the Law is holy. In fact, on several occasions God told the Hebrews to be holy in the same way that He was **holy** (Leviticus 11:45; 19:2; 20:26).

This body of law is recorded in the first five books of the **Bible.** The law included the **Ten Commandments** and religious, social, and dietary rules. The purpose of the Law was to direct the nation in how to live in relationship with God and each other. It was there to provide guidance, as its name in

Hebrew, *Torah* (meaning "instruction"), suggests. In Israel's law books, **Exodus** to **Deuteronomy,** there are three main collections of laws. The first follows the Ten Commandments in Exodus and deals with moral, civil, and religious laws (Exodus 21–23). In Leviticus (17–26), the second collection, known as "holiness" laws, focuses on worship rituals. The third collection, in Deuteronomy (12–25), emphasizes the detailed commands given in Exodus and Leviticus, and spells out the responsibilities of the king. The third set includes encouragement to the people to keep the law. Christians believe that **Jesus** marked the fulfillment of the Law.

Leibniz, Gottfried Wilhelm (1646–1716)

German philosopher, mathematician, and logician, regarded as one of the supreme intellects of the seventeenth century. Leibniz is probably best known for having invented differential and integral calculus (independently of Sir Isaac **Newton**). His principal works include: *De Arte Combinatoria* (On the Art of Combination), 1666; *Hypothesis Physica Nova* (New Physical Hypothesis), 1671; *Discours de Métaphysique* (Discourse on Metaphysics), 1686; unpublished manuscripts on the calculus of concepts, c. 1690; *Nouveaux Essais sur l'Entendement Humaine* (New Essays on Human Understanding), 1705; *Théodicée* ("**Theodicy**"), 1710; *Monadologia* ("The Monadology"), 1714.

Leibniz argued that a necessary being exists which carries within itself its reason for existence and is the sufficient reason for the existence of all contingent beings. Leibniz identified the necessary being as **God.** Says Leibniz, "God is at least possible since the concept of Him as the Infinite implies no contradiction; but if He is possible He must exist because the concept of Him involves existence."

Lewis, C(live) S(taples) (1898–1963)

English critic and novelist. Considered one of the most eloquent Christian apologists of his generation. He is well known to many through his books, which include *The Screwtape Letters, Mere* **Christianity,** *Surprised by Joy,* and his ever popular series for children, *The Chronicles of Narnia.* Born in Belfast, Ireland, Lewis was the son of a solicitor. He was educated privately and at the University of Oxford. Says Lewis of **God:** "God whispers to us in our pleasures, speaks in our conscience, but shouts in our pains: it is His megaphone to rouse a deaf world." He also comments, "The hardness of God is kinder than the softness of men, and His compulsion is our liberation."

Leza

The **supreme god** (also called a creator god) in Central **Africa.**

Libanza

Supreme god of the Upotos peoples of the Congo.

Life of Adam and Eve

One of the books found in the **Pseudepigrapha.** It relates the tale of the **fall** of the **angels.** According to the account, when **Adam** was created, **God** placed him above the angels, and instructed the angels to bow down to him because Adam had been created in the **image of God. Satan** refused to bow down to the newly created **man.** Afterward, Satan became the leader of other angels who also refused to bow down to Adam. Because of this act of disobedience, Satan and his followers were cast out of **Heaven,** and thrown down to the Earth. Satan blamed Adam for his ouster and set out for revenge. It was then that he assumed the guise of the serpent, entered the garden, and tricked **Eve** into **sin**.

Light

The light of **God** is a brilliant white light which radiates and filters down through the heavens, the **angels,** and the hierarchies. This Light is said to be filled with the knowledge, power, and wisdom of God, as well as His all-encompassing **love**. We all carry the Light of God inside us. The further away from God we are, the less we feel it. Both angels and mankind are said to carry the Light of God within them to remind them of God's love. The angels receive more of this light than we do, but we carry a portion of this light within us.

The Light of God is symbolically represented in most religions. Some religions use candles during their **prayer** and ceremonies, while others have incorporated stained glass, gem-stones, and skylights into their religious buildings. In addition, the Light of God has appeared to many **prophets**, saints, and mystics. Saul of Tarsus had a dra-matic encounter with God's Light on the road to Damascus (Acts 9:3). **Moses** witnessed it in the burning bush (**Exodus** 3:2). Revelation 21:23 speaks of the city of New Jerusalem having no need for lamps, a sun, or a moon to light it, because God will be its light.

Angels who have appeared to people on Earth are said to radiate a brilliant bright white light about them, the likes of which have not been seen on Earth before. This seems appropriate since darkness is usually associated with **evil** and light with goodness. Throughout history, God's Light has been depicted around images of **holy** people and in illustrations of angels, often referred to as a halo or aureola.

Today, many such as Betty J. **Eadie** refer to this light in popular books about near-**death** experiences. After her "death," Eadie found herself inside a tunnel. At the end of the tunnel was a brilliant light. In her book, *Embraced by the Light,* Eadie writes, "As I got closer the light became brilliant—bril-liant beyond any description, far more brilliant than the sun—and I knew that no earthly eyes in their natural state could look upon this light without being destroyed." Thomas **Aquinas**, widely considered to be one of the greatest Christian philosophers who ever lived, believed that in **Heaven** human **souls** have glorified bodies that are "brighter than the sun." These radiant bodies are similar to the angels who naturally reflect God's glory. He thought that since humans were "created in God's likeness," their heavenly bodies must reflect God's brilliance. The **Bible** tells us, "God is light and in him there is no darkness at all (1 John 1:5).

Lincoln, Abraham (1809–1865)

Sixteenth president of the U.S. (1861–1865). He steered the Union to victory in the American **Civil War** and abolished slavery. Early in life Lincoln's mother, Nancy Lincoln, introduced him to the **Bible,** spending Sunday after-noons with him on her knee as she read to him from the Bible, stressing the great need to follow the **Ten Commandments.** Her final words to him, when he was nine, were these: "Abe, I'm going to leave you now and I shall not return. I want you to be kind to your father and live as I have taught you. Love your Heavenly **Father** and keep His commandments." Abraham Lincoln often drew on his early teach-ings. He once stated: "My concern is not whether **God** is on our side. My great concern is to be on God's side." In his second inaugural address, Lincoln spoke of the fight between the Confede-racy and the Union saying: "Both read the same Bible, and pray to the same God; and each invokes His aid against the other. It may seem strange that any men should dare to ask a just God's assistance in wringing their bread from the sweat of other men's faces; but let us judge not, that we be not judged. The **prayers** of both could not be answered—that of neither has been answered fully."

Lion of God

The famous Spanish poet Miguel de Unamuno writes that **Christ** is the "lion of **God**." The lion represents God's **divine** presence on the Earth; He is the protector, giver, and the keeper of order on Earth.

Lion's Den

In the **Old Testament**'s Book of **Daniel**, the **prophet** Daniel was thrown into a lion's den for not obeying a king's edict, ordering everyone to pray to the King or the King's gods only. Daniel refused and continued to pray to the **Hebrew God**. For this reason, he was thrown into the lion's den. After he was thrown into the den, he was rescued by an **angel** who was sent by God to close the mouths of the lions. In Daniel 6:22, Daniel says to the King, "My God sent his angel and shut the lions' mouths so that they would not hurt me."

Locke, John (1632–1704)

English empiricist philosopher. He argued that the rights to life, liberty, and property are **God**-given to all men and women.

Locusts

Long-winged insects similar to grasshoppers. Locusts are the insects most often mentioned in the **Bible** and have nine different **Hebrew** names. A plague of locusts was one of the punishments of **God**. The locusts were also one of the **plagues** sent to **Egypt** by God in order to convince Pharaoh to free the Hebrews. When Pharaoh wouldn't agree to let the **Israel**ites leave Egypt, God sent him ten plagues so that he might change his mind. The account at **Exodus** 10:13–15 states, "So **Moses** stretched out his staff over the land of Egypt, and the **Lord** brought an east wind upon the land all that day and all that night; when morning came, the east wind had brought the locusts. The locusts came upon all the land of Egypt and settled on the whole country of Egypt, such a dense swarm of locusts as had never been before, nor ever shall be again."

Logos (The Word of God)

According to Philo **Judaeus**, the Logos is an intermediate class of beings of **God**. It is God's creative force, and also called the "the **image of God**." Philo believed the Logos to be beings with active powers, surrounding God as a number of attendant beings. In rabbinic mysticism, **Metatron** (sometimes referred to as "the Lesser **Yahweh**" or Lesser God) is the incarnate Logos. Both the Archangel **Michael** and the **Messiah** have been identified as the Logos, as well as God's **Holy Spirit**. The word "Logos," is said to have been used in the original Greek translation of John1:1 in the **New Testament**. Reading the word Logos in place of "word" in the English translation, John 1 reads, "In the beginning was the Logos, and the Logos was with God, and the Logos was God. He was in the beginning with God. All things came into being through Him, and without Him not one thing came into being. What has come into being in Him was life, and the life was the **light** of all people. The light shines in the darkness, and the darkness did not overcome it" (John 1:1–5).

Long-Suffering

An attribute of **God**. The term is used in referring to God in some **Bible** translations. The term applies to God being slow to anger, patient, and slow to punish. It is listed as a quality for humans to exemplify in the naming of the **fruits of the spirit** given in the **New Testament** (Galatians 5:22).

Lorber, Jakob (1800–1864)

Australian musician, author of *The New Revelation. The New Revelation* was dictated to Jakob Lorber by unseen spiritual beings. On March 15, 1840, Lorber heard a voice that told him to pick up a pen and write. From that day forward, he spent every day writing what the voice dictated. Part of the manuscript contains information on a scientific level; another part contains information of a spiritual nature and is called the "New Revelation." It tells of **God's divine** purpose, and reveals the meaning behind the scriptures. It talks extensively about the **fall** of **Satan** and the fall of the **angels**. It also speaks of a divine plan to bring back the **fallen angels** into a favored state with God.

Lord

One who has authority over persons or things. Therefore, **God,** the Supreme Authority, is the Lord. In the **Old Testament,** when large and small capital letters are used (LORD), the original text contained the **Tetragrammaton** (the four letters **YHWH**) which form the sacred name of God. God's name was removed by rabbis of the period because of their belief that God's Name was too sacred to be spoken. The words "LORD" and "GOD" placed in capital letters sets them apart from the common words "lord" and "god."

Lord of Spirits

In the Book of **Enoch,** God is referred to as the "**Lord** of Spirits."

Lord, Angel of the

See Angel of the Lord.

Lord's Prayer, The

A **prayer** taught by **Jesus** to his disciples. It was designed as an example of how to approach **God** in prayer and is widely used by Christians. It appears in two forms: A longer form in Matthew 6:9–13 is a part of the teaching on prayer in the Sermon on the Mount; a shorter form in Luke 11:2–4 is given as a response to the disciples' request for Jesus to teach them to pray.

The prayer opens by calling on God. The version in Luke states, "**Father,** hallowed be your name. Your kingdom come. Give us each day our daily bread. And forgive us our **sins,** for we ourselves forgive everyone indebted to us. And do not bring us to the time of trial." The version in Matthew is: "Our Father who art in **heaven,** Hallowed be thy name. Thy kingdom come, Thy will be done, On earth as it is in heaven. Give us this day our daily bread; And forgive us our debts, As we also have forgiven our debtors; And lead us not into temptation, But deliver us from **evil.**" A closing **doxology** was added to the prayer in ancient times. However, it does not appear in most versions of the **Bible.** It reads, "For thine is the kingdom and the power and the glory." In Matthew the prayer is composed of an invocation and seven petitions. The style of the petitions is modeled on the Psalms. The first three are concerned with revering God, and the last four are requests for God's assistance to humanity.

Lot

The nephew of **Abraham.** In the **Bible, angels** visited Lot because he was the nephew of the **prophet** Abraham. He was also a good and faithful servant of **God.** He was the only godly **man** to be found in the city of **Sodom.** The angels came to remove Lot and his family from Sodom because God had decided to destroy it. When the angels arrived, Lot insisted that they stay with him and his family. He invited them in, served them dinner, and offered them a place to sleep. However, before they could lie down, the men of Sodom surrounded the house and formed a mob. They called out to Lot to send out the men who were visiting him, so that they could have sex with them. Finally, Lot went outside and begged the mob to disperse and leave the visiting angels alone. He even offered them his two virgin daughters to have sex with instead. He explained to the mob that their conduct was the reason the angels had come. Angrily, the mob accused Lot of judging them. They threatened to do worse to him than what they had planned for his guests. The mob moved toward Lot, nearly breaking in his door.

The angels put out their hands and the door opened. They brought Lot quickly back inside the house and closed the door. They then struck the men with blindness. The angels told Lot to take his family out of Sodom because God had condemned the city and all in it, and they were going to destroy it. At dawn the angels told Lot to take his wife and daughters and leave Sodom. Lot lingered for a time. The angels finally grabbed hold of his hand, and the hands of his wife and two daughters, and escorted them out of the city. They told him to escape to the **mountains.** Lot said that he did not want to go to the mountains, but that he wanted to go to a nearby city. The angels gave their consent but told him to hurry because they could not destroy the city until he and his family were clear of danger. Once they were safe, fire and sulfur were rained upon Sodom (**Genesis** 19:1–26).

Love

The primary attribute of **God. Old Testament** writers emphasized God's loving care for the **Hebrews.** The most common word for love in the **New** Testament is *agape.* It is a Greek word for love, seldom used in classical Greek; however, it is found in the New Testament to describe God's love.

Lucifer
See Satan.

Luonnotar
Finnish creator **goddess.**

Luther, Martin (1483–1546)
"**A mighty fortress is our God,**" said Martin Luther, the German leader of the Protestant Reformation, said to be the greatest figure of the sixteenth century. An excommunicated member of the Roman Catholic **Church,** Luther and other Protestants believed that the Catholic Church no longer taught the concept of **Christianity** as given in the **Bible.** This launched their efforts to start a new movement, bringing people "back to the Bible." This new movement became **Lutheranism.** In the process, Luther produced many theological writings and commentaries on the Bible.

Salvation, according to Lutheran doctrine, does not depend on deeds, but is a free gift from **God.** In addition, Lutherans believe that trust in God is the only way for humans to be saved. This idea was controversial during Luther's time because Christianity teaches a responsibility to do good works and that individuals will reap the rewards after **death.** The following is Martin Luther's famous song, "A Mighty Fortress is Our God." It has been called "the greatest hymn of the greatest man of the greatest period of German history." It was sung at the funeral of American President Dwight Eisenhower at the National Cathedral in Washington, DC, March 1969.

A MIGHTY FORTRESS IS OUR GOD
A mighty fortress is our God, a bulwark never failing;

Our helper He, amid the flood of mortal ills prevailing:
For still our ancient foe doth seek to work us woe;
His craft and power are great, and, armed with cruel hate,
On earth is not his equal.

Did we in our strength confide, our striving would be losing;
Were not the right **Man** on our side, the Man of God's own choosing:
Dost ask who that may be? **Christ Jesus,** it is He;
Lord Sabaoth, His Name, from age to age the same,
And He must win the battle.

And though this world, with **devils** filled, should threaten to undo us,
We will not fear, for God hath willed His truth to triumph through us:
The Prince of Darkness grim, we tremble not for him;
His rage we can endure, for lo, his doom is sure,
One little word shall fell him.

That word above all earthly powers, no thanks to them, abideth;
The Spirit and the gifts are ours through Him Who with us sideth:
Let goods and kindred go, this mortal life also;
The body they may kill: God's truth abideth still,
His kingdom is forever.

Lutheranism

See Luther, Martin.

M

God is subtle, but he is not malicious.
—*Albert Einstein*

Madonna

The name used in **Catholicism** when referring to the **Virgin Mary.** As a girl, she was chosen by **God** to be the mother of **Jesus.** According to lore, the Madonna is one of the highest **angels** in **Heaven.** She belongs to the class of angels called the **Virtues.** She is also called: Blessed Mother, Queen of Angels, and Queen of Peace.

Magen

Ancient **Hebrew** name for **God.** It means "Shield."

Magnificat, The

The name popularly given to the song of **Mary** in the **Bible's New Testament** (Luke 1:46–55). According to the Bible, Mary sang a song of thanksgiving when she realized **God's** intention to redeem the people. The song is as follows: "And Mary said, 'My **soul** magnifies the **Lord,** and my **spirit** rejoices in God my Savior, for he has looked with favor on the lowliness of his servant. Surely, from now on all generations will call me blessed; for the **Mighty One** has done great things for me, and **holy** is his name. His **mercy** is for those who fear him from generation to generation. He has shown strength with his arm; he has scattered the proud in the thoughts of their hearts.

He has brought down the powerful from their thrones, and lifted up the lowly; he has filled the hungry with good things, and sent the rich away empty. He has helped his servant **Israel,** in remembrance of his mercy, according to the promise he made to our ancestors, to **Abraham** and to his descendants forever.'"

Mahatala

God of the Ngadju Dayak people of Borneo.

Maimonides, Moses (1135–1204)

Great medieval **Hebrew** scholar who was an authority on philosophy, medicine, and the **Torah** (Jewish **divine law**). Maimonides was known in his own time as Rabbi **Moses** Ben Maimon. His contributions to the development of **Judaism** earned him the title "Second Moses." He wrote extensively on the Hebrew law, and made important contributions to the fields of logic, law, medicine, mathematics, philosophy, and **theology.** Maimonides' fame as a physician equaled his fame as a philosopher and authority on Judaic law. He also produced writings on astronomy, logic, and mathematics.

Born in Cordoba, Spain, when Arabs ruled most of Spain, he lived during a time of great advancement in education, music, and art. A brilliant student, Maimonides was educated by his father in Judaism and the study of Jewish texts, medicine, and philosophy. However, it was also a time of great religious tension. The more conservative Arab groups who controlled Cordoba made it difficult for **Jews** to practice their **faith.** As a result, Maimonides moved several times, first to Fez in North **Africa** and then later to Cairo in **Egypt** where he did most of his important work.

His greatest work in the field of Jewish law is the Mishneh Torah, arranged in fourteen books and written in Hebrew (1170–1180), which he continued to revise until his **death.** In addition, he formulated the "Thirteen Articles of Faith," one of several creeds to which many Orthodox Jews still adhere. He wrote several studies of Jewish texts but is best known for the *Guide for the Perplexed* (1190). Earlier chapters in the *Guide* discuss the nature of **God** and the nature of belief. In the *Guide*, Maimonides' belief in God is firm and critical to all his thoughts.

It has been argued that the underlying purpose of *Guide for the Perplexed* is to show that God created the world as asserted by the **Abraham**ic religions (Judaism, **Christianity,** and **Islam**) as opposed to the view that God and the cosmos are co-**eternal,** as championed by **Aristotle.** In the *Guide,* he expresses his beliefs and ideas on God. He believed that God is incorporeal; that to say God has a human form belittles Him. He taught that God is Eternal and Infinite; that He was not begotten and will never see death. Maimonides believed that the reward for being faithful to God is to dwell with Him forever in **Heaven.** Those who did not follow God, the unrighteous, suffered the punishment of not residing with God. This belief differed from the traditional idea of an eternal hellfire. Maimonides died in Cairo, December 13, 1204, and was buried at Tiberias in Palestine.

Maker

A term sometimes used in the **Bible** when referring to **God.** It means "one who brings into being" and "one who creates." The term is used in parts of the Bible almost as a title. Scriptures supporting this idea are as follows:

Job 4:17 asks: "Can human beings be pure before their Maker?"

Job 36:3: "I will bring my knowledge from far away, and ascribe righteousness to my Maker."

Hosea 8:14: "Israel has forgotten his Maker . . ."

Isaiah 17:7: "On that day people will regard their Maker."

Isaiah 45:9: "Woe to you who strive with your Maker."

Isaiah 45:11: "Thus says the **Lord,** the **Holy** One of **Israel,** and Its Maker . . ."

Isaiah 51:13: "You have forgotten the Lord, your Maker, who stretched out the heavens and laid the foundations of the earth."

Isaiah 54:5: "For your Maker is your husband, the Lord of **hosts** is his name; the Holy One of Israel is your Redeemer, the God of the whole earth he is called."

Proverbs 14:31: "Those who oppress the poor insult their Maker."

Proverbs 17:5: "Those who mock the poor insult their Maker."

Psalms 95:6: "O come, let us worship and bow down, let us kneel before the Lord, our Maker!"

Psalms 149:2: "Let Israel be glad in its Maker."

Malachi

The word Malachi has two meanings. In **angelic** lore, it means "angel of

God," and was considered in ancient times an angel of **Jehovah (God)**. The second meaning of Malachi is in the **Old Testament**, where Malachi was the last of the minor **prophets** and in this case the name meant "My **Messenger.**" In the Book of Malachi, the prophet challenges **Israel** to keep God's commandments and encourage the people to rely on God for future **blessings**. The first two chapters proclaim God's **love** for Israel and give an account of the people's transgressions. The attack is particularly directed toward the **priests**, who have been unfaithful in their service to God. The second half of the book concerns God's judgment and blessings. It tells of the coming day of God, admonishes the people for not tithing, and promises God's deliverance for the righteous.

Mamre

A place in the district of Hebron associated with **Abraham**. It was under the oaks of Mamre that Abraham was first visited by three **angels** sent from **God** with a message. The angels informed him of the coming birth of his son **Isaac** and the destruction of **Sodom** and **Gomorrah.**

Man

Man is the **creation** of **God**. According to **Judaism, Christianity,** and **Islam**, the first man, **Adam,** was made in God's image (**Genesis** 1:26, 27) and placed in a **paradise** garden. According to Genesis chapter 1, the high point of God's creation of all things was the creation of Man. God told man to "be fruitful and multiply, and fill the earth, and subdue it; and rule over the fish of the sea and over the birds of the sky, and over every living thing that moves on the earth" (Genesis 2:28). When **Adam and Eve** (Adam's wife) sinned, all of humankind fell with them (Romans 5:12–21). Psalms 8:5 states,

"For thou hast made him a little lower than the **angels**, and hast crowned him with glory and honour."

Man Clothed in Linen

In the ancient world, linen symbolized purity. The **priests** wore linen in the temple. The **angels** wore linen to stand out among the humans of Earth and to symbolize their **holy** position. The **Old Testament** mentions two accounts of angels who are dressed in linen. The first account is found in **Ezekiel** 9:3–4. The angel had been sent by **God** to mark the righteous people of Jerusalem so that they would be saved from destruction. The **Bible** says, "The **Lord** called to the **man** clothed in linen and said to him, 'Go through Jerusalem, and put a mark on the foreheads of those who sigh and groan over all the abominations that are committed in it.'" The second account occurs in **Daniel** (10:5–6) when a man in linen appears to Daniel. "I looked up and saw a man clothed in linen, with a belt of gold from Uphaz around his waist. His body was like beryl, his face like lightning, his eyes like flaming torches, his arms and legs like the gleam of burnished bronze, and the sound of his words like the roar of a multitude." The angel had been sent by God in answer to Daniel's **prayers** and to inform him about the future of the **Hebrews.**

Manichaeism

Ancient religion named after its founder, the **Persian** visionary and **prophet**, Mani (or Manes), c. 216–c. 276 A.D. Manichaeism originated in **Babylonia** in the third century A.D. Mani proclaimed himself the last prophet in a succession of prophets that included **Zoroaster**, Buddha, and **Jesus Christ**, whose partial revelations were, as he taught, contained and completed in his own dogma. At around the age of twenty-four, Mani is said to have received a special revelation from **God** which came in the form of visions in which an **angel** designated him the prophet of a new and ultimate revelation. This revelation was a calling to him to perfect the incomplete religions founded by earlier prophets such as Zoroaster, Buddha, and Jesus Christ. About the year 242, Mani undertook an extensive journey as an itinerant preacher, proclaiming himself the "**Messenger** of Truth," the Paraclete promised by Jesus. Traveling throughout the Persian Empire and as far as **India**, he gathered a large following.

During ancient times, Manichaeism was popular in **Rome** and Asia. It carried elements of Zoroastrianism, **Gnosticism,** and **Christianity.** Vital to the teachings of Manichaeism was dualism. Mani believed that the universe and all creatures are a part of an ongoing battle between good (God) and **evil** (the **Devil**).

He held that in the spiritual realm these two energies exist independent of one another, but in our world they are intertwined. He taught that the majority of humans carry the evil energy within them, but in every individual there is a part of God, a part of His **divine light.**

Manna

The food that **God** sent from **Heaven** to feed the **Hebrews** as they traveled across the desert. **Exodus** 16:31 describes it as being similar to white coriander seed and tasting like wafers (or thin cakes) made with honey.

Manoah

Biblical character; the father of **Samson.** In the Book of Judges (13:1–5), Manoah and his wife received two visitations from an **angel** with a message from **God**. The angel informed them that they would have a son who was to be "dedicated to God as a Nazirite." The angel told them that Samson would deliver the **Israel**ites from the Philistines.

Mantra

A mantra is a word or phrase used in ritual and **meditation,** most commonly found in **Hinduism** and **Buddhism.** The mantra is chanted repetitively in an effort to attain mental peace and raise one's consciousness toward the self or **God.** It is a sound or group of sounds that are believed to have the exceptional power to restore people to a state of perfect harmony. In Hinduism, a mantra is a magic phrase or **prayer.** Mantras of different types accompany Hindu ceremonies and are often used as a means of asking the god to give a desired blessing.

Marduk

Mesopotamian high god. He was the **god of light** and life and the ruler of destinies. He was believed to be the creator of the universe and of humankind. He rose to such prominence that he claimed fifty titles. Eventually, he was called simply Bel, meaning "**Lord.**"

Mari

Supreme being in Basque beliefs.

Martyr, Saint Justin (c. 100 A.D.–c. 165 A.D.)

Philosopher and theologian. Martyr made it his mission to reconcile **Christianity** with **paganism.** He was born in Flavia Neapolis (now Nabulus, West Bank), a Roman city built on the site of the ancient Shechem in Samaria. His mother and father were both pagans. As a youngster Justin dedicated himself to the study of Greek philosophy and was particularly interested in the works of **Plato** and the Stoic philosophers. Martyr was first introduced to Christianity in Ephesus. He converted to Christianity and eventually moved to **Rome,** where he started a school. He later died in Rome as a martyr. His works include: *Apologies for the Christians* and *Dialogue with Trypho the Jew.* In the latter, he wrote: "There will be no other **God,** O Trypho, nor was there from eternity any other existing . . . but He who made and disposed all this universe. Nor do we think that there is one God for us, another for you, but that He alone is God who led your fathers out from **Egypt** with a strong hand and a high arm. Nor have we trusted in any other, for there is no other, but in Him in whom you also have trusted, the God of **Abraham,** and of **Isaac,** and of **Jacob.**"

Mary

The mother of **Jesus.** According to the **Bible,** Mary was a young **Hebrew** woman chosen by **God** for her **faithful**ness and piety to become the mother of the **Messiah.** In the **New Testament,** God sent an **angel** (the Archangel **Gabriel**) to tell Mary that she would conceive a son whom she was to call Jesus. Shocked at this revelation, Mary asked the angel how it was possible, since she was a virgin. The angel went on to inform her that she would conceive through the **Holy Spirit** and that the child would be the **Son of God.** Later, she was joyful at the revelation, realizing that through this act, God was redeeming the people. She then sang a song to God which is commonly called the **Magnificat.**

Roman Catholics (as well as members of some other Christian groups) believe that Mary was transported bodily to **Heaven** by God. She is believed to have been **sin**less and therefore did not have to suffer **death,** the punishment for sinning against God. This supernatural event, called the **Assumption of Mary** or the Assumption of the Blessed **Virgin Mary,** was made official doctrine by Pope Pius XII on November 1, 1950.

Massim-Biambe

Omnipotent creator god of the Mundang people of the Congo.

Maury, Matthew (1806–1873)

Founder of oceanography. He strongly believed in **God's** Word, so much so that he took the scripture in Psalms 8:8 literally where it speaks of "paths of the seas." He believed that there must be paths in the seas if the **Bible** said so. He devoted his life to proving the scripture to be true. By charting the winds and currents of the Atlantic Ocean, he was finally able to prove that the sea does have "paths."

Mayans

South American Indian people. The sun god, the maize god, the planet Venus, and numerous **death** gods were among the deities that watched over the Mayan world. The Mayan religion also centered on the worship of a large number of nature gods. Among their supreme deities were Kukulcan, a creator god closely related to the Toltec and Aztec Quetzalcoatl, and Itzamna, a **sky god.** Chaac, a god of rain, was especially important in popular ritual.

Mayin

Supreme god of the Siberian Tungus.

Mbotumbo

God of the Baule Negritos of the Ivory Coast.

Mecca

The location where **Muhammad** received **God's** revelation (the **Koran**) from the Archangel **Jibril** (also **Gabriel**). Once a year nearly two million **Muslims** travel to Saudi **Arabia,** to the city of Mecca (and also Medina) to perform the *Hajj*. It is a way of paying tribute to God and allows them to carry out the last of the **Five Pillars** of **Islam.** The **pilgrimage** to Mecca is one which every Muslim must attempt once. However, it is to be tried only if it does not involve hardship for the traveler and his or her family. It was at Mecca that **Abraham** and his son **Ishmael** reportedly built the "House of God," also referred to as the Kaaba. The House of God holds the very important, very sacred black stone that, according to tradition, was given by the Archangel Jibril to Ishmael as a sign of God's **covenant** with Abraham. Muslim pilgrims from around the world come to Mecca. No matter what their backgrounds or social status, they are all the same in the eyes of God. Their time there ends with a magnificent feast called the Feast of **Sacrifice** *(id al-Adha)*, one of the **holy** days of Islam. The feast observes God's command to Abraham to offer his son Ishmael as a sacrifice.

Mechtild of Magdeburg (1210–1285)

Famous medieval mystic. Born into an aristocratic family in Saxony, Germany, Mechtild began experiencing visions from **God** at the age of twelve. From that time forward, her visions continued on a daily basis. Because of her unusual experiences, she left home to become a Beguine (a member of a Roman Catholic lay sisterhood) at Magdeburg, Germany, in 1230. There, she led a life of contemplation and **prayer.** As she grew older, her heavenly visions became more frequent and by the order of her confessor, she wrote down her visions. Shortly after 1270, she joined the Cistercian nuns at Helfta (a Cistercian monastery near Eisleben, southwest of Magdeburg), where she spent the remaining twelve years of her life. There she was highly regarded as one favored by God. Mechtild wrote what has been called "a most wonderful

book," in which she recorded her many visions. She said that God ordered the title of the book, which was "**Light** of my **divinity,** flowing into all hearts that live without guile." Mechtild wrote: "Of all that God has shown me I can speak just the smallest word, not more than a honey bee takes on her foot from an over spilling jar." She died at Helfta in 1285.

Mediator(s)

One who acts as a go-between in making an agreement between two parties. The word mediator is not found in the **Old Testament,** though its principle is. In the Old Testament, **Moses** was the mediator in the **covenant** made at Sinai between **God** and the chosen people. In the **New Testament, Jesus** became the mediator between humanity and God. In **Judaism,** Zoroastrianism, **Christianity,** and **Islam,** the **angels** act as mediators between God and humankind, carrying **divine** messages and revelations to humans for God, and acting as protectors. In Islam, the angels listen to the **prayers** of humans and present them to God. The Archangel **Michael** mediated for the **Hebrews, Gabriel** mediated for the Christians and the **Muslims;** in Zoroastrianism, the **Amesha Spentas** were mediators for the **Persians.**

Meditation

A deep reflection on sacred matters as a devotional act. **Plato** called the **mystery** of meditation *theoria,* while early Christians called it *contemplatio.* The great mystics tell us that meditating bestows three gifts: peace and tranquility of mind; great insight and wisdom; and most important, a direct experience of **God.** They believed that by developing the habit of quietness of mind we could hear messages from God.

Medjugorje

A small town in Bosnia where **God's** presence is seen and felt. Since 1981, the **Virgin Mary** has been appearing on a daily basis to six young people who have become known as the "visionaries." Through these visionaries, the Virgin Mary communicates with the world, bringing revelations and messages of hope and encouragement from God. She also shares extraordinary secrets about the final outcome of the history of the world. She appears to the visionaries every day at 6:40 P.M. When she comes, she is said to be surrounded by **angels.**

Melchizedek

There are two different Melchizedeks associated with **God.** The first is the Melchizedek from the story in **Genesis** 14, where he was king of Salem (Jerusalem) and "a priest of God **Most High.**" He pronounced a blessing on **Abraham,** and Abraham gave him a tithe of all he had. In the second story, he is a great and powerful **angel** from the class of **Virtues.** Melchizedek is to the angels what **Jesus** is to humankind.

Legend has it that around two thousand years prior to the coming of Jesus, Melchizedek descended to Earth in the form of a **man.** He set up a school in which he taught for a hundred years. He also started an evangelistic school in Salem in which he trained students for missionary work. From his school, hundreds of missionaries graduated, and were sent to preach around the world about God. **Dionysius the Pseudo-Areopagite** once wrote that Melchizedek was the angel most loved by God. Later, during the third century A.D., a group called the Melchisedans said that they were in communication with a great power named Melchizedek. He is credited with delivering God's **covenant** to the **prophet** Abraham, bringing **light** to the world during a spiritually dark period on Earth, and for laying the foundation for Jesus' coming. According to one account, Melchizedek is the father of the seven **Elohim,** also known as angels of the **divine** presence. In Phoenician **mythology** he was called Sydik.

Melekh

Ancient **Hebrew** name for **God** meaning "king."

Mercy

One of the characteristics of **God,** meaning that He is forgiving, unwilling to punish. In **Judaism,** God's mercy is displayed when the **Israel**ites continually broke their **covenant.** Instead of abandoning them, God offered them His patient **love** and ready forgiveness. In Christian beliefs, God's mercy is offered through **Jesus** to the whole of humankind. **Hebrews** 4:16 states, "Let us therefore draw near with confidence to the throne of **grace,** that we may receive mercy and may find grace to help in time of need" (Hebrews 4:16).

Mercy Seat

The lid on the **Ark of the Covenant.** **God** spoke to the people from above it. Regarding the **Mercy** Seat, God said to the **Hebrews,** "There I will meet with you, and from above the mercy seat, from between the **cherubim** that are on the ark of the covenant, I will deliver to you all my commands for the **Israel**ites" (**Exodus** 25:22).

Mesopotamia

Region between the Tigris and **Euphrates** rivers, now in Iraq. It was made up of three cultures: **Babylo**nians, Assyrians, and **Sumerians.** In Mesopotamian beliefs, the principal gods were identified with the forces of nature, such as **Anu (sky god),** Sin (moon god), Enki (water god), and Enlil (wind god). Anu, the sky god, was originally the supreme god of the pantheon and was mainly concerned with rulership. When the nearby city of Nippur conquered Uruk, their own god, Enlil, became the primary object of worship. He was god and ruler of the atmosphere, the sun, moon, plant life, and necessities to human control of the Earth. Enlil was also considered the supreme god of Sumer and held the tablets on which were written of the fates of all people. By the middle of the second **millennium** B.C., Enlil's position was taken over by the god **Marduk** within Babylonia and by Ashur in Assyria.

Messengers

The **Koran** states, "**God** sends forth the **angels** as His messengers, with two, three, or four pairs of wings." The idea of God having messengers can be found in numerous religious traditions of many cultures. In Judaic lore they were angels who brought messages to **prophets** such as **Abraham** and **Daniel**. The Christians had **Gabriel**, the angel of revelation, who delivered messages regarding important births such as those of **John the Baptist** and **Jesus Christ**. In **Islam**, **Jibril** (Gabriel) brought **Muhammad** a revelation from God. The Babylonians had the *sukalli,* which translates into "angelic messengers." The Greeks had Hermes, the winged messenger of **Zeus** (**Supreme Being** in Greek **mythology**). The Greeks also had Iris who was messenger for Hera (Zeus' wife). In **Rome** there was Mercury, the messenger of **Jupiter**.

Messiah

A **Hebrew** word meaning "**anointed one** of God." In **Christianity** it is believed that the messiah came in the form of **Jesus** (Matthew 3:16). The messiah was the one prophesied by the **Jews** who would come to save his people and introduce a new world order.

Metatron

An **angel** from ancient Judaic lore. He is referred to as the "Lesser **YHWH**." The name YHWH is made of the four letters of the original (unspeakable) name of **God**.

Micah

Old Testament Hebrew prophet (the sixth of the twelve minor Prophets). His prophecies were recorded in the Book of Micah. Micah predicted **God's** judgment on Samaria and Jerusalem, the return from the captivity, and God's ultimate **blessings** on His people in the Final Days. One of the well-known predictions of the birth of **Christ** is found in Micah 5:2. The book closes with praise for God's **mercy**.

Michael (Who Is As God)

One of the seven **archangels**, he is **God's** warrior who leads the celestial army and is the ruler of the **seventh heaven**. In art, he is depicted as being muscular, youthful, handsome, wearing the breastplate of righteousness and the shield of **faith**. His sword is the **Word of God**. The **Bible** tells us that it was Michael and his army who defeated **Satan** and his hordes in the **war in Heaven**, throwing them out of **Heaven** and down to Earth. The Bible states, "And war broke out in heaven: Michael and his **angels** battled with the dragon and the dragon and its angels battled but did not prevail, neither was a place found for them any longer in heaven. So down the great dragon was hurled, the original serpent, the one called **Devil** and Satan, who is misleading the entire inhabited earth; he was hurled down to the earth, and his angels were hurled down with him" (Revelation 12:7–9).

It is also Michael who will descend from Heaven with the key to the **Abyss**, and will lock Satan away for a thousand years: "And I saw an angel coming down out of heaven with the key of the abyss and a great chain in his hand. And he seized the dragon, who is the Devil and Satan, and bound him for a thousand years. And he hurled him into the abyss and shut it and sealed it over him" (Revelation 20:1–3).

According to ancient Judaic lore, it was Michael who prevented **Abraham** from sacrificing his son **Isaac.** Legend has it that it was also Michael who appeared to **Moses** in the **burning bush.** He has been credited with freeing the apostle Peter from prison, and rescuing **Daniel** from the **lion's den** (Acts 5:19; Daniel 6:22). In **Islam,** Michael is called **Mikhail.** In the **Koran,** the **Cherubim** are created from the tears of Mikhail. During the Middle Ages the **church** portrayed Michael as a psychopomp (an escort of **souls** to the spiritual world, an idea found in the ancient beliefs of Zoroastrianism and **Greece**) in order to attract non-Christians into the Church.

In the Dead Sea **Scrolls,** Michael is the Prince of **Light,** battling against the sons of darkness. He leads the good angels against the **fallen angels,** which are led by Belial. Joan of Arc named him as one of the angels who encouraged her to help the Dauphin. In 1950, Pope Pius XII declared him "Protector of Police Officers." In the **Book of Raziel** he is listed as an amulet angel who is summoned in childbirth for a safe delivery. The depiction of the Archangel Michael battling the great dragon (Satan) has been portrayed in art by several artists. These paintings were inspired from the account in Revelation (12:7–9) where Michael battles the dragon and casts him out of Heaven.

Michelangelo (1475–1564)

Great Italian sculptor, painter, and poet. Michelangelo's religious beliefs can be viewed in his art. It has been said that **God** communicates with humankind through music, poetry, and art. If this is the case, then he most definitely used Michelangelo Buonarroti. Michelangelo was born in the small village of Caprese and grew up in Florence, the artistic center of the early Renaissance. He was a true Renaissance man whose art was deeply influenced by the **Bible.** An extremely religious man, his personal beliefs did not truly become evident until his later works. His late drawings are introspective meditations on Christian themes such as the Crucifixion, and in some works he inserted his own image as an onlooker in a religious scene. An intellectual and a profoundly educated man, he was also a spiritual person. He was keenly aware of the spiritual significance of beauty. Beauty was to him **divine,** one of the ways that God communicated Himself to humankind.

One of Michelangelo's most memorable early works displaying his **faith** and spirituality is his *Pietà* (1497–1500, St. Peter's Basilica, Vatican City). The Pietà theme shows **Christ** in his mother's lap, just after his Crucifixion. Michelangelo shows **Mary** grieving silently and makes Christ's wounds barely visible. Mary calls attention to her dead son with her left hand, while her right arm embraces him gently, lifting his arm slightly so that it hangs lifelessly before us. Mary's full robe forms a broad base for **Christ's** limp body, which curves slightly to wrap around hers, making the group graceful and compact.

Another famous work taken from the Bible is his sculpture of *David* (1501–1504, Galleria del l'Accademia, Florence). The subject of this work is the **Old Testament** story of David and Goliath, in which the young David flings a stone from his sling, killing the giant Goliath and saving his nation. The statue expresses the daring of young

David and his faith in God. The implicit sense of God's majesty is made explicit in much of Michelangelo's work, including the Tomb of Julius II, *Last Judgment*, and his paintings in the **Sistine Chapel.**

Michelangelo made some of his finest sculptures for the Julius Tomb, one of the most memorable of which is that of **Moses,** the central figure in the monument. Michelangelo created a muscular Moses who sits alertly in a shallow niche, holding the tablets of the **Ten Commandments** given to him by God. He looks off into the distance as if listening to God. For the Sistine Chapel, Michelangelo worked high above the chapel floor, lying on his back on scaffolding. What he produced has been hailed as some of the finest pictorial images of all time, and remains a huge testimony to Michelangelo's faith and belief in God. On the vault of the papal chapel, he created nine scenes from the Book of **Genesis,** including the Separation of **Light** from Darkness; **Creation** of the Sun, Moon, and Planets; Separation of the Earth from the Waters; Creation of **Adam;** Creation of **Eve;** The **Fall** and Expulsion from the **Garden of Eden;** the **Sacrifice** of Noah; The Deluge; and the Drunkenness of Noah.

Michelangelo was again called to work in the Sistine Chapel in 1534, when Clement VII commissioned him to paint the wall above the altar. *The Last Judgment* (1536–1541), taken from Revelation, takes up one entire wall of the Sistine Chapel. It portrays Christ's second coming in the last days. The scene focuses on Christ, whose right arm is positioned to strike down the unrighteous, while the left arm seems to beckon the righteous toward him. At his side is Mary, who silently looks down toward those being resurrected from their graves. There are saints and figures ascending to **Heaven,** and a scene of **Hell** that is based on the description of the Inferno from Dante's *Divine Comedy.* In addition, Michelangelo portrays the seven Angels of the **Apocalypse** blowing their **trumpets** from the four corners of the Earth, and calling the dead to the Last Judgment. The great Renaissance poet Ludovico Ariosto wrote succinctly of this famous artist, "Michael, more than mortal, divine angel." Indeed, Michelangelo was widely awarded the epithet "divine" because of his extraordinary accomplishments.

Middle Knowledge

A theory developed by the Jesuit Luis de Molina (Spanish Jesuit theologian, 1535–1600). It is the belief that **God** has prior knowledge of future events; that He knows beforehand how each individual will cooperate with **grace.**

Mighty One

One of **God's** many titles.

Mikhail

One of the four **archangels** of **Islam.** It is the Islamic name for the Archangel **Michael.** In Islam, Mikhail is the **angel** "who provides men with food and knowledge." The **Koran** describes him as having wings of green emerald and hair of saffron. Each hair has a million faces with a million mouths and tongues. He is said to speak in many languages. In these languages, he begs **God** for the pardon of mankind's many transgressions. Variations of the name Mikhail are: Mikail and Mikal.

Millennium

Literally, this word means 1000 years. In the study of end times doctrines **(eschatology),** the millennium is the duration of **Christ's** rule over the Earth. In some facets of **Christianity** it is believed that the millennium will be ushered in once the preaching of **God's** word reaches the entire world, a doctrine called **Postmillennialism.** The idea of Postmillennialism is that everyone will get a chance to learn of God and His coming kingdom and decide which way he or she would like to go. Do they want to be with God and part of His Kingdom or not? Those who choose to be part are thought to be granted **eternal life** in God's kingdom. Those who do not, according to tradition, will remain separated from God forever. Some teachings suggest that those who refuse God's word, rejecting what they hear, will be the ones destroyed in **Armageddon.** Afterward, it is believed that for the next thousand years God's Kingdom will rule.

Milton, John

See *Paradise Lost.*

Ministering Angels

Angels who attend to **God's** immediate wishes. God is said to have ministering angels surrounding His throne day and night to do His bidding. According to lore, there are many hundreds of thousands of ministering angels who act as **messengers** and **mediators** between God and humans. They are considered by some to be a separate class of angels. According to Judaic lore, it is the duty of the ministering angels to instruct the **nations** who are the offspring of **Noah.**

Miracle(s)

An extraordinary event in the world, believed to be caused by an act of **God.** Examples would be the parting of the **Red Sea** and **Jesus** walking on water. These kinds of events are thought to be a natural manifestation of God's work. By definition, a miracle is an event that exceeds the known **laws** of nature and science. They are usually acts of God accomplished through human agency. They are also known as powers, signs, and mighty works. They are a manifestation of the power of God over the universe and his creations.

THE **BIBLE.** In Biblical times miracles seemed common. Both the Old and New Testaments of the Bible tell of numerous miracles performed by God. Miracles of the **Old Testament** include: Lot's wife becoming a pillar of salt (**Genesis** 19:26); the **burning bush** unconsumed by fire (**Exodus** 3:2); the **ten plagues of Egypt** (Exodus 7:14–12:30); the parting of the Red Sea (Exodus 14:21–31); **Manna** from **Heaven** (Exodus 16:1–36); **Aaron's** rod bearing fruit (**Numbers** 17:8); the falling of the walls of Jericho (**Joshua** 6:1–27); the strength of **Samson** (Judges 14:1–16:22); **Elijah** taken up by a whirlwind (2 Kings 2:11); Elisha reviving a dead child (2 Kings 4:8–37); three men saved from a fiery furnace (**Daniel** 3:19–30); Daniel saved from the lion's den (Daniel 6:18–28); **Jonah** saved inside the fish (Jonah 2:1–10).

New Testament miracles of Jesus include: healing the leper (Matthew 8:1–4; Mark 1:40–45; Luke 5:12–16); healing the centurion's servant (Matthew 8:5–13; Luke 7:1–10); stilling of a storm (Matthew 8:23–27; Mark 4:35–41; Luke 8:22–25); sending the **demons** into swine (Matthew 8:28, 9:1; Mark 5:1–20; Luke 8:26–39); healing the mute (Matthew 9:32–34); feeding of the five thousand (Matthew 14:13–21; Mark 6:20–44; Luke 9:10–17; John 6: 1–15); walking on the water (Matthew 14:22–33; Mark 6:45–52; John 6:16–21); feeding the four thousand (Matthew 15:32–39; Mark 8:1–10); cleansing of the lepers (Luke 17:11–19); changing the water into wine (John 2:1–12); the raising of Lazarus from the dead (John 11:38–44); the gift of tongues (Acts 2:1–13); Peter's raising of Tabitha (Acts 9:36–43); Peter delivered from prison (Acts 12:6–19); Paul's raising of Eutychus (Acts 20:7–12).

Traditional **Judaism** and **Christianity,** in accepting the Bible as God's word, accepts that these events occurred, and were direct events from God. In **Islam,** the **prophet Muhammad** recorded the entire **Koran** despite his not being able to read or write. The Koran was revealed to him during a series of visions.

Mithra/Mithraism

In Zoroastrianism, Mithra was the **Angel of Light.** He was also the angelic **mediator** between **God** and mankind, and held the title of Guardian of the World. In addition, he was one of the twenty-eight *izeds* of **Ahura Mazda,** and one of the Adityas (**angels** of Vedic beliefs). He later became the **Persian god of light** and wisdom. In ancient art he was portrayed as young, handsome, and strong, and was often shown slaying bulls. The religion of Mithraism started in the second century A.D. It was based on the worship and following of Mithra. Mithraism taught of the dualistic conflict between the celestial forces of good and **evil.**

Modalism

An ancient Trinitarian belief dating back to the third century. The doctrine teaches that there is only one person in the Godhead, whereas the **Trinity** doctrine teaches three separate individuals. Modalism argues that one person (generally the **Father**) has manifested Himself at different times under "modes." As a result, Father, Son, and the **Holy Ghost** are three names for the same Being. The basic idea is that sometimes **God** exists in the form of the Father, sometimes as the Son, and sometimes as the **Holy Spirit,** but never all three at the same time.

Monarchianism

A third-century doctrine which argued that because **God's** nature is one, He cannot exist forever in three persons as the teaching of the **trinity** asserted. Popular forms of Monarchianism were dynamic Monarchianism and **Modalism.**

Monergism

The Christian teaching that **God** alone is the one who saves. It is opposite to **synergism** which teaches that God and **Man** work jointly to achieve **salvation.**

Monks

In **Catholicism** monks serve **God** by applying the vows of poverty, chastity, and obedience. These ideas were implemented during the medieval period. The thought behind the vows stems from God's relationship with the **angels.** The monks attempt to resemble the angels as closely as possible in their service to God. In **Heaven** the angels do not own possessions; thus the vow of poverty (in medieval times the monks had to give everything but a begging bowl away). Also, angels do not marry, nor do they reproduce. They were created directly by God, so because of this, the monks take a vow of chastity. Angels receive their orders from and obey God, so monks are obliged to respect and obey the abbot (the chief monk and the father of the community) of the monastery. Therefore, they take a vow of obedience.

Monolatry

The veneration of one god, even though several gods are thought to exist.

Monotheism

The belief that there is only one **God. Jews,** Christians, and **Muslims** worship one God as the creator and ruler of the universe. Although each of these religions is different, the concept of God is similar in all three. All three share the same fundamental doctrine that there is only one omnipotent God who is the source of everything that exists. They view him as having perfect **attributes** such as infinitude, **immutability,** eternity, goodness, knowledge, and power. While many religions ascribe certain human characteristics to God, the nature of God does not change from **Judaism,** through **Christianity** and into **Islam.** Zoroastrianism, **Sikhism,** and **Baha'ism** are also monotheistic religions.

Moody, D(wight) L(yman) (1837–1899)

American evangelist who has been hailed as one of the most important and fascinating people in America's religious history. He is founder of the Northfield Schools in Massachusetts, Moody **Church** and Moody **Bible** Institute in Chicago, and the Colportage Association. Although he was never ordained, his **faith** in **God** led him to become a famous minister. He told others that God had given him a lifeboat and said, "Moody, save all you can." His faith in God was so strong that Moody made this stirring comment: "Some day you will read in the papers that D. L. Moody of East Northfield, is dead. Don't you believe a word of it! At that moment I shall be more alive than I am now; I shall have gone up higher, that is all, out of this old clay tenement into a house that is immortal—a body that **death** cannot touch, that **sin** cannot taint; a body fashioned like unto His glorious body. I was born of the flesh in 1837. I was born of the **Spirit** in 1856. That which is born of the flesh may die. That which is born of the Spirit will live forever."

Mormonism (Church of Jesus Christ of Latter-Day Saints)

Major world religion, founded in the U.S. by Joseph Smith (known as "the

Prophet") in 1830. The Mormon beliefs are based on the **Bible,** *The Book of Mormon,* writings by Smith, and sayings collected in *The Pearl of Great Price.* Mormons perceive **God** as an exalted **Man** in the most literal, anthropomorphic terms. They believe that humans are created in God's image, but they differ from other Christian groups in their belief that God has a physical form and image. Mormon doctrine holds that God evolved from Man and that men might evolve into gods. They believe that persons of the **trinity** are distinct beings, and that human **souls** preexisted in **Heaven** before coming to Earth. Mormons believe that God is **endless and eternal,** a **God of love** who is all-knowing and all-powerful. God's "glory" is a central attribute of God, which Mormon scriptures associate with **divine law** and with God's power and **Spirit.** Ultimately, Mormons believe in God, the **Eternal Father;** in His Son, **Jesus Christ;** and in the **Holy Ghost.**

Moses

Hebrew prophet, leader, Lawgiver, and founder of **Israel.** He is presumed to be the author of the first five books of the **Old Testament** (or **Torah**). Moses was unique in that he spoke with **God** "face to face." God chose Moses to deliver the Hebrews from **Egyptian** slavery. The story of his life and his extraordinary relationship with God is set forth in the Old Testament books **Exodus,** Leviticus, Numbers, and **Deuteronomy.**

According to the account, Moses was born in Goshen, a part of ancient Egypt. At that time, the Hebrews lived in Egypt as slaves of the Egyptian Pharaoh. Just before Moses was born, Pharaoh ordered all Hebrew male infants be put to **death.** In order to save her child, Moses' mother placed him in a basket made of papyrus and set it floating on the Nile River in the presence of his older sister, Miriam (see Exodus 2:4; Numbers 26:59). He was rescued by the daughter of Pharaoh, who brought the infant up as her own child. She named him Moses because she took him out of the water (Exodus 2:5–10). As a result, Moses was reared in the Egyptian court. As an adult Moses was angered by the oppression of the Hebrew people. He killed an Egyptian taskmaster whom he had seen beating a Hebrew slave. He then fled Egypt in order to escape Pharaoh who sought to kill him as a result of the incident. He settled in Midian where he became a shepherd and eventually the son-in-law of a Midianite priest named Jethro.

Moses was a shepherd until he was eighty years of age. While tending his flocks one day, he saw a **burning bush** that remained unconsumed and heard there a call from God who identified Himself as the God of **Abraham, Isaac,** and **Jacob.** He informed Moses that He had heard the cries of the Hebrews and was aware of their oppression and that He was sending Moses as His representative to Pharaoh in order to rescue His people from bondage. God also disclosed that the divine name was **"I Am."** Moses was said to have a speech impediment; therefore his brother Aaron was to be his spokesman, but Moses would be the one representing God. Once Pharaoh had let the people go, Moses was to lead them to a land chosen by God, "a **land flowing with milk and honey.**"

Ramses II who reigned from 1279–1213 B.C. is believed to have been the pharaoh of Egypt during that period. He did as God had stated to Moses: he rejected the demand of this unknown God and responded by increasing the oppression of the Hebrews. God then brought on miracles to convince Pharaoh to let the Hebrews

go, such as changing the water of the Nile to blood and bringing **plagues** upon the Egyptians. At last, after God struck down all of the firstborn of Egypt, Pharaoh consented, and Moses led the Hebrews out of Egypt toward Canaan. Pharoah later changed his mind and sent his army to recapture the Hebrews. As they neared the **Red Sea,** Pharaoh's army came upon them from the rear. Moses stretched out his arm, whereupon the Red Sea rose up in two walls, leaving dry land between them. The Hebrews crossed on the land safely, but when the Egyptians tried to pursue them, the walls of water broke upon them, and they were engulfed.

Moses then led the people to **Mount Sinai.** When the Hebrews reached Sinai, Moses ascended the mountain to speak with God. God appeared to Moses there in a terrific storm. He spent forty days and nights with God, out of which came the **covenant** between God and the people of Israel. It was during this time that he received two tablets of stone on which were inscribed the **Ten Commandments,** which thereafter constituted the fundamental laws of the Hebrews. After leaving Mount Sinai and continuing the journey toward Canaan, Moses faced increasing resistance and frustration despite God's miracles such as the parting of the Red Sea and the gifts of **manna,** quails, and water in the desert—all signs that God was leading His people. Moses once became so angry at the people that he failed to honor God for providing water from a rock. God accounted it as a lack of **faith** and denied him entrance into Canaan.

After forty years of wandering in the wilderness and desert under Moses' leadership and enduring much adversity, the Hebrews at last came to Canaan. Moses was permitted by God to view Canaan, the **Promised Land,** from the top of Mount Pisgah, then he died. The account found in Deuteronomy

34:1–5 states, "Then Moses went up from the plains of Moab to Mount Nebo, to the top of Pisgah, and the **Lord** showed him the whole land. The Lord said to him, 'This is the land of which I swore to Abraham, to Isaac, and to Jacob, saying, "I will give it to your descendants"; I have let you see it with your eyes, but you shall not cross over there.' Then Moses, the servant of the Lord, died there in the land of Moab, at the Lord's command." Before he died, Moses turned the leadership of the people over to **Joshua.** Although the dates of Moses' birth and death are difficult to establish, many contemporary authorities believe that the Exodus took place in the thirteenth century B.C.

Most High

A title used to refer to **God.**

Most Holy Place

In the **Old Testament** of the **Bible,** it is the innermost room of the Tent of **God's** Presence (also called the **Tabernacle**). It was a section of about fifteen square feet, containing only one object, the **Ark of the Covenant** (the sacred chest that held the Tablets of the **Law** given to **Moses** by God). Only the High Priest could enter the Most Holy Place which he did once a year on the **Day of Atonement.** It is also referred to as **Holy of Holies.** Later, the **Hebrews'** ceremonies and rituals were held at the temple located in Jerusalem. The temple also had a Most Holy Place.

Mount Carmel

A beautiful, lush, forested mountain seventy miles north of Jerusalem. In the **Bible,** the **prophet Amos** tells of God roaring like a lion from Jerusalem because he is so angry at the **Hebrews.** God's roar was so severe that it caused the peak of Mount Carmel to shrivel. God's breath not only reached Carmel, but it also scorched the shepherd's

pastures between these two points (Amos 1:2). See Mountains.

Mount Hermon

A 9,100-foot mountain in the Anti-Lebanon Range. It is the highest mountain in the neighborhood of Palestine. According to 1 **Enoch** 6:6, it is where the **angels** of **God** known as the **Watchers** descended when they came to Earth to have sexual relations with mortal women. See Daughters of Men.

Mount Kenya

Extinct volcano in central Kenya, just south of the equator. It is the second highest after Mount Kilimanjaro. The mountain reaches high into the sky, giving it an image to the locals of reaching into the **heavens.** Neighboring villagers believe that **God** dwells there, and from Mount Kenya's peak, oversees human events. Upon **death,** it is believed that good people go there to dwell forever with God.

Mount Moriah

The place where **Abraham** took his son **Isaac** to offer him as a **sacrifice** to **God.** Just as Abraham was about to slay his son, an **Angel of the Lord** called out to him from **Heaven** to stop him. This **angel** is sometimes referred to as the Angel of Mount Moriah. See Mountains.

Mount Olympus

The home of **Zeus** (supreme god) and the major gods of Greek mythology. See Mountains.

Mount Sinai

The mountain in the **Old Testament** where **Moses** first encountered **God** in a **burning bush.** It is also the place where Moses received the tablets that held the **Ten Commandments** from God. About Mount Sinai, Psalms 68:17 says, "The chariots of God are twenty thousand, even thousands of **angels:** the **Lord** is among them, as in Sinai, in the **holy place**." It is also called Mount **Horeb** and the **Mountain of God**. See Mountains.

Mountain of God

Mount Sinai is sometimes referred to as the Mountain of **God**. See Mountains.

Mountains

To many, mountains provide the perfect setting for direct communication with **God**. They offer a natural place for **prayer, meditation,** reflection, and contemplation that enables people to feel closer to God. Mountains also play important roles in many religions and systems of belief as places of vision and higher consciousness. Mountains have long been viewed as the home of God or the gods and have also served as **altars** and places to offer **sacrifices** to God.

In the **Old Testament**, in Jewish tradition, **Mount Moriah** was the place where **Abraham** took his son **Isaac** to offer him as a sacrifice to God. **Mount Sinai** (also called Mount **Horeb**) was known as the **Mountain of God** or God's Mountain. It is where **Moses** first encountered God in a **burning bush**. It is also the place where Moses received the tablets that held the **Ten Commandments** from God.

Mount Carmel is also found in the Old Testament. It is a lush, wooded mountain seventy miles north of Jerusalem. It was sacred to both **Baal** (Canaanite God) and **Yahweh** (Hebrew God), and in the sixth century B.C. it was sacred to **Jupiter** (Roman supreme god). In the Bible, the **prophet Amos** tells of God roaring like a lion from Jerusalem because he is so angry at the Hebrews. The blast of his roar was so severe that it caused the peak of Mount Carmel to shrivel (Amos 1:2). It was Mount Carmel on which **Elijah** challenged the prophets of Baal to see whose god could answer their prayers with fire.

In early Greek **mythology, Mount Olympus** was home to **Zeus** and the major gods. It is the loftiest point in **Greece,** on the boundary between Thessaly and Macedonia, near the Aegean Sea. On its summit were the palaces of the gods. The entrance to Olympus was through a gate of clouds. Zeus had his throne on Olympus, where the gods feasted on nectar and ambrosia. In **Islam,** the prophet **Muhammad,** while meditating on a mountain, was first visited by an **angel** from God sent with a message. That message turned out to be the **Koran,** the **Holy** Book of Islam. In **Japan,** Mount Fuji is held in the Shinto religion to be the physical embodiment of a **divine spirit,** and members of the Fujuiko sect believe it to possess a **soul.** Several North American tribes, including the Lakota Sioux and the Cheyenne, visit Bear Butte, a sacred mountain ridge on the plains of South Dakota to pray and undertake vision quests.

Muhammad (570–632)

A great **prophet** of **God** and the founder of **Islam**. He is of key importance to **Muslims** as a living example of the "ideal Muslim," the model for all to emulate. Muhammad was born in **Mecca,** a commercial, cultural, and religious center in Saudi **Arabia,** in the year 570. He was raised by an uncle from the tribe of Quraysh after the **death** of his mother (his father died before Muhammad's birth). Growing up, Muhammad became known for his sincerity, honesty, and generosity. Historians describe him as calm and meditative, a man of a deeply religious nature who had long detested the decadence of his society. It became his habit to meditate from time to time in the Cave of Hira near the summit of Jabal al-Nur, the "Mountain of **Light**" near Mecca.

At the age of forty, while meditating one day, he heard a voice that commanded him, "Recite!" Muhammad, stunned and confused, wondered if he was hearing voices and worried that there was something wrong with him. Frightened and bewildered, he responded that he had nothing to recite. The voice was that of the **angel Jibril** who again commanded him to recite. Finally, the words came to him: "Recite in the name of your **Lord** who has created **man** out of a blood clot. Recite for your Lord is the Most Gracious One Who has taught by the pen, Taught man what he did not know!" Afterward, Muhammad began to receive a series of revelations from God through the angel Jibril (this vision is said to have occurred around the year 610).

Like the biblical prophets, Muhammad spent many years communicating the message he received from God, calling upon the people to repent their **sinful** ways and to return to the worship of the one true God. Over the next twenty-three years, Muhammad wrote under **divine** dictation a book so beautiful that people wept upon hearing it. The **Koran** affected the lives of all the Arab tribes in his region, and in only a few generations spread across all of North **Africa** and as far east as **India.** These revelations continued until shortly before Muhammad's death at the age of sixty-two. See Allah.

Mulungu

The **Supreme being** in some East **African** beliefs is Mulungu. Specifically he is the creator god of the Yao of the African nation Malawi.

Muslim(s)

See Islam; Muhammad.

Mysteries of Heaven

A term used in scripture when referring to knowledge that is known only by higher beings that exist in the spiritual realm. In the chronicles of **Enoch, God** informs Enoch that the mysteries of **Heaven** were no longer accessible to the group of **angels** called **Watchers** because of their **sin** with the women of the Earth. He accused the Watchers of broadcasting the mysteries of Heaven to women. Some of these mysteries that God referred to were also mysteries that were "rejected" in Heaven. God said that the people of Earth would use this knowledge to perform **evil** deeds. In 1 Enoch the angels **Michael,** Surafel, and **Gabriel** tell God about the events that took place on Earth after the angels had descended to be with women. They say to God, "You see what Azaz'el [Chief of the Watchers] has done; how he has taught all forms of oppression upon the earth. And they [the Watchers] revealed **eternal secrets** which are performed in heaven and which **man** learned." Another name for mysteries of heaven is eternal secrets.

Mystery

Many religious thinkers have held that **God** is so different from humans that He should be looked upon as a mystery that is beyond our understanding. However, many theologians, philosophers, and other great thinkers have assumed that a small amount of knowledge of God is feasible. Due to this line of thought, many have devised their own theories of Him in terms of godly qualities and paths of knowledge.

Mystical Experience

A direct encounter with **God.**

Mythology

Legends of gods that help shape a culture's standards. Mythology is generally made up of traditional stories about God or the gods. Myths often relay the stories of the **creation** of the world and humankind.

N

Be still and know that I am God.

—*Psalms 46:10*

Nahum

Book of the **Bible** written by Nahum, the seventh of the twelve minor **prophets**. Nahum prophesied in Judah in the late seventh century B.C. He was a contemporary of **Jeremiah, Habakkuk,** and **Zephaniah.** Nahum's message was a **prophecy** of doom against Nineveh, the capital of the oppressive Assyrian empire. In the book, Nahum proclaims that **God** is slow to anger but great in power, and He will take vengeance upon His adversaries. The first chapter praises God for His goodness and **mercy,** but stresses His great power and His ability to overthrow the wicked. Chapter 2 tells how Nineveh will be attacked and plundered; chapter 3 tells of the wickedness of Nineveh, comparing it with Thebes, a once-great city that fell to the Assyrians. Nahum tells the people that God will justly bring about Assyria's downfall.

Says Nahum of God: "A jealous and avenging God is the **Lord,** the Lord is avenging and wrathful; the Lord takes vengeance on his adversaries and rages against his enemies. The Lord is slow to anger but great in power, and the Lord will by no means clear the guilty" (Nahum 1:1–3).

Nations

According to the Book of **Isaiah, God** is not impressed with the great nations. As far as God is concerned, "The nations are like a drop in a bucket; they are regarded as **dust** on the scales" (**Isaiah** 40:15).

Native Americans

Ancient Native Americans worshipped an all-powerful, all-knowing creator or master spirit generally referred to as the **Great Spirit.** They also recognized a host of lesser entities. Even though the Great Spirit was prominent among their beliefs, they also perceived themselves as living in a universe permeated with powerful, mysterious spiritual beings. They believed that in order to continue to exist, it was essential that they recognize these beings in all areas of life. They did so by addressing them in music, **prayer,** gifts, ceremonies, and by handing down information about them to succeeding generations. These beliefs continued to be an essential part of the native North American civilization from the Stone Age (30,000 B.C.–2500 B.C.) until the end of the nineteenth century, when the European settlement of North America was completely established.

Native Americans also believed in **spirit** helpers they called guides or familiars. These spirits helped with problems and chores. When in need of help or guidance, Native Americans communed with these spirits privately. In addition, each tribe is said to have been protected by a guardian spirit. Personal guardian spirits were sought after by individual members of a tribe, and through vision quests they were able to learn their power animal and the names of their spirit helpers and guardians. Many of these beliefs are still practiced by Native Americans today.

Neolithic Peoples

The people of the cultural period beginning around 10,000 B.C. in the Middle East and later elsewhere. The period is characterized by the appearance of farming, ceramics, and the invention of technically advanced stone implements. As production grew in scope, people's conceptual thinking was gradually enhanced, and primitive forms of art and religion developed steadily. Eventually, the Neolithic peoples came to worship the Earth **goddess** in great seasonal festivals.

New Age

The term new age means a new era or new consciousness for humankind. It is an age where people will become more enlightened spiritually and will be brought closer to a relationship with **God.** The new age movement is a mixture of various religious practices with influences both modern and ancient. There is no main idea of God in new age beliefs; here, God is many things to many people. Some new-agers have simply incorporated their beliefs about God into their new-age style of thinking. They continue to see God as they always have depending upon their religions. Others envision God in a different **light.** Some believe that God is a "state of higher consciousness" while others believe that each individual is God.

There are also those who view all people as a part of the **divine,** as sparks from God that have gone out into the universe to experience, learn, and grow, and then when their lifespan is over, return to God with the knowledge and information they received. In other words, it is thought that we are all a part of God—all are a mini-God, so to speak—because we all came from the divine source, which some call God. New-age terms for God vary. Some refer to God as "God," others use such terms as "Godforce," "energy," "the divine source," "the All," or even "the universe."

New Testament

See Bible, The.

New Thought Alliance

In the early 1900s a number of schools of spiritual thought came together and formed the New Thought Alliance. This alliance wrote a declaration of truths, affirming that disease, sickness, sorrow, unhappiness, and self-guilt could be cured if people would apply two principles of truth every day. The first principle stated that there is one **divine God** who is All in All; the second said that God dwells inside all human beings. The basic idea was that by believing we are all a part of God and not separate from Him, we will be healed of maladies of the body and mind. New Thought Alliance followers proclaimed that our thoughts lack thoughts of God and that makes us break down and become ill. They taught that if we believe that we are apart from God, we will feel anxiety, uneasiness, weakness, powerlessness, attachment to the past, bitterness, a sense of being trapped, and hopelessness. It is because humans believe they are separate from God that they are incapable of freeing the God-given healing power that dwells within everyone.

Newton, Isaac (1642–1727)

English physicist, mathematician, and natural philosopher. He is considered one of the most important scientists of all time, and has major contributions to his credit. Newton strongly believed in **God, Jesus Christ** as his Savior, and the **Bible** as God's word. He wrote many books on these topics.

Newton, John (1725–1807)

English author of the beloved hymn "Amazing Grace." He was a self-proclaimed wretch who once was lost but then was found, saved by amazing **grace.** Newton, whose despicable life as a slave trader was turned around by **God**'s amazing grace, wrote of the night he found God. It began on a journey home aboard a ship. During the trip, he had to steer the ship through a horrendous storm; one so brutal that he felt he would surely die. He exclaimed, "**Lord,** have **mercy** upon us." Later, after the storm had calmed, he thought about the events. He believed that during the storm God had spoken to him, and he began to believe God's grace had begun to work in his life. Newton called this his "great deliverance." In "Amazing Grace" Newton speaks of God's mercy and grace:

Amazing grace! (how sweet the
   sound)
That sav'd a wretch like me!
I once was lost, but now am found,
Was blind, but now I see.

'Twas grace that taught my heart to
   fear,
And grace my fears reliev'd;
How precious did that grace appear,
The hour I first believ'd!

Thro' many dangers, toils and
   snares,
I have already come;

'Tis grace has brought me safe thus
   far,
And grace will lead me home.

The Lord has promis'd good to me,
His word my hope secures;
He will my shield and portion be,
As long as life endures.

Yes, when this flesh and heart shall
   fail,
And mortal life shall cease;
I shall possess, within the veil,
A life of joy and peace.

The earth shall soon dissolve like
   snow,
The sun forbear to shine;
But God, who call'd me here below,
Will be forever mine.

Nicholas of Cusa (1401–1464)

German cardinal, scholar, mathematician, scientist, and philosopher. He contended that true wisdom lies in recognizing human ignorance and that knowledge of **God** is only achievable through mystical **intuition,** an advanced state of intelligence.

Noah (Rest)

Biblical character. He was the patriarch chosen by **God** to build the **ark.** Noah and his family were spared by God because of his righteousness and **faith**fulness. At God's command Noah built a great ark that saved his family and various **animals** from the **Flood** brought about by God. Noah lived during a period on Earth when humans had become **evil** and **sinful,** about 1056 years after **creation.** The **Bible** states that all of their thoughts were evil. It was so bad that God came to regret having created humankind, and in His anger, decided to destroy all living things. He choose to do this through a great flood.

The Bible states that Noah was blameless among the people of his time, and that he walked with God. God said to Noah, "I am going to put an end to all people, for the earth is filled with violence because of them. I am surely going to destroy both them and the earth" (**Genesis** 6:13). However, he chose to spare Noah and his family saying, "So make yourself an ark of cypress wood." "I am going to bring floodwaters on the earth to destroy all life under the **heavens**, every creature that has the breath of life in it. Everything on earth will perish. But I will establish my **covenant** with you, and you will enter the ark—you and your sons and your wife and your sons' wives with you. You are to bring into the ark two of all living creatures, male and female, to keep them alive with you."

He gave Noah instructions for building an ark, and when the ark was completed, God sent the rains. Noah and all inside the ark were saved, but the rest of humanity was destroyed. After seven months, the ark came to sit on the top of Mount Ararat. At that point Noah sent out a **dove** and it brought back an olive leaf so that Noah knew that the Flood had subsided.

GOD'S COVENANT WITH NOAH. After the rain stopped, God said to Noah, "I now establish my covenant with you and with your descendants after you and with every living creature that was with you—the birds, the livestock and all the wild animals, all those that came out of the ark with you—every living creature on earth. I establish my covenant with you: Never again will all life be cut off by the waters of a flood; never again will there be a flood to destroy the earth." And God said, "This is the sign of the covenant I am making between me and you and every living creature with you, a covenant for all generations to come. I have set my **rainbow** in the clouds, and it will be the sign of the covenant between me and the earth. Whenever I bring clouds over the earth and the rainbow appears in the clouds, I will remember my covenant between me and you and all living creatures of every kind. Never again will the waters become a flood to destroy all life. Whenever the rainbow appears in the clouds, I will see it and remember the everlasting covenant between God and all living creatures of every kind on the earth." So God said to Noah, "This is the sign of the covenant I have established between me and all life on the earth" (Genesis 9:8–16).

Numbers

The finding of hidden meanings in numbers and letters in the **Hebrew** alphabet is called gematria. In Hebrew, each letter has a numerical value, so gematria is the calculation of the numerical equivalence of letters, words, or phrases. For instance, **God's** Name was interpreted by gematria. The four letters of God's Name (Y-H-W-H) have numerical values as follows: 10, 5, 6, 5. The sum of their squares is 186, which is the numerical value of M-Q-W-M, which means "place." This reminded the ancient rabbis that God is omnipresent (in every place).

O

He is the Living One; there is no God but He; call upon
Him, giving Him sincere devotion. Praise be to God,
Lord of the Worlds.

—*Koran*

Oaths

A request to **God** to observe the certainty of a statement or contract. An oath phrase which is found in the **Old Testament** is "as surely as the **Lord** lives." The **Hebrews** took oaths seriously, and it was written in the **Ten Commandments** not to take God's Name in vain.

Obadiah (Slave of God)

Hebrew prophet of **God**. The fourth of the twelve prophets. In the **Old Testament**, the Book of Obadiah contains a brief prophetic vision against the Edomites, a people that had taken advantage of Jerusalem. Obadiah warns the Edomites that God will destroy Edom. The book finishes with a prophesy of the restoration of **Zion**.

Obassi Osaw

High god of the Hausa people of the Niger.

Odin

The chief **divinity** and creator god in Norse **mythology**. Legend has it that Odin existed before time. He is said to have created the heavens and the Earth and all the creatures to mirror his glory. The **creation** of the Earth and humans were his definitive work.

He created humans with an **eternal soul**. As a result, at **death** the "good" go to reside forever with Odin in his glorious **paradise** called Gimli. There, they find lush meadows and banquet and ballrooms where great celebrations are held. The "bad" are destined to spend eternity tormented in the palace of Hel. Odin's wife was the Mother of all and protector of **children**.

Oh, God! (1977)

Film comedy directed by Carl Reiner, starring George Burns as **God**. In the movie, God is made visible to a supermarket manager (John Denver) and tells him to spread the word. People have a difficult time believing this and the manager must face a judge to vindicate himself. God shows up in the courtroom to offer a helping hand. Other cast members include: Teri Garr, Paul Sorvino, Ralph Bellamy, and George Furth.

Ohrmazd

Another name for **Ahura Mazda**, **God's** Name in Zoroastrianism.

Old Testament

See Bible, Torah.

Old Testament Names for God

Elohim (God); Jehovah/Yahweh (the self-existent one: I AM); Jehovah-jireh (the Lord will provide); Jehovah-rapha (the Lord Who heals); Jehovah-nissi (the Lord, our banner); Jehovah-Shalom (the Lord, our peace); Jehovah-ra-ah (the Lord, my shepherd); Jehovah-tsidkenu (the Lord, our righteousness); Jehovah-shammad (the Lord is present); Jehovah Elohim (the Lord God); Jehovah-Sabaoth (the Lord of Hosts); El Elyon (the Most High God); Adonai (our master); El Shaddai (Almighty God, the Strength Giver); El Olam (Everlasting God).

Oludumare

The supreme God of the Yoruba people of Africa. It was believed that Oludumare could be communicated with through the *orisa* which are the four hundred and one forces of nature. These would carry a person's prayers to Oludumare.

Om

A sanskrit word for the supreme entity.

Ometeotl

A primordial creator god of the Aztecs. He was believed by the Aztecs to be present in all things.

Omnibenevolence

See Divine Attributes.

Omnipotence

See Divine Attributes.

Omnipresence

See Divine Attributes.

Omniscience

See Divine Attributes.

Ontological Argument

One of the arguments in the proof of God's existence. The Ontological Argument is the attempt to prove God's existence through discussion of His nature and necessity. It is especially associated with the scholastic theologian Anselm of Canterbury. The Ontological Argument is based purely on reason. Saint Anselm developed the Ontological Argument for the existence of God in his book *Faith Seeking Understanding.*

Anselm argued: "Men believe God to be the Being than which none greater can be thought. It is greater to exist in reality and in the understanding than to exist in the understanding alone. Therefore, it is contradictory to hold that God exists only in the intellect, for then the being than which none greater can be thought is one than which a greater can be thought, namely, one that exists both in reality and in the understanding." The basic, more easily understandable structure of the argument is this: God is a being than which nothing greater can be conceived. It is greater to exist than not to exist. Therefore, God exists.

Oracles

Divine announcements given to God's people. God's way of imparting these oracles were diverse, ranging from dreams and visions to divination (see Urim and Thummim). God's way of communicating these oracles are not given in any detail in the Bible.

Origen (c. 185–c. 254)

Christian philosopher and scholar, considered to be one of the most distinguished of the Fathers of the early Church, as well as one of the most brilliant Christians of his time. His full name was Origines Adamantius. He was instructed by his father, Leonides, in the Bible and in elementary studies.

When he was young, his father was martyred. At the age of seventeen, Origen became head of the catechetical school of Alexandria in **Egypt,** where he had studied under Clement of Alexandria. Origen taught in Alexandria for twenty-eight years, and wrote hundreds of works of **theology** and Biblical commentary, becoming famous for his interpretation of the scriptures. His writings were widely read. Most of his teachings were Bible-based and his piety was never an issue. However, there were parts of his teachings which created controversy. These included his thoughts on **reincarnation** and whether or not it was real; also controversial were his thoughts on **universalism** (universal **salvation** and **eternal** progress of all **souls**), which held that all could come to **God** and achieve salvation. Origen held that **Satan** and his **demons** could be saved. These ideas were proclaimed heretical by the church, and eventually, Origen died from injuries inflicted under Roman persecution.

On God, Origen once commented: "Since our mind is in itself unable to behold God as he is, it knows the **Father** of the universe from the beauty of his works and from the elegance of his creatures. God, therefore, is not to be thought of as being either a body or as existing in a body, but as a simple intellectual being, admitting within himself no addition of any kind" (*Fundamental Doctrines* 1:1:6 [225 A.D.]).

Original Sin
See Adam.

Osanna of Mantua
See Andreasi, Osanna.

Osiris
Chief **Egyptian God** and the supreme god of the ancient Egyptian pantheon. He presided over the dead, the netherworld, and the **spirit** world. In him came the hope of continued life after **death,** based on the lifestyle to which people had been accustomed. He was associated with the Nile, whose yearly rise brought renewed life to the Earth. His cult probably came the closest to a universal Egyptian religion in pre-Christian times.

P

God enters by a private door into every individual.
—*Ralph Waldo Emerson*

Paganism

A term used to refer to belief in a god or gods other than the Jewish, Christian, or **Muslim God.**

Palet

Ancient **Hebrew** name for **God.** It means "Deliverer."

Paley, William

See Teleological Argument.

Panentheism

The belief that **God** is *in* all (not to be confused with **pantheism** which means God *is* all). The word Panentheism is taken from the Greek words *pan,* meaning all; *en,* meaning in; and *theos,* meaning God. The idea is that God encompasses the whole universe within Himself, and yet is also more than the universe. As a result, God is believed to be evolving along with **creation.**

Pantheism

The belief that **God** *is* all (not to be confused with **Panentheism** which means God is *in* all). The word Pantheism comes from the Greek word *pan,* meaning all and *theos,* meaning God. The idea is that God and universe are one and the same.

Paradise

The **Garden of Eden.** The English word paradise is derived from the old **Persian** word **pairidaeza,** which means pleasure park or garden. According to **Genesis, God** created a beautiful paradise (also known as the Garden of Eden, or Eden) and placed the first **man** and woman there. He told them to be fruitful there and multiply. He also instructed the couple to cultivate the garden so it would grow and flourish and be filled with their happy offspring. However, paradise was lost when the two committed a forbidden act and they were cast out of Paradise forever. Later, after **Adam and Eve** were cast out of Paradise, God placed two **Cherubim** and a turning flaming sword as guards to the entrance. See also Heaven; Djanna.

Paradise Lost

An epic poem written by John Milton in 1667. It has been hailed as the greatest epic ever written in the English language. It is the story of **Adam and Eve's** expulsion from **Paradise.** In it, Milton writes about the **fallen angels** and the effect their **rebellion** had on mankind's destiny. It begins with **Satan's** revolt against **God** and the banishment of Adam and Eve from the **Garden of Eden.** It also tells how **Jesus** overcame the temptations of the **Devil.** It describes the great **war in Heaven,** which Milton depicts as occurring for three days, after which the **Son of God** intervened. Satan is then cast out of Heaven, taking with him one third of the **angels,** whom Milton portrays as angels from the **Cherubim** and **Seraphim** classes. According to Milton, after he was cast out of Heaven, Satan recovered for nine days, then he went after Adam and Eve. The sequel to *Paradise Lost* was named *Paradise Regained.*

Paradise Regained

A sequel to the classic *Paradise Lost,* written by John Milton in 1671. The sequel continues the exploits of humankind after their expulsion from **Paradise.** Milton follows with biblical stories from the emergence of the **Hebrew prophets** through to the life of **Christ.** Throughout it all, **God** sits above overlooking humanity, protecting it, all the while promising to welcome it home to **Heaven.**

Pascal, Blaise (1623–1662)

French philosopher, mathematician, and physicist. He laid the foundations for hydrostatics, hydrodynamics, differential calculus, and the theory of probability. He is considered one of the great minds in Western intellectual history. He is credited with the famous "Pascal's Wager." Pascal's Wager is the name given to an argument for believing, or taking steps to believe, in **God.** Pascal's Wager as summarized by Tim Stout, chairman of the board and chief scientist for T & G Technologies, Inc., basically says this: "How can anyone lose who chooses to be a Christian? If, when he dies, there turns out to be no God and his **faith** was in vain, he has lost nothing—in fact, has been happier in life than his nonbelieving friends. If, however, there is a God and a **heaven** and **hell,** then he has gained heaven and his skeptical friends will have lost everything in hell!"

Passover

A celebration of **Judaism.** The Passover is an eight-day observance commemorating the **Israel**ites' escape from **Egypt.** About 3,000 years ago the Israelites were enslaved by the Egyptians under the rule of Ramses II, pharaoh during that time. According to the **Bible**'s Book of **Exodus, Moses,** working as a shepherd, was instructed by **God** to go to Pharaoh and demand freedom for the Israelites. Moses did as he was told and went to Egypt to speak with Pharaoh and to relay all that God had told him. Moses' plea of "Let my people go" was ignored by Pharaoh, who protested that he did not know this God. No, he would not let the **Hebrews** go. Moses warned Pharaoh that God would send severe punishments to the people of Egypt if the Israelites were not set free. Still Pharaoh did not relent. In response, God unleashed a series of ten **plagues** on the people of Egypt including: **Blood,** Frogs, Lice (vermin), Wild Beasts (flies), Blight (cattle disease), Boils, Hail, **Locusts,** Darkness, and the Slaying of the First Born.

The holiday's Hebrew name *Pesach,* meaning "passing over," stems from the directions given to Moses by God. In order to convince Pharaoh to free the Hebrews, God intended to strike down the first-born of the Egyptians and their livestock. To achieve this, He planned to send an **angel** to do the killing. To protect themselves, the Israelites were instructed by God to mark their homes with lamb's blood so that they would be passed over by the Angel of **Death.** After the final plague, Pharaoh released the Hebrews. Upon hearing this, the Israelites left their homes so quickly that they had no time to let their bread rise.

Pharaoh later had a change of heart and sent his army to retrieve the Hebrews. The army chased them through the desert towards the **Red Sea.** When the **Jews** reached the sea they were trapped. God intervened and rescued them, parting the Red Sea to allow the Israelites to cross to the other side. As soon as they reached the other side, the opening in the Red Sea closed, trapping the Pharaoh's army as the waves engulfed them. As the Israelites watched the waters of the Red Sea sweep away Pharaoh's army, they realized they were finally free. It is this history and the Hebrews' great relationship with God that Passover commemorates.

Pasteur, Louis (1822–1895)

World-famous French chemist and biologist. The founder of the science of microbiology, he established the germ theory of disease, invented the process of pasteurization, and produced vaccines for a number of diseases, including rabies. He is said to have had a strong belief in **God** and very strong religious convictions.

Patriarchs

The word "patriarchs" in relation to **God** applies to the ancestors of God's Chosen People, the **Children of Israel.** Though there were several biblical patriarchs, the most important were **Abraham** (originally Abram), the one whom God would make the father of a great nation, receive a land, and bring **blessings** to all **nations; Isaac** (Abraham's son); and **Jacob** (Isaac's son, whose name later became **Israel**). These ancient biblical figures were especially important because of God's special promises to them and their **children.**

Pelagianism

The philosophy of Pelagius, a British Christian (thought by some to

be a monk), active in **Rome** in the late fourth and early fifth centuries. Pelagius was a theologian and biblical interpreter who stressed the human ability to fulfill **God's** commandments. According to Pelagius, humans are able to keep the commandments of God because God has given them that ability. He therefore felt that there is no need of **salvation,** saying that **Jesus' death** was simply a supreme example of **love,** humbleness, obedience, and **sacrifice.** Pelagius' opinions were fiercely opposed by Saint **Augustine** who believed that each person requires the aid of God's **Grace** if he or she is to do good. In 417, Pelagius was excommunicated by Pope Innocent I, and his ideas were condemned by a series of **Church** councils.

Pentateuch

The first five books of the **Bible** (**Genesis, Exodus,** Leviticus, Numbers, and **Deuteronomy**). In Jewish tradition they are called the **Torah,** which means "instruction." These are the books of **God's Law.** The books were traditionally written as a single unbroken **scroll.** It was divided into the five books that we have today sometime before the second century B.C. According to tradition, God instructed and gave laws to **Moses** on how the **Israel**ites should live, and Moses wrote these commands as the Pentateuch. Today, some scholars believe that there were several authors of the Pentateuch, not just Moses. They note several distinct styles to the writings of the books. For example, one writer used the name **"Yahweh"** for God; another used the term **"Elohim."** Exactly who these other writers were and when they lived is unclear. Even though the five books are very different, they all tell the story of God, His **creation,** His work, His purposes, His relationship with humankind, and His **call** to a nation to become His chosen people.

People of the Book

A term used by some **Muslims** (followers of **Islam**) when speaking of **Jews** and Christians. Muslims worship the same **God** as the Jews and the Christians. They regard them more than those who are outside of the two religions. Muslims believe that the **holy** scriptures of the Jews and Christians were inspired of God; however, they feel that these books have been corrupted. Muslims believe that the **Koran** is the same as it was since it was first given by God to the prophet **Muhammad.**

People of the Covenant

A term used by **Muslims** when referring to **Jews.** This stems from the belief that the Jews are a chosen people of **God** with whom God once made a covenant.

Perendi

Old Illyrian name for **(Jehovah) God.**

Perseity

See Aseity.

Persia

Ancient Persia's rich religious background was deeply rooted in beliefs in **God.** Before the Arab invasion, the main religion of Persians was Zoroastrianism, a religion founded by **Zarathustra.** In Zoroastrianism, the supreme God is **Ahura Mazda (or Ohrmazd),** the greatest Persian god of antiquity, known as "the god of **Light** and Wisdom." Considered a great **spirit,** he is the creator of the world and sees into the depths of our hearts. His **law** demanded followers to give love and respect to the Wise **Lord** and his **priests,** the **Amesha Spentas.**

Modern Persia (Iran) is made up mostly of **Muslims** who believe in **Allah.** Allah is the **Islam**ic name for "the One and Only God," the creator and sustainer of the universe. With the advent of **Islam,** the majority of the Persian people accepted the religion of Islam and the worship of Allah. Christians are mainly concentrated in Djolfa near Isfahan and Urumieh, and a minority of **Jews** are concentrated in Hamedan and Isfahan. All three religions worship the same God, as the God of the Jews, the God of the Christians, and the God of Islam is the same. See Khoda.

Petty, William (1623–1687)

One of the founders of the science of statistics and the modern study of economics. In addition, he was a strong supporter and defender of **Christianity,** writing several works on **God's creation.**

Peyotism

The largest religion started, organized, and directed by and for **Native Americans.** Peyotism uses the peyote plant in its rituals. The name comes from the Aztec word *peyotl* which designates a small spineless psychedelic cactus *(Lophophora williamsii)* native to southern Texas and north-central Mexico. Members believe peyote is a sacred plant placed on Earth by **God** to help the Native Americans. They view it as a **divine** instructor and medicine that helps true believers to receive knowledge from God.

Philosophes

See Age of Enlightenment.

Pilgrimage

In many **faiths,** devout believers travel to the sacred cities of their faith: **Jews** and Christians to Jerusalem; Catholics to **Rome,** Fatima, and Lourdes; Hindus to Benares; Sikhs to Amritsar; and **Muslims** to **Mecca.** They commemorate and often ritually reenact important moments from their sacred history, thus helping them to feel closer to **God.** Pilgrimages turn away from the real world of manifestation, traveling through unfamiliar territory in search of God and **enlightenment.** In some cases, pilgrims are deprived of their comfortable home lives and subjected to trial and peril. Every pilgrimage is part of the **eternal** striving of the human **soul** toward God.

Most world religions revere certain temples, cities, or natural features because they are historically linked to God or His **prophets.** Sometimes, as with Jerusalem, sites are important to more than one religion, perhaps suggesting that they have a fundamental, even intrinsic, sacredness and closeness to the **Supreme Being.** Buddhists and Jains visit the Ganges Basin, where both the historical Buddha and Mahavira, the Jain saint, lived, taught, and died. The river Ganges is sacred to Hindus, and millions each year cleanse themselves in its waters, hoping to wash away their **sins.**

Some pilgrims, believing that their **prayers** are more likely to be heard by God if offered in a **holy** place, will travel hundreds of miles to make a specific request. During the Middle Ages, many thousands of Christians undertook pilgrimages to Jerusalem, Rome, Santiago de Compostela, Canterbury, and Walsingham. Since then, other destinations such as Lourdes in France have gained a reputation for granting wishes or for healing. Certain religions demand that specific pilgrimages are undertaken by their worshippers. The last of the **Five Pillars** of **Islam,** for example, states that every Muslim who is physically able should journey to Mecca in Saudi **Arabia** at least once in his or her lifetime. The *hajj,* as this pilgrimage is called, is believed to bestow great merit and to wash away all sins.

Pillar of Fire

The **Bible** tells us that when the **Hebrews** left **Egypt, God** lead them through the wilderness with a pillar of cloud by day and a pillar of fire at night. The account in **Exodus** 13:21–22 said: "During the day the **LORD** went in front of them in a pillar of cloud to show them the way, and during the night he went in front of them in a pillar of fire to give them **light,** so that they could travel night and day." The pillar of cloud would stand over the **tabernacle** when God met **Moses** there. When Moses went into the Tent, the pillar of cloud would come down and stay at the entrance while God spoke with him. The account at Exodus 33:9 states: "After Moses had gone in, the pillar of cloud would come down and stay at the door of the Tent, and the LORD would speak to Moses from the cloud. As soon as the people saw the pillar of cloud at the door of the Tent, they would bow down. The LORD would speak with Moses face-to-face, just as a **man** speaks with a friend."

Place(s) of Worship

Religions all over the world have houses of worship where the **faithful** go to revere **God.** In **Judaism,** they are synagogues; in **Christianity,** they are called **churches;** in **Islam,** they are mosques. The style of building tells much about a each religion's traditions and concepts of God.

Plagues

See Ten Plagues of Egypt; Seven Plagues.

Plato (c. 427–347 B.C.)

Greek philosopher. In his writings, Plato referenced mediating spirits that existed in both the physical and spiritual realms. He believed that there are many spirits of different kinds. One of these spirits was Eros (the god of **love** in Greek **mythology**). According to Plato, Eros had the duties of translating and showing the gods the thoughts of humans; he also communicated to humans what the gods required. According to Plato, the gods do not communicate directly with humans. He held that **mediators** were necessary to converse between the two realms. Plato said: "He best keeps from anger who remembers that **God** is always looking upon him."

Polytheism

The belief in more than one god, in contrast to **monotheism** (one **God**) or **atheism** (no God or gods). The word polytheism is taken from the Greek word *poly* which means "many," and the Greek word *theos* which means "God." In monotheistic religions, God is worshipped as the One, the **supreme being** that has created all things; however, in polytheism, which has also flourished throughout history, there are many **holy** beings, each manifesting a specific **divine** attribute or taking care of some aspect of nature or human affairs. Polytheism was the most common form of religion in the ancient world and was well developed in **Egypt, Mesopotamia, Greece, Rome,** and elsewhere.

The gods of a polytheistic culture were usually conceived of existing in a familial relationship which ensured a sense of their unity. There was usually a father God and a female consort who ruled supreme over the other gods. Some see the gods of polytheism as a breakdown from the one God. These gods are thought to have represented the divine personality of the one God and were a way for humans to worship and cope with such an enormous, vast, spiritual personality. It is thought that when they personalized the unseen forces associated with nature such as the wind, sun, sea, and stars, and assigned them human characteristics, humans were expressing their sense of closeness to nature, to the All, and to God, seeing Him manifest in the many aspects and personalities of the divine beings of the various pantheons.

Ponticus, Evagrius (346–399)

Christian mystic, writer, disciple, and teacher of the ascetic life. Evagrius created a **theology** of meditative **prayer** and asceticism that was the foundation for a tradition of spiritual life in both Eastern and Western **churches**. His writings deeply influenced many later theologians and leaders of monasticism, including John Cassian, Dionysius the Areopagite, Maximus the Confessor, John Climacus, and Simeon the New Theologian. Evagrius stressed that the basic function of spiritual beings is to experience oneness with **God**, the transcendent One, expressed as pure **light**. Of God, Evagrius wrote in his *Dogmatic Letter on the Trinity*: "To those who accuse us of a doctrine of three gods, let it be stated that we confess one God, not in number but in nature. For all that is said to be one numerically is not one absolutely, nor is it simple in nature. It is universally confessed, however, that God is simple and not composite."

Postmillennialism

The idea that through the teaching of **God's** word, people all over the world will be converted to **Christianity**. This world conversion will then usher in the kingdom of God.

Powers

The Powers are said to be the first **angels** created by **God**. They are guardians of the passageways leading to **Heaven**. They also act as guides to lost **souls**. It is the job of the Powers to bring balance to the Earth. It is because

163

of them that humans are able to maintain balance within their spirits. It is also the job of the Powers to record the history of mankind, and they are said to prevent the efforts of **demons** to take control of the world.

Prayer

The act of talking to **God**. Prayer may be individual or group, formal or spontaneous, silent or spoken, but all religions have some form of prayer. The **Israelites** in the **Old Testament** prayed three times every day; **Jesus** taught his followers how to pray; **Muslims** pray five times a day. It is believed that God desires people to pray and is moved to act through the prayers of his people. In biblical times, people prayed at any time of the day or night, and there were formal prayers for morning and evening services in the temple. The **prophet Daniel** prayed three times a day in his bedroom; Nehemiah prayed while he was working. On several occasions he uttered quick, impromptu prayers under his breath when a crisis arose. Jesus also prayed often—from early morning to late at night.

The Christian God is said to be one who listens and responds to prayer. While praying was to be practiced at any time, it was to be done respectfully and with purpose. Jesus warned about idly repeating meaningless expressions in prayer. He even gave an example of how to pray to his followers. This prayer was to aid those who did not know how to pray. This is what is now called the **Lord's Prayer.**

In **Islam**, prayers are believed to be a direct link between the worshipper and God. Muslims pray five times a day. The prayers contain verses from the **Koran** and are said in Arabic, the language in which the Koran was first given through revelation to **Muhammad**. However, personal prayers may be offered in one's own native language.

Prayers are said at sunrise, noon, midafternoon, dusk, and nightfall. Muslims pray almost anywhere, including schools, work, or wherever they may be.

The Koran states that such a inflexible program of prayer encourages worshippers to obey God completely. **Angels of Islam** are said to sit in the mosques listening to and recording the prayers of men. A general translation of the "Call to Prayer" is:

God is most great.
God is most great.
God is most great.
God is most great.
I testify that there is no god except God.
I testify that there is no god except God.
I testify that Muhammad is the messenger of God.
I testify that Muhammad is the messenger of God.
Come to prayer!
Come to prayer!
Come to success (in this life and the Hereafter)!
Come to success!
God is most great.
God is most great.
There is no god except God.

Predestination

The teaching that **God** has preordained all things and events. It is also believed that certain of God's people have their fates predetermined and that good works will make no difference.

Priests

In worship, rituals, and ceremonies in various religions around the world there is often a priest or priests. The priest acts as the **mediator** between the people and **God** or the gods.

Principalities

The Principalities are the angelic guardians of all large groups on the Earth including **nations**, great cities, religions, even large corporations. They are said to be empowered with greater strength by **God** than the **guardian angels** and thus are more frequently involved in human affairs, using their incalculable strength from God to move the hearts and minds of mortals and to perform **miracles.**

Promised Land

The region of land which **God** gave to the **Israelites**. It was said to be "a **land flowing with milk and honey.**"

Prophecy

A message sent by **God** to humans, generally communicated through a **mediator,** usually in the form of a **prophet** or **prophetess.** The prophecy may contain revealing information of a future event, a warning, encouragement, or some other information. Some prophetic messages are relayed directly through **meditation**, a voice, or through a dream. Prophecy often includes some form of **divination** or **oracles** from which the will of the gods is interpreted.

In Judaic beliefs, a prophet is a person selected to take God's messages to his people. Often the **Hebrew** prophets prophesied under enormous pressure and trepidation, often needing God's encouragement and motivation to continue. The concept of prophecy was handed down from **Judaism** to **Christianity. Jesus** is considered both a prophet and the fulfillment of the prophecy of the coming **Messiah.** Indeed, in many respects, Jesus was a typical Judaic prophet. In Judaism and **Islam,** Jesus is looked upon as a prophet from God. Christian visionaries throughout the ages have been thought of as prophets from God, however, they were never quite seen in the same **light** as the prophets of Biblical times. Muslims worship the same God revered by Christians and **Jews,** and recognize the same biblical prophets. They especially consider **Moses** and Jesus to be great prophets who received revelations from God. They consider **Muhammad** to be the final prophet of God, the last in a long line of prophets running from **Adam** through to Muhammad.

Prophet/ess

A person called by **God** to speak on His behalf. According to scripture, certain people were chosen by God to become prophets to remind the people of God's great **love** for them, and of the need to follow His **law.**

Prophetic Books

Religious books that reveal prophecies of **God**.

JUDAISM. In Judaism, the last part of the **Old Testament** consists of sixteen prophetic books. The titles of the books are the name of the **prophet** whose words are recorded within. **Isaiah, Jeremiah, Ezekiel,** and **Daniel** are known as major prophets. The other twelve are referred to as the minor prophets. God called upon the prophets to be His servants and gave them special skills to perform their assignments. Messages of the prophets included words of **faith** from God and encouragement to trust in God alone. The prophets brought messages to God's people, and these were messages of hope, faith, warning, and revelation about the future. They also emphasized that God **(Yahweh)** was **Lord** of all **Creation.**

BOOKS OF THE PROPHETS. The **Hebrew** books of the Prophets given in the Old Testament include Isaiah, Jeremiah, Ezekiel, Daniel, **Hosea, Joel, Amos, Obadiah, Jonah, Micah, Nahum,**

Habakkuk, **Zephaniah**, Haggai, **Zecha-riah**, and **Malachi**.

CHRISTIANITY. In Christianity, **Jesus** brought revealing prophecies about God and the future of humankind, and these are found throughout the books of the **New Testament**. Perhaps the best-known prophecy and prophetic book of the New Testament is Revelation, which announces God's Kingdom, the destruction of the Earth, and the future of the universe.

ISLAM. In Islam, the entire **Koran** is considered one long revelation from God. It was originally recorded in Arabic, and great pains have been taken to ensure the original meaning is maintained. It was revealed to **Muhammad** over a period of twenty-three years and is regarded by **Muslims** as the word of God and his final revelation to humankind. Its basic theme is the relationship between God and His creatures.

Protestantism

A movement that came out of **Christianity**. It came about as an objection to the political power of and corruption within the Roman Catholic **Church**. Concerned followers saw an excessive emphasis on works and on physical representations, while the church was losing sight of what should be of more importance: the direct human relationship to **God** through **faith** in **Jesus**. Protestants rejected the idea that God was a harsh God as had been portrayed for centuries. They no longer believed that **sin** would keep one away from a relationship or favor with God. They rejected the idea that **salvation** would be granted by good works alone. They believed that God was forgiving and all that was needed for salvation was faith in God. This doctrine became known as Justification by Faith. Protestants made certain that God's Word was available to all.

Pseudepigrapha

A group of scriptures not included in the **holy** canon. The Pseudepigrapha contains a substantial amount of information on **God, Heaven,** and God's **angels.** The scriptures were left out of the holy canon because of their questionable authorship. There is also speculation that the scriptures were left out because of the number of angels listed. The rabbis of the period thought the writings bordered on **paganism** because angels represented every function of the universe, just as did the pagan gods and **goddess**es of the day.

Q

O mankind! We created you from a single soul, male and female, and made you into nations and tribes, so that you may come to know one another. Truly, the most honored of you in God's sight is the greatest of you in piety. God is All-Knowing, All-Aware.

—Koran

Qadosh

A **Hebrew** name for **God.** It means "the **Holy** One."

Qormusta

High god of the Mongols.

Quamta

Supreme god of the Xhosa, a Bantu-speaking people of the Transkei in South **Africa.**

Questioning of the Dead

An ancient Islamic belief. In **Islam,** there are said to be two **angels,** Munkar and Nakir, who are assigned by **God** to question the dead to determine whether or not their **souls** will go to **Paradise** or **Hell.** The angels visit the tombs of those who have recently died and ask several questions: "Who is God?" "What is the name of God's **prophet?**" "What is the true religion?" Souls responding with such answers as "**Allah** is God," "**Muhammad** is God's prophet," and "Islam is God's true religion," are considered righteous individuals and are immediately allowed entrance into Paradise. The unrighteous souls, those who did not respond correctly and did not lead lives that served God, are left at the gates of Hell. **Muslims** now believe that God (Allah) keeps detailed accounts of the deeds of all humans and therefore would not rely on a system of questioning.

R

God does not pay weekly, but he pays at the end.
—*Dutch proverb*

Rainbow

According to Judaeo-Christian beliefs, the rainbow is a sign of one of **God's covenants** with **Man**. See Flood; Noah.

Ramakrishna (or Sri Ramakrishna Paramahansa) (1836–1886)

Hindu mystic who spent his entire life contemplating **God**. He reached a depth of God-consciousness that transcends all time and place and has a universal appeal. He was born of a poor Brahman family in Bengal. In about 1855 he became a devotee of the Hindu **goddess** Kali. Over the next fifteen years he immersed himself in extensive spiritual study, including **Christianity, Islam,** and Hindu yoga. From his studies he had a tremendous revelation that all religions have something to offer, all are legitimate in God's view, and all are a means of coming to and approaching God. Eventually, he began to teach. After his **death** his ideas were spread by his wife and followers. Through Ramakrishna's piety, wisdom, and knowledge, he attracted a tremendous following. Today, seekers of God of all religions are drawn to his teachings. His message is God-consciousness and universal religion. Quotes from Ramakrishna follow:

"One cannot have the vision of God as long as one has these three—shame, hatred and fear."

"Live in the world like an unchaste woman. She performs her household duties with great attention, but her mind dwells day and night on her paramour. Perform your duties in the world. But keep your mind always fixed on God."

"The world is a mixture of milk and water, the bliss of God-consciousness and the pleasure of sense enjoyment. Be a swan and drink the milk, leaving the water aside."

"The darkness of centuries is dispersed as soon as a **light** is brought into a room. The accumulated **sins** of countless lives vanish by a single glance of God."

"One cannot realize God without sincerity and simplicity. God is far away from the crooked heart."

Raphael (Shining One Who Heals)

One of **God's** seven **archangels.** According to tradition, his original name was Labbiel. God changed his name from Labbiel to Raphael when he sided with God on the issue of creating **Man.** He is charged with healing mankind and the Earth. It was Raphael who healed **Abraham** of the pain from being circumcised. He also cured **Jacob** after his hip was dislocated while wrestling with an **angel**. He is said to have given **Noah** a medical book containing cures for diseases; legend has it that this was the **Book of Raziel**. In the Book of Tobit, Raphael travels with the young Tobias under the alias of Azarias; as Azarias he acts as a guide and protector to Tobias while on the journey. The Book of Raziel lists Raphael as an amulet angel who is summoned at the time of childbirth. In his play, *The Nativity,* the poet Henry Wadsworth Longfellow refers to Raphael as the "Angel of the Sun." Raphael is said to be especially concerned about those who make religious **pilgrimages** for God.

Ravens

The raven is the largest member of the crow family. It is considered to be an unclean animal (Leviticus 11:15). In the **Bible's Old Testament** some of its features are used for illustrations: the black locks of hair, its nesting in lonely places, its being fed by **God** (Song of **Solomon** 5:11; **Isaiah** 34:11; Psalms 147:9). In addition, **Jesus** used the ravens to illustrate God's provision (Luke 12:24). God's care for the raven was a symbol of His care for His people, and it also was a symbol of judgment and desolation. It was a raven that was sent out first from **Noah's ark (Genesis** 8:7), and **Elijah** was fed by them (1 Kings 17:4-6).

Rebellion

See War in Heaven.

Reconciliation

The bringing together of two or more for the improvement of a relationship. **God** and **Man** are believed in the Christian religion to have been reconciled through the sacrifice of **Jesus.** The belief is that humankind can now have a relationship with God, whereas

before Jesus came, this was believed not to have been possible due to the **sin** of **Adam**. After Jesus' **death** everything changed.

Red Sea

In the **Bible, God** parted the Red Sea in order for the **Hebrews** to cross as they fled Pharaoh's soldiers. See Moses.

Redemption

A term meaning the spiritual **salvation** through **God's sacrifice (Christianity)** or **mercy.**

Reese, Della (1932–)

Star of the hit television series, *Touched by an Angel.* Della Reese is also an ordained minister who has always maintained a strong **faith.** She refers to **God** as her "partner" in life and credits her mother for her close relationship with God. She speaks of this in her autobiography, *Angels Along the Way, My Life with Help from Above.* She writes, "Mama made God one of the family. He wasn't distant or remote or mysterious. He lived with us, inside us, ever-present. This was a fundamental gift my mother bestowed on me, giving me a personal relationship with God that has sustained me through my life and continues to do so today."

Reincarnation

Being reborn in different forms for spiritual development. In some metaphysical beliefs, it is believed that the **soul** comes to the Earth in a variety of lifetimes to learn and to grow spiritually. Each of these lifetimes is a contract or an agreement with **God.**

Rock

A term used in referring to **God.** The word rock refers to the strength one finds in God. In the **Bible,** He is referred to as the Rock of **Israel.** King **David** once said, "The **Lord** is my rock

Rolle, Richard

and my fortress and my deliverer" (2 Samuel 22:2). Psalms 18:31 says, "Who is a rock, except our God."

Rolle, Richard
(Richard Rolle of Hampole)
(c. 1290–c. 1349)

The first of the great British mystics. Rolle was a prolific writer and quite popular in his day. A learned man, he wrote both in Latin and English. At nineteen, Rolle dropped out of his studies at Oxford University to become a hermit. However, he received opposition on the matter from his father, so he decided to leave home. Even though a new hermit should be mentored by a spiritual director, Rolle had no intention of getting one. He was convinced that he had no need of human advice because he was instructed directly by **God,** who, Rolle claimed, made His presence felt in his life in strange but wonderful experiences. After being a hermit, Rolle spent the rest of his life praying, writing, and offering spiritual guidance to others. Rolle's writings are extremely personal, dramatic, and passionate in describing the profundity of his **faith** and his experiences of God.

In his treatise *Fire of Love,* Rolle tells of a strange feeling of heat in his breast. He worried about it but determined that it was from God because it brought with it an abundance of enjoyable and calming emotions. He believed that this experience was a sign of God's special favor. Rolle also spoke of hearing sweet heavenly music that he alone could hear. It was so beautiful that he was unable to tolerate even **church** music. This music, which sometimes came with the heat in his chest and sometimes came separately, brought a flood of pleasurable emotions that Rolle identified with the love of God. In addition to his prose treatises, Rolle also composed a number of lyric poems in which his emotional relationship with God finds its fullest expression.

Roman Catholics

The Roman Catholic **Church** is the oldest Christian church in the world. It was begun around 312 A.D. by the Roman Emperor Constantine, and is headed today by the Pope, the Bishop of **Rome.** The term "Roman Catholic" is a nineteenth century British coinage, but is now in common use among English-speaking people. Because of its enormity (about a billion people worldwide in membership), the actual beliefs held by Catholics worldwide are extensive and diverse. However, one important doctrine unifying all Catholics is the belief that the Pope is the highest representative of **God** on Earth. From its earliest roots, the Church has always considered itself blessed by God, through **Jesus.** The Church believes that God is triune, one God in three **Divine** Persons: the **Father,** the Son, and the **Holy Spirit.**

Rome

See Jupiter.

S

God does not see all things in their particularity or separately, as if He looked first here and then there; but He sees all things together at once.

—Saint Augustine

Sabbath

A day of rest in Jewish tradition. The seventh day of the week became a day of rest for **God's** people, since God had rested from **Creation** on the seventh day. The account in **Genesis** tells us, "By the seventh day God had finished the work he had been doing; so on the seventh day he rested from all his work. And God blessed the seventh day and made it **holy** because on it he rested from all the work of creating that he had done" (Genesis 2:2).

The day of rest was very important to the **Hebrews** because in ancient times life was difficult and people labored hard. The Sabbath as a day of rest was a time once a week when they could rest and regroup. The Jewish Talmud recognized thirty-nine main categories of work that were to be avoided on the Sabbath and devoted one extensive discussion to how the Sabbath should be observed. In modern times, the Sabbath celebration begins at sundown on Friday evening. At that time Jewish families gather for a specially prepared meal. On Saturday morning, they go to the synagogue, and the rest of the day is spent relaxing, eating, and reading the scriptures.

Says Richard John Neuhaus, presi-dent of the Institute on Religion and Public Life, of the Sabbath: "The Jewish understanding of the Sabbath is not connected with the need for relaxation but with the need for intensification, of heightened awareness, that anticipates the hope of cosmic healing." In addition, **Heaven** is viewed as a sort of **eternal** Sabbath. After toiling in this life, many look forward to a never ending Sabbath after **death.**

Sacred Name Movement

A religious movement that began in the U.S. in the late 1920s and early 1930s. The movement asserts that **God** must be addressed by a form of the **Divine** Name from the **Bible's Old Testament** (i.e., **Yahweh, Jehovah, Yah,** Yahvah), and that **salvation** depends upon calling on God by His proper name.

Sacrifice(s)

Something of value offered as an act of worship or devotion to **God.** Sacrifices to God or the gods can be found in religions all over the world. Objects have been offered to the gods for centuries in exchange for power, fertility, plentiful food supplies, or victories in battle. In the **Bible,** the story of

Adam and Eve's sons, **Cain** and **Abel**, introduces the issue of sacrifice. **Genesis** tells us that God favored Abel's sacrifice over his brother Cain's. This was because Abel brought the very finest from his flocks, while Cain brought an average offering from his crops. In ancient times, it was common among the **Hebrews** to use **animals** as sacrifices to God, and the Hebrew **priests** made **atonement** for people through the **blood** of animals. **Moses** also used the blood of animals to seal the **covenant** between God and the Hebrews. In addition, if people wanted to give something to God, they had to put it on an **altar.** They sometimes offered grain, bread, oil, or wine to God.

A famous account about sacrifice in the Hebrew scriptures is that of the **Binding of Isaac** or the *Akedah.* In the story God tests **Abraham's faith** by commanding him to offer his son **Isaac** as a sacrifice, whom Abraham loved greatly. Abraham put Isaac on the altar as instructed, but when he was about to sacrifice him, God sent an **angel** to stop him.

In **Babylon,** sacrifices were offered to the gods on a daily basis. Their sacrifices included meat, vegetables, libations of water, wine, and the offering up of **incense.** In **Hinduism,** sacrifice was important in the Vedic period. Only gods directly connected with sacrifices such as **Agni** (the god of fire), Soma (the god of sacrificial libation or the pouring of drinks), and Brahaspati (the **divine** priest and **lord** of **prayer**) retained the interest of the later Vedic **priests**. In this later era, the gods **Varuna, Indra,** and others only received minor sacrifices. In Christian beliefs **Jesus** gave the ultimate sacrifice, offering himself up as a sacrifice for the **salvation** of humankind.

Salvation

The deliverance of **Man** or his **soul** from the penalty of **sin.** In nearly all religions, salvation is attained through human effort. In the Christian religion, however, salvation is solely a gift from **God.** This is referred to as **Salvation by Grace.**

Salvation by Grace

See Salvation.

Samson

An **Israelite** hero whose birth was foretold by an **angel** in the Book of Judges, chapter 13. Samson's birth was foretold by an **Angel of the Lord** who first appeared to Samson's mother. He told her that she would become pregnant and give birth to a son. He instructed her not to drink any alcohol and not to eat unclean foods. He told her never to cut the child's hair and that the boy would be "dedicated to **God** as a Nazirite." Worried about the angel's revelation to her, she told her husband **Manoah.** Manoah prayed to God, and later the angel reappeared to both Manoah and his wife together, bringing the same message that he had delivered earlier. When Manoah asked the angel what his name was, the angel said that it is "unknowable."

Sandage, Alan Rex (1926–)

U.S. astronomer and winner of the Crawford Prize in astronomy. Sandage discovered the first quasi-stellar radio source (quasar), a star-like object that is a strong emitter of radio waves. He made the discovery in collaboration with the U.S. radio astronomer Thomas A. Matthews. On the subject of **God,** Sandage states: "I find it quite improbable that such order came out of chaos. There has to be some organizing principle. God to me is a **mystery** but is the explanation for the **miracle** of existence, why there is something instead of nothing."

Sarah

Biblical wife of **Abraham.** In **Genesis,** three **angels** sent from **God** visited Abraham. The angels informed him that God would bless him and his wife Sarah with a son. God promised this even though Sarah was barren and old. One of the angels said, "Nine months from now I will come back, and your wife Sarah will have a son." When Sarah heard the angel reveal this to Abraham, she laughed, saying to herself. "Now that I am old and worn out, can I still enjoy sex? And besides, my husband is old too." The angel asked Abraham, "Why did Sarah laugh? Is anything too hard for God? As I said, nine months from now I will return, and Sarah will have a son." Because Sarah was afraid of the angel, she denied it, saying, "I didn't laugh." But the angel said, "Yes, you did. You laughed" (Genesis 18:9-15).

Satan (Opposer)

God's adversary, also known as the **Devil.** According to lore, he was once one of God's perfect **angels,** who eventually came to think a great deal of himself. He was the anointed Cherub and was considered the most beautiful of all the angels. He was so spectacular that he thought he should be worshipped as a god. In order to achieve this, he sought out the newly created humans, **Adam and Eve.** Knowing that the whole Earth would eventually be filled with worshipers of God, he sought to have this worship for himself. He used the guise of a serpent to trick **Eve** into disobedience to God. When he spoke to her, he accused God of lying to her and **Adam.** He also accused God of holding back knowledge from them. This was a lie and it made him the Devil, which means slanderer, and Satan, which means opposer. Ever since then, Satan has been competing with God for the worship of humans. He does this by attempting to lead them into wrongdoing and away from God. This in itself is believed to be a form of worship to him. He has been so successful in getting humankind to worship him that he was able to offer **Jesus** all the kingdoms of the world if he would fall down and perform an act of worship to him (Matthew 4: 8, 9). In 2 Corinthians 11:14 we read that Satan can appear as an angel of **light.** It says, "Even Satan disguises himself as an angel of light."

In **Islamic** beliefs, Satan **(Iblis)** became God's adversary when he refused to bow down and worship Adam, whom God had placed above the angels. Iblis is said to have loved God most of all the angels. When God created Adam, he told the angels to bow down and worship him. Iblis refused. Because of this disobedient act, God ordered him from his presence. The **Koran** states that when Adam was created, God told the angels to prostrate themselves saying, "Fall ye prostrate before Adam! And they fell prostrate, all save Iblis, who was not of those who make prostration. He said: What hindered Thee that thou did not fall prostrate when I bid thee? [Iblis] said: I am better than he. Thou createdst me of fire, while him Thou didst create of mud. He said: Then go down hence! It is not for Thee to show pride here, so go forth! Lo! Thou art of Those degraded" (Koran, VII).

In Dante's **_Divine Comedy,_** Satan is portrayed as the greatest of all the **Seraphim.** In Revelation he is referred to as the "great dragon" (Revelation 12:3, 7–9) and is defeated by God. In the Kaballah he is called Samael. In Zoroastrianism he is **Ahaitin** (also **Angra Mainyu**), the opposer to **Ahura Mazda** (God).

Schaefer, Henry F. (1944–)

Graham Perdue Professor of Chemistry and director of the Center for Computational Quantum Chemistry at the University of Georgia. He has been nominated for the Nobel Prize and was recently named the third-most cited chemist in the world. About **God,** Dr. Schaefer states: "The significance and joy in my science comes in the occasional moments of discovering something new and saying to myself, 'So that's how God did it!' My goal is to understand a little corner of God's plan."

Schawlow, Arthur L. (1921–1999)

Professor of Physics at Stanford University, 1981 Nobel Prize-winner in physics. On **God** he says: "It seems to me that when confronted with the marvels of life and the universe, one must ask why and not just how. The only possible answers are religious. I find a need for God in the universe and in my own life."

Scroll(s)

An ancient book in the form of a rolled manuscript. In biblical times sacred books were largely written and stored in the form of scrolls. In the **Bible** there were two occurrences in which scrolls containing **God's** words were eaten. They are found in both the Old and New Testaments. In both instances, God's words tasted as "sweet as honey." In the **Old Testament** it is the **prophet Ezekiel** (3:2) who partook of a scroll. The account states: "Then he said to me, 'Son of **man,** eat this scroll I am giving you and fill your stomach with it.' So I ate it, and it tasted as sweet as honey in my mouth." Also, in the **New Testament,** John in Revelation (10:10) ate a scroll. Revelation states: "I took the little scroll from the **angel's** hand and ate it. It tasted as sweet as honey in my mouth, but when I had eaten it, my stomach turned sour." The eating of the scrolls acted as a symbol of internalizing God's words.

Sea of Galilee

Freshwater lake in northeastern **Israel** through which the Jordan River flows. There is an old rabbinic saying that **God** "has created seven seas, but the Sea of Galilee is His joy." This idea is obviously taken from the majestic beauty and natural qualities of the Sea. Located about 685 feet below sea level, it is of a lovely deep blue color, with cool clear water. Magnificent rugged hills rise up from its eastern and western shores, approximately 2,650 feet above the surface. With its location below sea level and its wall of high mountains on the east, it is especially susceptible to severe weather changes. Great storms can come up quickly, turning smooth waters rough in just a few minutes. Some of these storms were recorded in the **New Testament,** where the lake is known for its association with the lives of **Jesus** and his disciples.

Seal of the Prophets

A term used in **Islam** for the **prophet Muhammad.** Muhammad is believed to be the Seal of the Prophets through whom **God** has sent the last, perfect revelation.

Searching for God

The Apostle Paul, in a discourse to the intelligentsia of Athens, once said: "From one ancestor [God] made all **nations** to inhabit the whole earth, and he allotted the times of their existence and the boundaries of the places where they would live, so that they would search for God and perhaps grope for him and find him though indeed he is not far from each one of us" (Acts 17:26, 27). In his book *Searching for God in America,* author and broadcaster Hugh Hewitt tells us, "According to this text, human groping for God is part of God's created design. Our search for God flows, not only from our individual createdness, but also from the very structure of the universe. . . . searching, even groping for God is part of the plan."

Sennacherib

In the Book of 2 Kings (19:35), Assyrian King Sennacherib's army is slayed by an **angel** after **Hezekiah** prays to **God** to save them from Sennacherib's threats. The account states, "That night an **angel of the Lord** went to the Assyrian camp and killed 185,000 soldiers. At dawn the next day there they lay, all dead!" According to lore, the angel who slew Sennacherib's army was the Angel of **Death**.

Seraphim

The highest order of **angels** in **Heaven.** They have been described as incorruptible, brilliant, and powerful. They are the closest angels to **God** and are in direct communication with Him. It is said that they are so radiant that not even the **Cherubim** and the Ophanim can look upon them. If humans stood in their presence, they would be incinerated. They control the motion of the Heavens as they flow out from God. Their essence is **love,** and they are called "Angels of Love." Through their purifying powers, they move humans to a love of God. They surround God's throne continuously singing the *Trisagion,* a song of celebration. 3 **Enoch** (26:9–12) says that there are four Seraphim corresponding to the four winds of the world. They each have six wings corresponding to the six days of **creation;** each has sixteen faces, facing in each direction, and each wing is the size of Heaven. The name Seraphim is a combination of the **Hebrew** word *Rapha,* which means "healer," and *ser,* which means "higher being."

They are also known as "living creatures," in the Book of Revelation (4:8). There, John makes reference to them, "And the four living creatures, each of them with six wings, are full of eyes all around and inside. Day and night without ceasing they sing, **Holy, holy, holy, the Lord** God the **Almighty,** who was and is and is to come." In his vision, the **prophet Ezekiel** also saw angels whom he referred to as living creatures. "I looked up and saw a windstorm coming from the north. Lightning was flashing from a huge cloud, and the sky around it was glowing. Where the lightning was flashing, something shone like bronze. At the center of the storm I saw what looked like four living creatures in human form, but each of them had four faces and four wings" (Ezekiel: 1:4–6). They are represented by the serpent, which is a symbol of healing. They are also called "Seraphs."

Seven

A symbol of **divine** perfection in the **Bible.** It is taken from the reference made to the seventh day in **Genesis,** "And on the seventh day **God** finished the work that he had done, and he rested on the seventh day . . . God blessed the seventh day and hallowed it . . ." (Genesis 2:2–3).

Seven Plagues

In Revelation (15:1,6,7,8) there are **seven angels** who carry seven **plagues.** The plagues are carried in seven vials that are opened at **God's** command and poured upon the Earth. Revelation states: "And I saw another sign in **heaven,** great and marvelous, seven angels having the seven last plagues; for in them is filled up the wrath of God" (15:1). "And the seven angels came out of the temple, having the seven plagues, clothed in pure and white linen, and having their breasts girded with golden girdles" (15:6). "And one of the four beasts gave unto the seven angels seven golden vials full of the wrath of God, who liveth forever and ever" (15:7). "And the temple was filled with smoke from the glory of God, and from his power; and no **man** was able to enter into the temple, till the seven plagues of the seven angels were fulfilled (15:8).

Seventh Heaven

See Arabot.

Shadrach, Meshach, and Abednego

Three **Hebrew** men who displayed unswerving **faith** in **God** in the **Bible's Old Testament.** Shadrach, Meshach, and Abednego obeyed God's commandments and would not worship another god. Nebuchadnezzar, the king of **Babylon,** didn't like their commitment to God and ordered that they be thrown into a furnace. God saved them from the fire by sending an **angel** to rescue them.

The account from the Old Testament states: King Nebuchadnezzar said: "Is it true, Shadrach, Meshach, and Abednego, that you will not serve my god, or worship the golden statue that I set up? Be ready now to fall down and worship the statue I had made, whenever you hear the sound of the **trumpet,** flute, lyre, harp, psaltery, bagpipe, and all the other musical instruments; otherwise, you shall be instantly cast into the white-hot furnace; and who is the God that can deliver you out of my hands?" Shadrach, Meshach, and Abednego answered King Nebuchadnezzar, "There is no need for us to defend ourselves before you in this matter. If our God, whom we serve, can save us from the white-hot furnace and from your hands, O king, may he save us! But even if he will not, know, O king, that we will not serve your god or worship the golden statue which you set up." Nebuchadnezzar's face became livid with utter rage against Shadrach,

Meshach, and Abednego. He ordered the furnace to be heated **seven** times more than usual and had some of the strongest men in his army bind Shadrach, Meshach, and Abednego and cast them into the white-hot furnace. Nebuchadnezzar rose in haste and asked his nobles, "Did we not cast three men bound into the fire?" "Assuredly, O king," they answered. "But," he replied, "I see four men unfettered and unhurt, walking in the fire, and the fourth looks like a **son of God.**" Nebuchadnezzar exclaimed, "Blessed be the God of Shadrach, Meshach, and Abednego, who sent his angel to deliver the servants that trusted in him; they disobeyed the royal command and yielded their bodies rather than serve or worship any god except their own God" (**Daniel** 3:14–20; 91–92; 95).

Shang Di (ShangTi)

Supreme god and an ancestral god of ancient Chinese beliefs.

Shaphat

An ancient **Hebrew** name for **God.** It means "Judge."

Shekinah

The female manifestation of **God.** According to the Zohar, the Shekinah created the world and all creatures within it. Judaic lore tells us that the **Torah** was created in order to bring the Shekinah back into a relationship with God.

Shema, The

A vital confession of **Judaism.** It is an affirmation of one's belief in only one true **God. Faithful Jews** are expected to recite the Shema each day. It is said as follows, "Hear O **Israel,** the **Lord** is our God, the Lord alone. You must **love** the Lord your God with all your heart and with all your **soul** and with all your might."

Shepherd

According to the New Revised Standard Version of the **Holy Bible,** a shepherd is "the ruler or king of a people." Therefore, the term shepherd when referring to **God,** denotes His authority and sovereignty over His people.

Shiang Ti

An ancient Chinese supreme ruler.

Shintoism (Way of the Gods)

Indigenous religion of **Japan.** A polytheistic religion, Shintoism recognizes a variety of gods created from the primordial coupling of a **divine** brother and sister named **Izanagi and Izanami** on the "floating bridge of **heaven.**" The gods (also referred to as Kami) of the Shinto religion are believed to have created Japan as their image of **paradise** on Earth. An old Shinto saying states: "Come near to **God;** He is your friend."

Shiva

One of the great gods of **Hinduism,** the third supreme god in the Hindu triad. He personifies the creative force, destruction, and the procreative forces of the universe.

Sikhism

A religion of **India,** that attempts to combine the teachings of **Hinduism** and **Islam.** Founded in the fifteenth century by **Guru Nanak,** Sikhism is based on his vision and teachings. Today it has over twenty million followers worldwide and is ranked as the fifth largest religion in the world. The Sikhs follow Sat Nam (True Name), whom they consider to be the one true **God.** Devotion and remembrance of God at all times is a key teaching in Sikhism. Their key scriptures are found in the *Granth Sahib* which means the "The Lord's Book," compiled by the **guru** Arjan.

To the Sikhs, **salvation** is a merging with the universal force. The Guru Amar Das states, "Deep within the self is the **Light** of God. It radiates throughout the expanse of His **creation.** Through the Guru's teachings, the darkness of spiritual ignorance is dispelled. The heart lotus flower blossoms forth and **eternal** peace is obtained, as one's light merges into the Supreme Light." A **holy** Sikh text speaks of God thus: "Completely fulfilled is myself, as the Master has granted a vision of the **Supreme Being** . . . With Him seated on the throne of eternal justice, ended is all wailing and crying" (Adi Granth, Majh, M.5).

Sin

The use of the word sin is primarily found in Judeo-Christian beliefs. It means to transgress against **God's laws** or to commit an offense against God. Christians believe that through **Jesus** their sins can be forgiven. On the subject of sin, John Bunyan (1628–1688), an English writer, Puritan minister, and author of the famous *Pilgrim's Progress,* once wrote: "Sin turns all God's **grace** into wantonness; it is the dare of His justice, the rape of His **mercy;** the jeer of His patience; the slight of His power; and the contempt of His **love.**"

Sinner's Prayer, The

A small **prayer** that originated from the **Bible.** Years ago, according to tradition, when a person was dying, they were encouraged to offer the **sinner's** prayer to God. It states simply, "God, have **mercy** on me, a sinner." It is taken from a parable of **Jesus** involving a tax collector. The parable says, "the tax collector stood at a distance. He would not even look up to **heaven,** but beat his breast and said, 'God, have mercy on me, a sinner'" (Luke 18:13).

Sioux Indians

A confederation of seven North American Indian tribes. They maintained a typical Plains culture, including buffalo hunts and the sun dance. The Sioux believed in one, all-pervasive, omnipotent god, **Wakan Tanka,** also referred to as the "Great **Mystery.**"

Sistine Chapel

See Michelangelo.

Sky

Genesis, in speaking of the creation of the sky, says, "And **God** said, 'Let there be a dome in the midst of the waters, and let it separate the waters from the waters.' So God made the dome and separated the waters that were under the dome from the waters that were above the dome. And it was so. God called the dome Sky. And there was evening and there was morning, the second day."

Sky Father

The **Sky** Father is generally known as a god who gives life in the universe. The idea of a Sky Father appears in the beliefs of many world cultures. The Sky Father is sometimes referred to as the **Sky God.**

Sky God

See Sky Father.

Smith, Joseph (1805–1844)

Founder of the **Church of Jesus Christ of Latter-Day Saints.** Latter-Day Saints (also called Mormons) refer to him as the **Prophet** because he, like the prophets of the **Bible's** Old and New Testaments, depended on revelations from **God** for his teachings. Members see Smith as an instrument used by God to restore to the Earth the "ancient truths" of the "**divine** gospel." There is a false impression that the Latter-Day Saints worship Joseph Smith. According to the *Encyclopedia of Mormonism,* the Latter Day Saints worship only "God the **Eternal Father.**"

Sodom

One of two cities described in the **Old Testament** that was destroyed by God because of the wickedness of its people (**Genesis** 19:24–28). The other city was called **Gomorrah.** See Fire and Brimstone.

Sola Gratia

A Christian belief that **God** pardons believers who commit wrongdoing without their doing anything to deserve it. God's excusing them is based purely on the sacrificial work of **Jesus.**

Sola Scriptura

A Christian belief that the Old and New Testaments hold all the required doctrine to obtain **eternal salvation** and living a proper life in the eyes of **God.**

Solomon (970–928 B.C.)

Judaic king. Solomon was the son of **David** and Bathsheba. He came to the throne aided by his mother, Nathan the **prophet,** and Zadok the priest. He was noted for his wisdom and his gift for expressing himself. The **Old Testament** books of Proverbs, Ecclesiastes, and Song of Solomon, as well as the 72nd and 127th Psalms, are attributed to him. The reign of Solomon was eminently peaceful, marked by foreign alliances, notably with **Egypt** and Phoenicia. He also developed trade and commerce. During his reign the kingdom reached its zenith.

SOLOMON'S TEMPLE. On the summit of **Mount Moriah** in Jerusalem, Solomon built a magnificent temple dedicated to **God.** After the temple was completed, Solomon held a grand dedication ceremony; all the spiritual leaders as well as the people of **Israel** were there. Many **animals** were sacrificed, the **Ark of the Covenant** was placed in the inner sanctuary, and the Cloud of God's magnificence filled the temple. It was a great moment for Israel. King Solomon led the worship, holding his hands spread out toward **Heaven.** He said to God, "O **Lord,** God of Israel, there is no God like you in heaven above or on earth beneath, keeping **covenant** and steadfast **love** for your servants who walk before you with all their heart, the covenant that you kept for your servant my father David as you declared to him; you promised with your mouth and have this day fulfilled with your hand" (1 Kings 8:22-26).

Solomon's Temple

See Solomon.

Son(s) of God

Son of **God** has several meanings. In the **Old Testament,** the term is used for **angels** or heavenly beings. It is also a title of **Jesus** used numerous times in the **Bible's New Testament,** and in *A Course in Miracles,* the term is used to refer to all of **Creation.**

Soul

The spiritual nature of humans regarded to be immortal and separable from the body at **death.** In **Judaism, Christianity,** and **Islam,** it is believed that once a person is deceased, if she has lived a good life in the eyes of **God,** then that person's soul (or **spirit**) will ascend to **Heaven** to live for eternity in **Paradise.** In **Hinduism,** the soul (or **Atman**) is seen as neither beginning nor ending. In some **new-age** and metaphysical beliefs, the soul existed before coming to Earth. The soul is believed to have been created by God in a perfect state of **grace.** However, the soul was also in a perfect state of ignorance, and God allowed individual souls to come to Earth to learn and grow and experience. This is God's true gift to us as

individual souls. God also gave us **free will** to choose what we please including choosing between being good or **evil.** Once the individual finishes his journey on Earth and experiences "death," the soul travels home only to decide whether or not it wants to come back into another lifetime.

It is believed that coming to Earth allows the soul to grow spiritually, by removing itself from a perfect home (Heaven) and being born into the not-so-perfect Earth. The Earth is believed to be the learning ground for the soul where it experiences all of the delights of being in the physical, and learning the difference between good and evil. The famous American poet Longfellow wrote of the soul:

Tell me not in mournful **numbers,**
Life is but an empty dream,
For the soul is dead that slumbers,
And things are not what they seem.
Life is real, life is earnest,
And the grave is not its goal.
Dust thou art, to dust returneth,
Was not spoken of the soul.

Spinoza, Baruch (1632–1677)

Jewish philosopher. Spinoza argued for an "intellectual **love** of **God**" in which he identified God as the entire universe. Spinoza believed that all that exists is God. He thought that God had boundless qualities, of which humans can distinguish only two, extension and thought. The highest good, he stated, was the knowledge of God, which brought genuine blessedness. Spinoza believed that God reveals Himself in the orderly harmony of what exists and is not a God who concerns Himself with the fates and actions of humans. Spinoza advanced such radical ideas about God, ethics, and nature that he was expelled from his congregation and **Judaism.** Though Spinoza founded no new school of philosophy, his influence on later philosophers and poets was enormous. Especially important are his works *Ethics* and *Theologico-Political Treatise*. Spinoza said: "God is a being absolutely infinite; a substance consisting of infinite **attributes**, each of which expresses His **eternal** and infinite essence."

Spirit

The part of a person that is considered to be the center of one's life. It is the part of a human that survives **death**. See soul.

Spirit Guides

Spirits from **Heaven** sent by **God** to act as personal instructors to humans on Earth. They come and go according to an individual's needs and the lessons that person is to learn while on Earth. In her book *Messengers of Light,* Terry Lynn Taylor says, "Spiritual guides come in and out of our lives according to need. They usually represent the essence of a particular culture, race, or religion, or they can represent a career or avenue of life. They are teachers." It is believed that there can be many **spirit** guides with an individual during a lifetime.

Spirit of God

The **Spirit** of **God** is considered to be the **divine** source of all life. It is also thought to be a special manifestation of God's presence. Other thought holds that the Spirit of God is God Himself.

Spirit of the Lord

See Spirit of God.

Spiritual Warfare

A term used in **Christianity** referring to the continuous battle between good and **evil**. This ongoing warfare is fought between **God** and His heavenly **angels** and **Satan** and his hordes. Those on Earth are to choose on whose side of the battle they will serve, God's or Satan's. In the end, good conquers evil and those on God's side will receive **everlasting** life while Satan and his followers will receive everlasting **destruction.**

Spokesman

In the **Bible**, the **Angel of the Lord** is God's "personal" spokesman. He is sometimes referred to as **Angel of God.** In the **New Testament** he is personalized as both **Gabriel** and the **Holy Spirit.**

Steward(s)

A person who manages a household or property. Spiritual and religious teachers are considered to be stewards for **God** because they are said to be guardians in the affairs of God.

Stoicism

A school of philosophy founded by Zeno of Citium c. 300 B.C. Influenced by Socratic ideals and by the thought of Heraclitus, **Aristotle,** and **Plato,** the Stoics held that all reality is material but is shaped by a universal working force **(God)** that pervades everything. They believed that only by putting aside passion, unjust thoughts, and indulgence, and by performing one's duty with the right temperament could a person live consistently with nature, thereby achieving true freedom. The school was especially well received in the Roman world. Cicero, Seneca, **Epictetus,** and Marcus Aurelius were all Stoics.

Sufism

A sect of **Islamic** mysticism, dating from the seventh century A.D. (the first century of Islam) and developed mainly in **Persia.** Followers of Sufism strive to find **divine love** and knowledge through direct personal experiences of **God.**

The term *Sufi* is Arabic and means "man of wool," probably in reference to the woolen garments worn by early Islamic ascetics. Yearning for a personal union with God, the Sufi claims to have found ways of finding mystical knowledge about God with the objective being to attain union with God. Before doing so, the Sufi embarks on a spiritual journey, one that requires **seven** steps along their path to oneness with God. The steps include: repentance, abstinence, renunciation, poverty, patience, trust in God, and submission to God's will. Once the journey is completed, with God's **grace**, the Sufi reaches an elevated level of consciousness; once this higher consciousness is achieved, the Sufi believes himself to be in union with God.

Suicide

The act of taking one's own life. In **Christianity** it is commonly believed that the act of suicide is the one act committed by a human that **God** will not forgive, although this idea is not biblically based. In fact, the **Bible** virtually says nothing on the subject of suicide. There were several people in the Bible, in both the Old and New Testaments, who took their own lives, including Judas Iscariot, **Samson,** and Saul; however, the Bible makes no comment on this act, speaking neither on whether it was right or wrong in God's eyes.

The position of most Christians, however, is that our lives are not our own to take. This is because we were given life by God, and it is only God who has the right to take life. Humans are required therefore to live out their lives on Earth until they reach the end. In addition, some believe that to take one's own life is an act of murder, a crime that in God's eyes will be punished.

In metaphysical thought it is believed that when a person commits

suicide they break a contract with God. This is a contract that allows the **soul** to come to Earth to learn, grow, and experience. The soul is to live out its life on the Earth until the time allotted for a physical **death.** When a person commits suicide and the contract with God is broken, it is believed that that soul is immediately sent back into another life to fulfill their contract that they established with God. This contract is said to be a spiritual agreement between God and each individual person and is not to be entered into lightly or broken.

Sumerians

The people of Sumer (an ancient country of western Asia, corresponding approximately to **Babylon**ia of biblical times). The Sumerians worshipped a pantheon of gods who were considered to be living beings that had human form. Immortal with supernatural abilities, the gods were unseen by humans. However, they were believed to rule the heavens and the Earth. The four principal deities who were also creator gods included: An (god of **Heaven**), Ki (**goddess** of Earth), **Enlil** (god of air), and Enki (god of water). To the Sumerians, Heaven, Earth, air, and water were the four key components of the cosmos and it is no wonder that, for them, there would be four major gods associated with these elements. It was believed that the gods created the heavens, the Earth, and humanity by simply speaking. As in Judaic, Christian, and **Islamic theology,** they believed that the gods fashioned humans from clay.

Summa Theologica

See Aquinas, St. Thomas.

Supralapsarianism (Before the Fall)

The view that **God** decreed the **Fall** of **Man,** and that the choosing of some individuals to **everlasting** life while rejecting everyone else was decided prior to the Fall.

Supreme Being

There are supreme beings in many cultures of the world. Supreme beings are generally viewed as the creators and rulers of the universe. The creator is believed to exist alone. His act of **creation** is believed to be a conscious effort in planning and deliberation. The term supreme being is another name for **God** or, in beliefs of those cultures with many gods, the primary or main god.

Swedenborg, Emanuel (1688–1772)

Swedish scientist, religious teacher, and mystic. His religious system is often referred to as Swedenborgianism. He published many works on religion and philosophy. In his later years he gave himself fully to the contemplation of spiritual matters believing that **God** had revealed the true inner doctrines of the **Divine** Word to him alone. Throughout his life, Swedenborg regularly communicated with **angels.** He held that angels, like humans, have bodies but in a spiritual form. He believed that humans cannot see angels with their physical eyes but only with the spiritual eyes. About angels Swedenborg once wrote, "I am well aware that many will say that no one can possibly speak with spirits and angels so long as he is living in the body. Many say it is all fancy, others that I recount such things to win credence, while others will make other kinds of objection. But I am deterred by none of these: for I have seen, I have heard, I have felt."

Swedenborg incorporated the information revealed to him from the angels in his many writings. His book *Heaven and Hell*, written while he was in his fifties, is recognized as his greatest work. The book reveals information about God, Heaven, Hell, **demons**, and angels, as communicated to him from the angels. Swedenborg firmly believed that God had called him to view and report on the unseen worlds of Heaven and Hell. Says Swedenborg, "Conscience is God's presence in **man**."

Synergism

The teaching that **God** and **Man** work jointly to achieve **salvation.** It is the opposite of **Monergism** that teaches that God alone is the one who saves.

T

God is, even though the whole world deny him.
—*Mahatma Gandhi*

Tabernacle

The place where the **Israel**ites worshipped **God** on their way from **Egypt** to the **Promised Land** (also called the **Tent of Meeting**). It was thought of by the Israelites as "God's Home." Since the Israelites were then still on the move, no permanent structure could be built, so the Tabernacle took the form of an elaborate (and **holy**) tent-structure that could be taken apart and moved. The tabernacle was set up by the priest when they camped. In it was stored the **Ark of the Covenant** and other holy items. The layout of the Tabernacle and the materials of its construction were specified in great detail to **Moses** by God at **Mount Sinai**. It was approximately 45 feet long, 15 feet wide, and 15 feet high. The west end of the interior contained a 15-foot square room, referred to as the **Most Holy Place**. This is where the Ark of the Covenant was kept. The tent also stored various articles used by the priests. The tabernacle became the center of Israel's religious life. It also served as a reminder to the people that God was with them, and was believed to be the dwelling place of God, a place where God's presence could be felt, and a place where God and His people came together.

Tagore, Rabindranath (1861–1941)

Indian writer, philosopher, and Nobel Laureate for literature. He was one of modern India's greatest poets and the composer of independent India's national anthem. He has been called "a towering and epochal figure of legendary proportions." Born in Calcutta into a wealthy Brahmin family, he was the youngest of fourteen **children**. He began writing at the age of **seven** and published his first book at seventeen. He studied **law** for a short period in England but later returned to India because he did not find the studies interesting. After returning home he became a popular and influential writer.

Multitalented, Tagore wrote poetry, short stories, novels, and plays. He later published songs as well. Tagore's writing expresses his feelings on **God** and is filled with his **love** of nature and India. Politically, Tagore admired **Gandhi** and stressed the need for a new world order based on transnational values and ideas. Much of Tagore's ideology comes from the teaching of the Upanishads and from his own belief that God can be found through personal purity and service to others.

About our relationship with God, Tagore said, "Our daily worship of God is not really the process of gradual acquisition of him, but the daily process of surrendering ourselves, removing all obstacles to union and extending our consciousness of him in devotion and service, in goodness and in love . . ." Tagore also states: "Religion, like poetry, is not a mere idea, it is expression. The self-expression of God is in the endless variety of **creation;** and our attitude toward the Infinite Being must also in its expression have a variety of individuality ceaseless and unending."

T'ai I

Chinese **high god** of the Han dynasty.

Tao(ism)

A Chinese religion and philosophy based on the teachings of Lao-tse. The term *Tao* is not easily understood and cannot be easily translated. In one sense it means the Way, as in "the way to **enlightenment**" or "the way to live." Some sections of the *Tao-te Ching* (the centerpiece of scripture and inspiration to Taoism) suggest that the Tao is the Allness of the universe, and possibly even a synonym for **God.**

Taylor, Hudson (1832–1905)

Missionary to China. Hudson Taylor was born in Yorkshire, England, in 1832. He had long sought the truth by studying Confucianism, **Buddhism,** and **Taoism.** However, it was not until he heard the gospel of **Jesus** that he had found the truth he had been searching for. Afterward, Taylor embarked upon a great mission to preach all he had learned to his fellow humans. Ultimately, however, he believed that the responsibility for the mission rested with **God** and not himself and saw himself as an instrument of God. Taylor sensed that God was calling him to

China, and living on as little as possible, Taylor trusted God for his every provision, saying, "God's work, done in God's way, will never lack for supplies." Ignoring the political restrictions of the land, Taylor traveled extensively along the inland Chinese canals preaching the gospel. About his relationship with God and his mission, Taylor commented: "There is a living God; He has spoken in the **Bible;** He means what He says and will do all He has promised." "God chose me because I was weak enough. God does not do his great works by large committees. He trains somebody to be quiet enough, and little enough, and then uses him."

Taylor, Jeremy (1613–1667)

English bishop, theologian, and devotional writer. Called the Shakespeare and Spenser of the pulpit, he is said to have written some of the greatest devotional works in the English language. His greatest works include: *A Discourse of the Liberty of Prophesying* (1646), a **call** for charity and tolerance; *The Golden Grove* (1655), a collection of daily **prayers**; and the *Unum Necessarium* (1655), a work on **sin** and repentance. His two famous books of devotion, *The Rule and Exercises of Holy Living* (1650) and *The Rule and Exercises of Holy Dying* (1651), are considered classics.

In *The Rule and Exercises of Holy Living,* Taylor comments on our relationship with **God.** He writes, "God hath given to **man** a short time here upon earth, and yet upon this short time eternity depends: but so, that for every hour of our life (after we are persons capable of **laws,** and know good from **evil**) we must give account to the great Judge of men and **angels.** And this is it which our blessed Saviour told us, that we must account for every idle word; not meaning that every word which is not designed to edification, or is less prudent, shall be reckoned for a sin; but that the time which we spend in our idle talking and unprofitable discoursings; that time which might and ought to have been employed to spiritual and useful purposes—that is to be accounted for."

Teleological Argument

An argument for proof of the existence of **God.** It is sometimes referred to as the **Argument from Design.** The Teleological Argument comes from William **Paley** (English theologian, 1743–1805). At a time when **Man** was discovering the wonders of mechanics, Paley sought to prove God's existence by comparing the world to the mechanisms and operations of a watch. According to Paley, the watchmaker is to the watch as God is to the universe. Just as a watch with its intelligent design and functions had a watchmaker, the universe, with all its complexity, design, order, and greatness, was created by an intelligent and powerful "**maker,**" God.

Ten Commandments

The ten rules for daily life given by **God** to **Moses** on **Mount Sinai.** The Ten Commandments were God's **covenant** with His people, and they form the core of **Old Testament law.** They are the main beliefs that the rest of the law expands upon. The commandments were, according to **Exodus,** written on two stone tablets by God himself. Moses later destroyed the tablets in anger over his people's desertion of their **faith.** God then ordered him to hew and inscribe new tablets. Those were put into the **Ark of the Covenant** for safe keeping.

There are two accounts of the Ten Commandments, Exodus 20:1–17 and **Deuteronomy** 5:6–21, but the substance is the same in both. The account at Exodus 20:1–17 says, "God spoke,

and these were his words: 'I am the **LORD** your God who brought you out of **Egypt,** where you were slaves. 1. Worship no god but me. 2. Do not make for yourselves images of anything in **heaven** or on earth or in the water under the earth. 3. Do not use my name for **evil** purposes, for I, the LORD your God, will punish anyone who misuses my name. 4. Observe the **Sabbath** and keep it **holy.** 5. Respect your father and your mother. 6. Do not commit murder. 7. Do not commit adultery. 8. Do not steal. 9. Do not accuse anyone falsely. 10. Do not desire another man's house; do not desire his wife, his slaves, his cattle, his donkeys, or anything else that he owns.'"

Ten Plagues of Egypt

In the **Old Testament, plagues** were the means by which **God** convinced Pharaoh to release the **Hebrews** from bondage. Pharaoh, who was stubborn, was not convinced that the Hebrews' God was the true God. He therefore refused to listen to **Moses** and his brother **Aaron** when they came with instructions from God to approach Pharaoh and tell him to release the Hebrews. Pharaoh mocked, scoffed, and refused. God then brought ten plagues, one at a time upon Pharaoh and the **Egypti**ans. The ten plagues were turning the waters to **blood,** frogs, lice, flies, a disease on the cattle, boils on **man** and beast, hail, **locusts,** darkness, and the **death** of the firstborn. The tenth plague finally convinced Pharaoh to release the Hebrews. Pharaoh later changed his mind and sent his army after the Hebrews to kill them. God parted the **Red Sea** so that the Hebrews could escape Pharaoh's army, and then once the Hebrews had reached the other side, closed the waters, drowning Pharaoh's army.

Tent of Meeting
See Tabernacle.

Teresa of Avila, Saint (1515–1582)
Spanish Carmelite, Doctor of the **Church**, and one of the great mystics. She is one of the Catholic church's most popular saints. Teresa de Cepeda y Ahumada was born in Avila on March 28, 1515. She was educated in an Augustinian convent and, about 1535, entered the local Carmelite Convent of the **Incarnation**. She was a leading figure in the Catholic Reformation. In 1562 she founded, at Avila, the convent of the Discalced, or Barefoot, Carmelites. In 1555, after many years marked by serious illness and increasingly rigorous religious exercises, she began experiencing visions and hearing voices. This deeply troubled her. However, in 1557 she began seeing Saint Peter of Alcantara for spiritual guidance. Saint Peter persuaded her that the visions and voices she heard were from the **angels** and were real. Afterward, she was visited frequently by angels and even reported a visitation from an angel who appeared in bodily form. This angel, whom she described as fiery and beautiful, plunged a golden spear into her heart, the tip piercing her heart, causing a pain in which Teresa could only describe as sweet. After that experience she realized that she could never want of anything except **God**. About God, Teresa commented, "Let nothing disturb you, let nothing frighten you: everything passes away except God; God alone is sufficient."

Tetragrammaton
See YHWH.

Theism
The belief that **God** exists and actively participates and sometimes intervenes in the affairs of the world.

The word is taken from the Greek word *theos* which means "God."

Theocentric
A word meaning **God**-centered. It means centering on God as the main concern.

Theodicy
The study of the problem of **evil** in the world. The term theodicy was coined by Gottfried **Leibniz** who published the book *Théodicée* in 1710, in which he tackled the problem of evil in a world created by a good **God**. Leibniz maintained that the universe had to be imperfect, otherwise it would not be different from God who is perfect. Leibniz was attempting to answer an age old question, one that has been debated for centuries, that is, how could a **holy** and loving God who is in control of all things allow evil to exist and continue? It is a question that the Christian **Church** has long debated and one that the Buddha sought a solution to; the answer he found he taught for the rest of his life. *A Course in **Miracles*** also speaks on the subject, teaching that the problem does not exist—that there is no evil. It is only an illusion.

Theology
The study of **God** and the relations between God and the universe. The term is taken from the Greek words *theos* which means God, and *logos* which means speech. Studies include religious doctrines, matters of **divinity**, as well as theories on God's nature, **attributes**, character, abilities, and revelations. Western thought distinguishes revealed theology (what can be known of God through revelation) and natural theology (what can be known of God through the **light** of reason and the use of the five senses). The study of theology has classically been seen as **faith** seeking understanding.

Theophany

The word theophany means "manifestation of **God**," or the "appearance of a god or God to **Man**." It is taken from the Greek words *theos* which means "God" and *phainesthai* which means "to appear."

Theopneustos

A word invented by the apostle Paul. It means "**God**-breathed."

Theos

Greek word meaning **God**. It is the equivalent to the **Hebrew** word **Elohim**. It can be found 1,000 times in the original Greek of the **New Testament**.

Theotes

A name for **God** meaning Godhead. It was found in the original Greek translation of the **Holy** Scriptures.

Throne of God

According to Jewish lore, the Throne of **God** is where God sits while the court of **Heaven** convenes, where the deeds of men are weighed, and where judgment is served. The **seven archangels** stand at the Throne of God. There are twenty-four **Elders** who also stand at God's Throne. The **Seraphim, Cherubim,** and **Thrones** encircle the Throne of God. When the court convenes to judge the deeds of mankind, the **Angels** of **Mercy** stand to God's right, the Angels of Peace to His left, and the angels of punishment stand in front of Him waiting to do His bidding. There, according to lore, the angel named Radweri'el **YHWH** takes out the **scroll** box in which the **Book of Records** (the record of mankind's deeds) is kept, and brings it into the presence of God. He breaks the seals of the scroll box, opens it, takes out the scrolls and puts them in the hand of God. God then places them before the scribes, so that they can read them out

to the great court of **law**, which is convened. The entire account can be found in the **Pseudepigraphal** Book of 3 **Enoch** 27:1–2. When the angels stand before God's Throne, they are in four rows. At the head of each row stands a great Prince of Heaven. In 3 Enoch, **Metatron** explains to Enoch how it is that so many angels are able to stand before God. Metatron responded, "just as a bridge is laid across a river and everyone crosses over it, so a bridge is laid from the beginning of the entrance to its end, and the **ministering angels** go over it and recite the song before God."

Thrones

The order of **angels** ranking third in the angelic hierarchy. It was from the **prophet Ezekiel's** vision that the medieval scholars derived the class of angels known as Thrones. The Thrones are said to wheel around the **Throne of God**. Their role is to inspire confidence in the power of **God**.

Tian

Supreme being in Chinese philosophy and religion. He rules over lesser gods, humankind, and controls the cosmos. The word *Tian* may also refer to **Heaven**. As a god, Tian is often seen as an impersonal power. He was initially the supreme god **Shang Di**, but eventually Tian replaced Shang Di as ruler of the universe.

Tien

See Tian.

Tillich, Paul Johannes (1886–1965)

German-American philosopher, writer, and theologian. He is hailed as one of last century's most outstanding and influential thinkers, and was known for his belief that all existence is based in **God**. Tillich was born in

Starzeddel, Brandenburg, Germany, on August 20, 1886, the son of a Lutheran pastor. In his day, Tillich was held in high esteem not only among theologians, but by experts in many different fields for his incredible breadth of knowledge, his insight into culture, and his humanity. After teaching **theology** and philosophy at various German universities, he came to the United States in 1933. For many years he was professor of philosophical theology at Union Theological Seminary in New York City, then university professor at Harvard University.

Among his best-known works are: *The Religious Situation, The Socialist Decision, On the Boundary, The Protestant Era,* and *Systematic Theology, Volumes I, II, III* which was one of the most important theological works of the twentieth century. Tillich developed ideas concerning the religious basis of life in works such as *The Religious Situation, The Interpretation of History, The Protestant Era,* and *Dynamics of **Faith.*** In *The Courage to Be* he argued that existence is rooted in God as the ground of all being. About God, Tillich stated, "The basic assertion about the relation of God to **love,** power, and justice is made, if one says that God is being Itself. For being Itself, according to our ontological analysis, implies love as well as power and justice. God is the basic and universal symbol for what concerns us ultimately."

Tloque Nahuaque

Aztec creator god.

Tomor

Illyrian father of the gods.

Tonacatecuhtli

Aztec creator god. In the Aztec **creation** beliefs, Tonacatecuhtli was the primeval male principle. He and his wife Tonacacihuatl, the female principle, created all life.

Torah

In **Judaism,** the word Torah refers to **God's** revelation to humankind. It is God's teaching (also referred to as the **law** or the "five books of **Moses**") to the Jewish people. The Torah represents the written account of the revelation of God. To the **Hebrews** (as well as the Christians and **Muslims** who came later) God is considered to have been a participant in the development and history of humankind. This is unlike many religions of that time, in which a god was worshipped but seen to be uninvolved in the affairs, lives, and development of humans. This in itself made the Hebrew God stand out among the **nations.** Never before had they seen or heard of a God who gave laws to its people. It was through the **prophet** Moses that God gave the Torah. Some **Jews** even believed the Torah to be the presence of God's **divine** wisdom on Earth.

The word *Torah* means "a teaching." In the Torah, God instructs the Jews on how to live. It is filled with commandments which are God's instructions to the Jews. It also contains stories which teach about the history of the Jews and their relationship with God. The Torah is broken into two sections, the Oral Torah or the *Torah Sheb'al Peh,* and the Written Torah, or the *Torah Shebiksav.*

Several things are not explained in the *Torah Shebiksav.* God gave the explanations to Moses on **Mount Sinai** together with the written Torah. These explanations are called the *Torah Sheb'al Peh,* the Oral Torah, because they were meant to be passed from teacher to student. The *Torah Shebiksav* has three parts. The first is the Torah which is made up of five books, each of which is called a *Chumash.* The books include: **Genesis** *(B'reishis),*

Exodus *(Shemos)*, Leviticus *(Vayikra)*, Numbers *(Bamidbar)*, and **Deuteronomy (Devarim)**.

The second part is *Nevi'im* (**Prophets**). The Prophets are believed to be great and saintly people who communicate with God. The books in *Nevi'im* are recordings of some of what God has said to His prophets. They include: **Joshua** *(Yehoshua)*, Judges *(Shoftim)*, Samuel *(Shmuel)*, Two books of Kings *(Melachim)*, Two books of **Jeremiah** *(Yirmiyahu)*, **Ezekiel** *(Yechezkel)*, and **Isaiah** *(Yeshayahu)*. The following twelve are combined in one book referred to as The Twelve *(Trey Asar)*. They include: **Hosea** *(Hoshaia)*, **Joel** *(Yoel)*, **Amos, Obadiah** *(Ovadiah)*, **Jonah** *(Yonah)*, **Micah** *(Michah)*, **Nahum** *(Nachum)*, **Habakkuk** *(Chabakkuk)*, **Zephaniah** *(Tzefaniah)*, Haggai *(Chaggai)*, Zachariah *(Zechariah)*, and **Malachi.**

The third section is *Kesuvim* (Writings). These include books that were written by prophets with God's guidance but are not direct prophecies. These three sections *(Torah, Nevi'im,* and *Kesuvim)* are often referred to by the acronym *TaNaKh* (or *Tanach*).

Tower of Babel

The tower built by Babylonian King Nimrod in defiance of **God**. The word Babel is the **Hebrew** form of the name **Babylon.** It has two meanings, *babili* which means "gate of God," and *balal* which means "confusion." Babel was the name of the city where according to the **Old Testament,** men built a tower to the **heavens** (it was probably constructed before 4000 B.C.). It was a ziggurat, a pyramid of sun-dried bricks with a temple at the top which is reached by a series of steps. The construction of the temple was left unfinished because **Yahweh** (the name of God in **Hebrew**) interrupted it by confounding the speech of the builders.

The tower came to be known as "Babel" or "Confusion." God then scattered these men and the different languages over the face of the Earth. The tower later became a symbol of confusion, especially a confusion of language.

The account found in the **Jerusalem Bible** at **Genesis** 11:1–9 states: "Throughout the earth men spoke the same language, with the same vocabulary. Now as they moved eastwards they found a plain in the land of Shinar where they settled. They said to one another, 'Come, let us make bricks and bake them in the fire.' For stone they used bricks, and for mortar they used bitumen. 'Come,' they said 'let us build ourselves a town and a tower with its top reaching heaven. Let us make a name for ourselves, so that we may not be scattered about the whole earth.' Now Yahweh (God) came down to see the town and the tower that the sons of man had built. 'So they are all a single people with a single language!' said Yahweh. 'This is but the start of their undertakings! There will be nothing too hard for them to do. Come, let us go down and confuse their language on the spot so that they can no longer understand one another.' Yahweh scattered them thence over the whole face of the earth, and they stopped building the town. It was named Babel therefore, because there Yahweh confused the language of the whole earth. It was from there that Yahweh scattered them over the whole face of the earth."

Tozer, A. W. (1897–1963)

Great American minister, known as the twentieth century **prophet.** His writings inspire readers to think of **God** as He is, to worship God as He is, and to develop a "personal heart religion" in keeping with who He is. Tozer used the power of words to nurture lost **souls,** pierce their hearts and minds, and turn people's thoughts toward God. Tozer's conversion to **Christianity** came when he was seventeen. One afternoon as he walked home from his job, he overheard a street preacher say, "If you don't know how to be saved . . . just call on God." When he got home, he climbed the narrow stairs to his attic where, heeding the preacher's words, Tozer launched himself into a relentless, lifelong, loving pursuit of God.

During his lifetime, Tozer pastured several Christian and Missionary Alliance (CMA) **church**es, authored more than forty books, and served as editor of *Alliance Life,* the monthly denominational publication for the CMA. At least two of Tozer's books are considered spiritual classics: *The Pursuit of God* and *The Knowledge of the Holy.* Tozer received no formal theological training; the presence of God was said to be his classroom. His notebooks and tools consisted of **prayer** and the writings of early Christians. For almost fifty years, Tozer worked diligently for God. Today, even though he is gone, he continues to speak and minister for God. As someone put it, "This **man** makes you want to know and feel God." The following are quotes on God by A. W. Tozer:

"Let a man set his heart only on doing the will of God and he is instantly free. No one can hinder him."

"I thank God that the **kingdom of God** is not divided into areas for big, important people and areas for little, unimportant people. Every one is just as needful in God's sight as any other!"

"The only fear I have is to fear to get out of the will of God. Outside of the will of God, there's nothing I want, and in the will of God there's nothing I fear, for God has sworn to keep me in His will. If I'm out of his will that's another

matter. But if I'm in His will, He's sworn to keep me."

"God being who He is must always be sought for Himself, never as a means toward something else."

"Whoever seeks God as a means toward desired ends will not find God. The mighty God, the **maker** of **heaven** and earth, will not be one of many treasures, not even the chief of all treasures. He will be all in all or He will be nothing. God will not be used."

"The greatness of God rouses fear within us, but His goodness encourages us not to be afraid of Him. To fear and not be afraid— that is the paradox of **faith**."

Transcendence
An attribute of **God**. The term transcendence means that God is completely unknowable and unreachable, that God transcends His **creation,** that He exists over and beyond it in every way.

Transcendentalism
A nineteenth-century American literary and philosophical movement that stressed the intuitive more than the scientific, the inspiration of the **spirit,** and the existence of an idyllic spiritual reality that transcends the world of space and time. In Transcendentalism, **God** is believed to be inherent in nature and in human beings. Each individual is thought to have to rely on his or her own conscience and intuition for spiritual truths.

Transgression
In **Judaism** and **Christianity**, a transgression is considered a **sin**. It is also a rebellion against **God's** Will.

Tree of Knowledge
The tree which bore the **forbidden fruit** in the **Garden of Eden** in the **Bible's** Book of **Genesis. God** placed the

Tree of Knowledge (of good and **evil**) in the Garden and instructed **Adam and Eve** not to eat from it. **Eve**, after being tempted by the serpent, tasted the fruit and convinced **Adam** to partake of it also. After Adam and Eve ate from the tree, their eyes were opened and God banished them from the Garden as a punishment and to prevent them from eating from the **Tree of Life**. He placed two **Cherubim** at the entrance of the Garden, along with a turning, flaming sword, to prevent them from reentering.

Tree of Life

A tree mentioned in the **Bible** Book of **Genesis** as one that **God** did not want **Adam and Eve** to partake from. After God created the **Garden of Eden**, he caused lots of trees to grow including two very special trees: the Tree of Life (in "the midst of the garden") and the **Tree of Knowledge** (of good and **evil**). Genesis (2:9) states, "Out of the ground the **Lord** God made to grow every tree that is pleasant to the sight and good for food, the tree of life also in the midst of the garden, and the tree of the knowledge of good and evil." The Tree of Knowledge is the tree that Adam and Eve ate from and caused a great disturbance with God. Once they ate from it, God removed them from the Garden, in order that they would not eat from the Tree of Life also. Genesis (3:22–23) says, "Then the Lord God said, 'See, the **man** has become like one of us, knowing good and evil; and now, he might reach out his hand and take also from the tree of life, and eat, and live forever'—therefore the Lord God sent him forth from the garden of Eden, to till the ground from which he was taken."

The Tree of Life is mentioned again much later, in Revelation's description of **Heaven** as the New Jerusalem. There it produces twelve kinds of fruit that the **faithful** are allowed to eat. The accounts states: "On either side of the river, is the Tree of Life with its twelve kinds of fruit, producing its fruit each month; and the leaves of the tree are for the healing of the **nations**" (Revelation 22:2). In the Kabbalah, the Tree of Life has ten circles referred to as the *Sephirot* (singular: *Sephira*). Each *Sephira* symbolizes a "**divine** emanation." In effect, it represents a map of the qualities of God.

Trinity/Trinitarianism

A Christian teaching adopted in the fourth century by the Catholic **Church.** The word was coined by Tertullian (Roman theologian and Christian apologist), and its doctrine teaches that **God** exists as three persons in one—the **Father,** Son, and the **Holy Spirit**—while being one substance. The doctrine is described as a **mystery** because it is not logical. The Trinity became official doctrine at Nicea in 325 A.D., though this doctrine is not followed in all facets of **Christianity.**

Triple Goddess

Triads involving gods and **goddess**es are older than the Christian archetype. In the beliefs of the Triple Goddess, the triad is symbolized by women in the form of a maiden, mother, and crone. The maiden represents a young woman, a virgin still in her youth between puberty and her twenties. The image of the mother depicts a woman in her thirties to mid-forties; she is nurturing, a protector of her family, caring, and fertile. The crone is an experienced older woman. She is someone who has been a maiden and a mother and has moved into the last phase of her life. She is a shrewd and wise counselor.

Trisagion

A song of celebration that is sung continuously day and night to **God** by the **Seraphim.** As they encircle God's throne they sing: "**Holy, holy, holy, the**

Lord God the **Almighty,** who was and is and is to come" (Revelation 4:8).

Trumpet(s)

In **Christianity** the trumpet represents the voice of **God.**

Turkish Proverb

"**God** postpones, he does not overlook."

Tutu, Desmond Mpilo (1931–)

South **African** clergyman, civil rights activist, and Nobel Peace Prize Laureate. Tutu was ordained as an Anglican priest in 1960. He has since become one of the great inspirational leaders of our time. For many he has come to symbolize the nonviolent struggle against apartheid, South Africa's system of racial separatism, which has since been dismantled, from his tireless work on behalf of blacks under the system. In 1984, he was awarded the Nobel Peace Prize in recognition of the courage and heroism shown by black South Africans in their use of peaceful methods in the struggle against apartheid. In November 1995, Nelson Mandela, president of South Africa, selected Archbishop Tutu to serve as head of the Truth and Reconciliation Commission, a panel established to investigate crimes committed during the apartheid era. In June 1996, Tutu retired from his position as head of the Anglican **church** in South Africa so that he could devote himself to his role on the commission.

About **God,** Tutu says: "God does take sides. Incredibly, he sides with those whom the world would marginalize, whom the world considers of little account. That was what he did in the founding of **Israel.** He took their side when they did not deserve it against the powerful, against Pharaoh. That was a paradigmatic act that gave an

important clue about the sort of God he is."

Twelve Stones

A reminder of **God's** power in parting the Jordan so that **Israel** and the **Ark of the Covenant** could cross. The account in **Joshua** 4:1–7 reads as follows: "When all the people were safely across, the **Lord** said to Joshua, 'Tell the twelve men chosen for a special task, one from each tribe, each to take a stone from where the **priests** are standing in the middle of the Jordan, and to carry them out and pile them up as a monument at the place where you camp tonight.' So Joshua summoned the twelve men, and told them, 'Go out into the middle of the Jordan where the **ark** is. Each of you is to carry out a stone on your shoulder—twelve stones in all, one for each of the twelve tribes. We will use them to build a monument so that in the future, when your **children** ask, "What is the monument for?" You can tell them, "It is to remind us that the Jordan River stopped flowing when the Ark of God went across!" The monument will be a permanent reminder to the people of Israel of this amazing **miracle.**'"

Tyndale, William (1492–1536)

English biblical translator, religious reformer, and writer. His translation of the **Bible,** along with earlier versions of John Wycliffe, formed the basis of the Authorized (King James) Version of 1611. On **faith,** Tyndale writes: "Note now the order: first **God** gives me **light** to see the goodness and righteousness of the **law,** and mine own **sin** and unrighteousness. Out of which knowledge springeth repentance. . . . Then the same **Spirit** worketh in mine heart, trust and confidence to believe the **mercy** of God and his truth, that he will do as he hath promised, which belief saveth me."

U

God does not forgive because He never has condemned.

—A Course in Miracles

Ulgen
Central Asian creator god.

Umvelinqangi
Zulu creator god.

Unitarianism
The belief that **God** is exclusively one Person.

Universalism
Term used for the belief in universal **salvation** and **eternal** progress of all **souls**. Universalists believe that all can come to **God** and achieve salvation. That there is no eternal punishment of **Hell**, and that all humans, lost souls, as well as **Satan** and the **demons**, can achieve redemption from God. This line of thought was taught by **Origen** as well as St. Gregory of Nyssa. The thought behind this belief is that since humans were created by a God of **love**, He in no way would torture them forever in a fiery Hell or by any other means. They believe a loving God would embrace His children and welcome them home.

Unmoved Mover
A portrayal of **God** by **Aristotle**. His theory was embraced by some of the more orthodox Jewish, Christian, and Islamic philosophers during the Middle Ages. The idea is that God is unchangeable in everything. However, God was still believed to be the cause behind changes that take place in the universe.

Uriel (Fire of God)
One of the **seven archangels** of Judaic and Christian beliefs. In Judaic lore he is believed to stand in the Presence of **God**. According to lore, Uriel is a great and powerful **angel** who holds the keys to **Hell**, and who will do away with the gates of Hell on **Judgment Day**. He is symbolized by the **scroll** and an open hand holding a flame. The flame represents the meaning of his name, which is "fire of God."

Urim and Thummim
Two small objects used by **Israelite priests** to determine **God's** Will. Urim and Thummim possibly mean "lights and perfections" or "lights and integrity" (the correct meanings of these words are dubious). They are first mentioned in the Book of **Exodus** (28:29–30) where it states: "Tie the rings of the breast piece to the rings of the ephod with a blue cord, so that the breast piece rests above the belt and does not come loose. When **Aaron** enters the **Holy** Place, he will wear this

breast piece engraved with the names of the tribes of Israel, so that I, the **Lord,** will always remember my people. Put the Urim and Thummim in the breast piece, so that Aaron will carry them when he comes into my holy presence. At such times he must always wear the breast piece, so that he can determine my will for the people of Israel."

The account does not give a description of the Urim and Thummim, nor does it tell how they worked. They are believed to have been precious stones or metal that were placed in the breastplate or pocket of the high priest.

There are two theories concerning their use. The first is that they were used as an oracular device (possibly in the form of lots) to determine God's Will. The second theory is that they served as a symbol of the high priest's authority to seek the Will of God. According to the *Dictionary of the Bible,* by John L. McKenzie, S. J.: The "Urim and Thummim were an extremely primitive device for ascertaining the will of the deity; indeed, their use can scarcely be distinguished from **divination.**" They were later discarded after the **Hebrews** came to the understanding that **Yahweh** disapproved of the use of divination.

V

To get into the core of God at his greatest, one must
first get into the core of himself at his least, for no one
can know God who has not first known himself.
—*Meister Eckhard*

Vaishnavism

A method of Hindu beliefs and traditions that revere **Vishnu/Krishna** as the Supreme **God. Bhakti yoga** is the main observance of Vaishnavism. The final reward of followers is an **everlasting** spiritual union with God. The most well-known names of this god are Vishnu, Narayana, **Hari,** Bhagavan, Krishna, and Rama.

Van Gogh, Vincent (1853–1890)

Dutch Postimpressionist painter. Van Gogh was born March 30, 1853, in Groot-Zundert, Holland, son of a Dutch Protestant pastor. Van Gogh spent some time as a theological student and evangelist minister among the miners at Wasmes in Belgium. His spirituality is reflected in his work. Said Van Gogh, "The best way to know **God** is to **love** many things."

Varuna (He Who Covers)

Vedic **God,** said to be the most important of the early Vedic gods. His personality and characteristics were close to that of **Yahweh,** the God of the **Jews. Ahura Mazda,** the God of Zoroastrianism is believed by some to have been patterned after Varuna. In pre-Vedic times Varuna was the overseer of cosmic, moral, and religious order, and was called omnipotent and omniscient. The following is a Vedic hymn to Varuna:

Forgive, O gracious **Lord,** forgive!
Whatever **sin** we
mortals have committed against the
people of the gods,
if, foolish, we have thwarted your
decrees, O god,
do not destroy us in your anger!
(Basham 240).

Vials of the Wrath of God

The Book of Revelation (16:1) makes reference to **seven angels** who carry vials of the Wrath of **God.** At God's command, these angels pour out the contents of these vials upon the Earth. The account tells us, "The first angel went and poured his vial on the earth, and a foul and painful sore came on those who had the mark of the beast. The second angel poured out his vial upon the sea and every living **soul** died in the sea. The third angel poured out his vial upon the **fountain**s of waters; and they became **blood.** The fourth angel poured out his vial upon the sun; and power was given unto him to scorch men with fire. The fifth angel poured out his vial upon the seat of the beast; and his kingdom was full of darkness; and they gnawed their tongues for pain. The sixth angel poured out his vial upon the great river **Euphrates;** and the water thereof was dried up, that the way of the kings of the east might be prepared. The seventh angel poured out his vial into the air; and there came a great voice out of the temple of **Heaven,** from the throne, saying, 'It is done.'"

Virgin Mary

See Mary.

Virtues

An order of **angels** ranking fifth in the angelic hierarchy. The Virtues are responsible for working **miracles** in God's name on Earth. They also look after the heroes of the world and those who champion for the good, and impart strength and courage to individuals on behalf of God when needed. It was two angels from the class of Virtues that escorted **Jesus** to **Heaven** in the **ascension.** The Virtues are also referred to as the Angels of **Grace.**

Vishnu

One of the great gods of **Hinduism.** He is one of the **trinity** of Hindu gods, representing **God** as the sustainer of the universe. He is also associated with the Avatars, which are ten semi-angelic beings of Hindu lore. Rama and **Krishna** are the best known of His incarnations.

Vishnu is seen as a force of transcendent **love.**

Voice of God

Gabriel, one of the four and perhaps the most well-known **archangels,** is referred to as **God's** "personal" **spokesman.** Because of this, he is sometimes referred to as the "Voice of God." In addition, **angels** are often depicted in art holding **trumpets.** The trumpet symbolizes the voice of God. The Archangel Gabriel is associated with the trumpet because he is the personification of the voice of God. In the Book of Revelation, there are **seven** angels holding trumpets. As each angel sounds his trumpet, an apocalyptic event takes place.

Voluntarism

The belief that **God's** ability to create and His knowledge of moral and physical **laws** originate from His will.

von Braun, Wernher (1912–1977)

Scientist. One of the most important rocket developers and champions of space exploration during the period between the 1930s and the 1970s. He once wrote: ". . . the vast mysteries of the universe should only confirm our belief in the certainty of its Creator. I find it as difficult to understand a scientist who does not acknowledge the presence of a superior rationality behind the existence of the universe as it is to comprehend a theologian who would deny the advances of science."

W

For what can be known about God is plain to them, because God has shown it to them. Ever since the creation of the world his invisible nature, namely, his eternal power and deity, has been clearly perceived in the things that have been made.

—*Romans 1:19–20*

Wak

Ethiopian supreme god.

Wakan Tanka

God in the Sioux Indian beliefs. He was an all-pervasive, omnipotent god, sometimes referred to as the "Great Mystery."

War in Heaven

War in **Heaven** is spoken of in the **Bible's New Testament.** The war began when **Satan** became an opposer to **God.** For this reason God enlisted the Archangel **Michael** to lead the battle against Satan and the other **angels** who chose to rebel against God's **laws.** The Bible states: "Then war broke out in heaven. Michael and his angels fought against the dragon, who fought back with his angels; but the dragon was defeated, and he and his angels were not allowed to stay in heaven any longer. The huge dragon was thrown out—that ancient serpent, named the **Devil,** or Satan, that deceived the whole world. He was thrown down to earth, and all his angels with him" (Revelation 12:7–9).

Warrior of God

A title held by the Archangel **Michael.**

Washington, George (1732–1799)

America's first president (1789–1797) and one of the most important leaders in the United States history. Said Washington on the subject of worshipping **God,** "Every **man** ought to be protected in worshipping the Deity according to the dictates of his own conscience."

Watchers

An order of **angels** also called **Grigori.** According to Judaic lore, the Watchers were given the responsibility by **God** to be guardians and teachers to humankind. They are also said to have worked with the **archangels** in creating **Paradise.** The Watchers fell from **grace** when they became attracted to the women of Earth (referred to in the **Bible** at the "**Daughters of Men**"). Twelve thousand years ago, two hundred of these Watchers left their positions in **Heaven** to come to the Earth to have sexual relations with women.

Because they feared God, the angels made a pact amongst themselves that they would go forward with this act.

1 **Enoch** 6:3–4 states, "And Semyaza, being their leader, said unto them, 'I fear that perhaps you will not consent that this deed should be done, and I alone will become (responsible) for this great **sin**.' But they all responded to him, 'Let us all swear an oath and bind everyone among us by a curse not to abandon this suggestion but to do the deed.' Then they all swore together and bound one another by (the curse)." They descended upon **Mount Sinai**, taking on fleshly bodies in the process. The Biblical account at **Genesis** 6:2 says, "When people began to multiply on the face of the ground, and daughters were born to them, the **sons of God** saw that they were fair; and they took wives for themselves of all that they chose." 1 Enoch 6:1–2 states, "In those days, when the **children** of **man** had multiplied, it happened that there were born unto them beautiful daughters. And the angels, the children of Heaven, saw them and desired them; and they said to one another, 'Come, let us choose wives for ourselves from among the daughters of man and beget us children.'"

It was an act God wholly disapproved of. According to 1 Enoch 3:6–7, God said to these angels, "For what reason have you abandoned the high, **holy**, and **eternal** heaven; and slept with women and defiled yourselves with the daughters of the people, taking wives, acting like the children of the earth, and begetting giant sons?" "Indeed, formerly you were spiritual, having eternal life, and immortal in all the generations of the world. That is why I did not make wives for you, for the dwelling of the spiritual beings of heaven is heaven."

From their union with women they produced children called the "Nephilim," who turned out to be **evil** giants. In **Genesis** (6:4) it states, "The Nephilim were on the earth in those days—and also afterward—when the sons of God went in to the daughters of humans, who bore children to them." The Nephilim were part of the reason that God sent the deluge. According to one account, the Watchers shed their bodies and returned to the spiritual realm once the great **flood** came. Azaz'el was the Chief of the Watchers. The leaders of the Watchers who came to the Earth were named: Azaz'el, Arakeb, Rame'el, Tam'el, Ram'el, Dan'el, Ezeqel, Baraqyal, As'el, Armaros, Batar'el, Anan'el, Zaqe'el, Sasomaspe'el, Kestar'el, Tur'el, Yamayol, and Arazyal. The leader of the leaders was named Shemyaza. While on Earth the Watchers taught their wives many things. Much of it was knowledge forbidden to humans. First Enoch talks extensively about this saying: "And they took wives unto themselves, and everyone chose one woman for himself, and they began to go unto them. And they taught them magical medicine, incantations, the cutting of roots, and taught them about plants" 1 Enoch (7:1–2). After their descending to Earth the Watchers were never allowed to enter Heaven again.

White Light
See Light.

Whitman, Walt (1819–1892)

One of the greatest American poets and considered by many to be the father of American poetry. In 1855 he self-published the volume that would bring him recognition: *Leaves of Grass*. Within it was the emblematic "Song of Myself," a poem in which Whitman's spiritual self and idea of who or what **God** is, is revealed. An excerpt of the poem follows:

> And I say to mankind, Be not curious about God,

For I am who am curious about
each am not curious about God,
(No array of terms can say how
much I am
at peace about God and about
death.)

I hear and behold God in every
object,
yet understand God not in the least,
Nor do I understand who there can
be more wonderful than myself.

Why should I wish to see God better
than this day?
I see something of God each hour of
the
Twenty-four, and each moment
then,
In the faces of men and women I see
God, and in my own face in the
glass,
I find letters from God dropt in the
street,
and every one is sign'd by God's
name,
And I leave them where they are,
for I know that wheresoe'er I go,
Others will punctually come for
ever and ever.

Wicca (Wise One)

Witchcraft also referred to as the
"craft of the wise." In Wiccan beliefs
God is the **divine spirit** or the **All.** This
divine spirit is the essence of every living form and is present in all creatures
and things. Wicca, like many religions,
recognizes the deity as dual, worshipping both the god and the **goddess.** In
some covens, both are celebrated
equally; in others, the goddess is given
precedence or even celebrated without
reference to the god. These deities are
equals, loving, warm, and omnipresent
throughout the universe. The aspects
most popular in Wicca are the **Triple
Goddess** (maiden, mother, and crone)
and the God of **death** and rebirth.
Wiccans do not believe in or worship
Satan.

Word of God

A term used when referring to the
Bible. The word of **God** is mediated
through the scriptures.

Word, The

A term found in the **Bible's New
Testament** used to refer to **Jesus** as the
comprehensible manifestation of **God
Almighty.**

Writing Case

The **Bible's Old Testament** Book of
Ezekiel mentions an **angel** sent by **God,**
dressed in linen and carrying a writing
case. He was to use the writing case to
mark the righteous people in the city of
Jerusalem. At Ezekiel 9:4 it states, "The
Lord called to the **man clothed in linen,**
who had the writing case at his side; and
said to him, 'Go through Jerusalem, and
put a mark on the foreheads of those
who sigh and groan over all the abominations that are committed in it.'"

Y

I want to know the face of God. Everything else is detail.

—Albert Einstein

Yah
A shortened version of the **Hebrew** name for **God (Yahweh)**.

Yahweh
Personal name of **God** in **Hebrew**. It appears in the Hebrew Scriptures as the four Hebrew letters **YHWH**, known as the **Tetragrammaton**. The name occurred 6,823 times in the original translation of the **Old Testament**. Ancient Hebrews considered the name too sacred to be uttered. It was therefore replaced with the word *Adonai*, meaning **Lord**. As a result the correct pronunciation of the name is believed lost. When vowel sounds were later added, the vowels from *Adonai* were used and the name appeared as Yahweh. In English versions of the **Bible** Yahweh is translated as "the Lord" or **"Jehovah"** (another form of Yahweh).

Yahweh Adonai
A **Hebrew** term meaning "Lord God" or "Sovereign Lord."

Yahweh Elohim
A Hebrew term meaning "Lord God."

Yahweh Elohim Israel
A **Hebrew** term meaning "Yahweh God of Israel."

Yahweh is Gracious
The meaning of the name John. It can also be translated as "**God** is gracious."

Yahweh Jireh
A **Hebrew** term meaning "**Yahweh** Our Provider."

Yahweh Maccaddeshcem
A **Hebrew** term meaning "**Yahweh** Our Sanctification."

Yahweh Nissi
A **Hebrew** term meaning "**Yahweh** Our Banner."

Yahweh Roi
A **Hebrew** term meaning "**Yahweh** Our **Shepherd**."

Yahweh Ropheka
A **Hebrew** term meaning "**Yahweh** Our Healer."

Yahweh Sabbaoth
A **Hebrew** term meaning "**Lord** of Hosts" or "**Yahweh** Our Commander."

Yahweh Shalom
A **Hebrew** term meaning "**Yahweh** Our Peace."

Yahweh Shammah

A **Hebrew** term meaning "**Yahweh** is There."

Yahweh Tsidkenu

A **Hebrew** term meaning "**Yahweh** Our Righteousness."

Yehovah

Another form of **Jehovah**, a form of the name of **God** in **Hebrew**.

YHWH

The **Tetragrammaton** (four letters) representing the name of **God**. YHWH has been variously transliterated as JHVH, IHVH, JHWH, and YHVH.

Yiddish proverb

"God is a **father**; luck, a stepfather."

Yom Kippur

Hebrew Day of Atonement. In **Judaism,** Yom Kippur is a commemoration and celebration of the day **Moses** descended from **Mount Sinai** carrying the second tablets of stone, on which **God** had commanded him to recarve the **Ten Commandments.** At that time, Moses informed the Hebrews that God had pardoned them for worshipping a false **idol,** namely the golden calf. Since that time, Yom Kippur has been a day of **fasting** and self-denial and petitioning of God to pardon **sins.** However, it is also a time of happiness, because during that time, God reestablished His **covenant** with the **Israel**ites.

Yotzrenu

The figure that **Ezekiel** saw on **God's** throne. *Shi'ur Qomah,* a Jewish mystical text from the fifth century, describes Yotzrenu this way:

A quality of holiness, a quality of power, a fearful
quality, a dreaded quality, a quality of awe, a
quality of dismay, a quality of terror—
Such is the quality of the garment of the Creator,
Adonai, God of **Israel,** who, crowned, comes to the throne of his glory;
His garment is engraved inside and outside
And entirely covered with **YHWH,** YHWH.
No eyes are able to behold it, neither the eyes of flesh and blood, nor the eyes of his servants.

Yu Huang

Ancient Chinese **high god** of the Sung dynasty.

Yu-di

Ancient Chinese supreme **lord** of **Heaven.**

Z

I am the Alpha and the Omega, the beginning and the end.

—Revelation 21:6

Zarathustra

See Zoroaster.

Zechariah (God Remembers)

A **prophet** of **God**. In the **Bible's Old Testament**, Zechariah is the eleventh of the minor prophets. The Book of Zechariah falls into two parts: Chapters 1–8 consist of visions of Jerusalem's restoration, and chapters 9–14 include prophesies about the day of God's victory. Zechariah prophesied in Jerusalem around 520–518 B.C. During a period in which some of the **Jews** who had been in exile in **Babylon** were returning. In Zechariah 1–8 there are visions of Jerusalem's restoration. A vision of a heavenly horseman proclaims that God will upset the **nations** and reestablish Jerusalem. Zechariah also prophesied that God would send a Davidic servant who would bring in peace and prosperity. Zechariah 9–14 includes prophesies regarding the imminent day of God's great victory. They pronounce the coming of God the warrior and a king who will bring peace. The book concludes with a prophecy regarding the day when God will triumph over **Israel's** enemies. Those who remain will worship God in Jerusalem.

Zend-Avesta

See Zoroaster.

Zephaniah

A **prophet** of **God** from the **Old Testament.** Zephaniah concerned himself with God's Judgment on a number of peoples and God's promise to send great deliverance through the later messianic age.

Zeus

Chief deity of the ancient Greeks. The Greeks were polytheistic in their beliefs, and their gods and **goddesses** were believed to exercise control over the world and the forces of nature. There were the celestial gods who were believed to dwell on **Mount Olympus** in Thessaly, and there were Earth deities thought to live under the Earth. The gods were immortal, and were believed to have had a beginning. According to the myths, in the beginning, the Earth was inhabited by monsters; however, in time, they were driven out by giants called Titans. The ruler of these Titans was named **Cronus**, and Rhea, his sister, was his queen. Cronus believed that one of his **children** would overthrow him. To prevent this, he swallowed each child after Rhea gave birth. However, when Zeus was born, Rhea hid him on the island of Crete, presenting Cronus with a stone wrapped in blankets instead of the baby. Cronus swallowed the stone. When Zeus grew into adulthood, he forced Cronus to disgorge his siblings. He then, along with his brothers and sisters, overthrew Cronus.

Zeus became the most powerful god in the universe, ruling over both gods and men. The eagle was his special messenger. Zeus poured the rain upon the Earth and, when he was angry, hurled thunderbolts. His sister Hera (goddess and guardian of the sanctity of marriage) became his wife, and together they ruled in a palace high up on Mount Olympus. They became the heads of the **divine** family which was made up of themselves and ten other gods and goddesses.

There were their brothers, Poseidon (ruler of the sea) and Hades (ruler of the Underworld), their sister Hestia (goddess of hearth and home), and their son Ares (god of war). Zeus had children other than those by Hera. There were Athena (the virgin goddess of wisdom and war), Apollo (god of the sun, poetry, and music), Artemis (goddess of wildlife and, later, of the moon), Aphrodite (goddess of **love**), and Hermes (the divine messenger, later, god of science and invention). Finally there was Hera's son Hephaestus (god of fire). The principal chthonic gods and goddesses were Hades (ruler of the Underworld) and his wife Persephone (daughter of Demeter); Demeter (goddess of the harvest); and Dionysus (god of the grape and wine). Other important deities included Gaea (the **Earth Mother**); Asclepius (the god of healing); and Pan (the great Arcadian god of flocks, pastures, and forests).

LESSER GODS AND GODDESSES. In addition to the divine gods and goddesses were lesser deities. Among them were Helios (the sun), Selene (the moon [antedating Artemis]), the Graces (the attendants of the Olympians), the Muses, Iris (goddess of the **rainbow**), Hebe (goddess of youth and cupbearer of the gods), and Ganymede (the male counterpart of Hebe). There was also the entourage of Poseidon and his wife Amphitrite which included the Nereids, Tritons, and other minor sea deities.

Zikr (Remembrance of God)
See Dhikr.

Zion
A hill in Jerusalem. According to the **Bible,** Zion is the place from which **God** rules over the Earth.

Zoroaster (dates uncertain; between 1000 B.C. and 550 B.C.)
Ancient **Persian prophet** who founded the first world religion, Zoroastrianism. Zoroaster, or **Zarathustra,** lived sometime between 1000 and 600 B.C. He was born in Medea and was active in Bactria, and was a **man** known for his devotion and obedience to **God.** According to the *Zend Avesta* (sacred book of Zoroastrianism), Zoroaster received a vision from God (**Ahura Mazda**), who called on him to preach. Zoroaster began preaching his message of conflict between Ahura Mazda, the god of **light,** and Ahriman, the principle of **evil.** He taught that the world is polarized in a perpetual battle between good and evil and that humans are supposed to choose between the two. Zoroaster emphasized good thoughts, good words, and good deeds. The end of the world would come when the forces of light triumphed and the saved **souls** rejoiced in the victory. Zoroaster's teaching became the guiding light of Persian civilization. The following are *Yasnas* (songs) written by Zoroaster to God (Ahura Mazda):

When I conceived of Thee, O Mazda, as the very **First and the Last,** as the most Adorable One, as the **Father** of Good Thought, as the Creator of Truth and Right, as the **Lord** Judge of our actions in life, then I made a place for Thee in my very eyes. —*Yasna,* 31–4.

Thus do I announce the Greatest of all. I weave my songs of praise for Him through Truth, helpful and beneficent to all that live. Let Ahura Mazda listen to them with His **Holy Spirit,** for the Good Mind instructed me to adore Him; by His Wisdom let Him teach me about what is best. —*Yasna,* 45–6.

Verily I believe Thee, O Ahura Mazda, to be the Supreme Benevolent Providence, when Sraosha came to me with the Good Mind, when first I received and became wise with Thy words! And though the task be difficult, though woe may come to me, I shall proclaim to all mankind Thy message, which Thou declarest to be the best. —*Yasna,* 43–11.

Zuhd

A term used in **Islam.** It means to abstain from everything that separates the individual from **God.**

Appendix
Quotes from Great Thinkers

Ambrose of Milan, Saint Augustine, Cyril of Alexandria, Rene Descartes, Didymus the Blind, Benjamin Franklin, Mahatma Gandhi, Patrick Henry, Heraclitus, Hildebert of Lavardin, Abraham Lincoln, Novatian, Origen, Ovid, Blaise Pascal, Seneca, Saint Prosper of Aquitaine, Tatian the Syrian, Tertullian, Voltaire, Walt Whitman

"God is of a simple nature, not conjoined nor composite. Nothing can be added to him. He has in his nature only what is divine, filling up everything, never himself confused with anything, penetrating everything, never himself being penetrated, everywhere complete, and present at the same time in heaven, on earth, and in the farthest reaches of the sea, incomprehensible to the sight."

—Ambrose of Milan

"Lord, who art always the same, give that I know myself, give that I know Thee."

—Saint Augustine

"We have even our good works from God, from whom likewise our faith and our love come."

—Saint Augustine

"When the divine Scripture presents sayings about God and remarks on corporeal parts, do not let the mind of those hearing it harbor thoughts of tangible things, but from those tangible things as if from things said figuratively let it ascend to the beauty of things intellectual, and rather than figures and quantity and circumscriptions and shapes and everything else that pertains to bodies, let it think on God, although he is above all understanding. We were speaking of him in a human way, for there is no other way in which we could think about the things that are above us."

—Cyril of Alexandria

"Whatever is contained in a clear and distinct idea of a thing must be predicated of that thing; but a clear and distinct idea of an absolutely perfect Being contains the notion of actual existence; therefore since we have the idea of an absolutely perfect Being such a Being must really exist."

—Rene Descartes

"God is simple and of an incomposite and spiritual nature, having neither ears nor organs of speech. A solitary essence and unlimitable, he is composed of no numbers and parts."

—Didymus the Blind

"I believe in one God, Creator of the universe."

—Benjamin Franklin

"To feel that we are something is to set up a barrier between God and ourselves; to cease feeling that we are something is to become one with God."

—Mahatma Gandhi

"God presides over the destinies of nations."

—Patrick Henry

"God is day and night, winter and summer, war and peace, surfeit and hunger."

—Heraclitus

"God is over all things, under all things; outside all; within but not enclosed; without but not excluded; above but not raised up; below but not depressed; wholly above, presiding; wholly beneath, embracing; wholly within, fulfilling."

—Hildebert of Lavardin

"We trust, sir, that God will be on our side. It is more important to know that we are on God's side."

—Abraham Lincoln

"God the Father, founder and creator of all things, who alone knows no beginning, who is invisible, immeasurable, immortal, and eternal, is one God. Neither his greatness nor his majesty nor his power can possibly be—I should not say exceeded, for they cannot even be equaled."

—Novatian

"A thing will not happen, because God knows it as future, but because it is future, it is on that account known by God before it exists."

—Origen

"John says in the gospel, 'No one has at any time seen God,' clearly declaring to all who are able to understand, that there is no nature to which God is visible, not as if he were indeed visible by nature, and merely escaped or baffled the view of a frailer creature, but because he is by nature impossible to be seen."

—Origen

"A God has made His abode within our breast: when he rouses us, the glow of inspiration warms us; this holy rapture springs from the seeds of the divine mind sown in man."

—Ovid

"The knowledge of God is very far from the love of Him."

—Blaise Pascal

"He who asks of God in faith things needful for this life is sometimes mercifully heard and sometimes mercifully not heard."

—Saint Prosper of Aquitaine

"Call it Nature, Fate, Fortune; all these are names of the one and selfsame God."

—Seneca

"God is a spirit, not attending upon matter, but the Maker of material spirits and of the appearances which are in matter. He is invisible, being himself the Father of both sensible and invisible things."

—Tatian the Syrian

"There is only one God, and none other besides him, the creator of the world who brought forth all things out of nothing through his Word, first of all sent forth."

—Tertullian

"I have never made but one prayer to God, a very short one: 'O Lord, make my enemies ridiculous.' And God granted it."

—Voltaire

"My reason tells me that God exists, but it also tells me that I can never know what He is."

—Voltaire

"In the faces of men and women I see God and in my own face in the glass, I find letters from God dropt in the street, and every one is signed by God's name, and I leave them where they are, for I know that wheresoever I go others will punctually come forever and ever."

—Walt Whitman

Bibliography

Al Hoad, Abdul Latif. *Religions of the World: Islam*. New York: The Bookwright Press, 1987.

Alighieri, Dante. *The Divine Comedy*. Austin, Texas: Holt, Rinehart and Winston, 1964.

Altea, Rosemary. *Proud Spirit: Lessons, Insights & Healing from "The Voice of the Spirit World."* New York: Published by Eagle Brook an imprint of William Morrow and Company, Inc., 1997.

Ariel, David S. *The Mystic Quest: An Introduction to Jewish Mysticism*. New York: Schocken Books, 1988.

Armstrong, Karen. *A History of God*. New York: Ballantine Books, 1993.

Audi, Robert, ed. *The Cambridge Dictionary of Philosophy*. Second Edition. Cambridge, United Kingdom: Cambridge University Press, 1999.

Birnie, W. A. H, ed., et al. *Family Songbook, Reader's Digest*. Pleasantville, New York: The Reader's Digest Association, Inc., 1969.

Blakney, Raymond B. *Meister Eckhart,* *A Modern Translation*. New York: Harper & Row, Publishers, Inc., 1941.

Bowker, John, ed. *Oxford Concise Dictionary of World Religions*. New York: Oxford University Press, 2000.

Bram, Leon L., ed., and, Norma H. Dickey, ed. *Funk & Wagnalls New Encyclopedia*. Volumes 1–16. USA: Funk & Wagnalls, Inc.,

Briggs, Constance Victoria. *The Encyclopedia of Angels*. New York: Dutton, published by Penguin Putnam Inc., 1997.

Brown, Stuart Gerry, ed. *We Hold These Truths: Documents of American Democracy*. New York: Harper & Brothers Publishers, 1948.

Browne, Sylvia. *The Other Side and Back: A Psychic's Guide to Our World and Beyond*. New York: Dutton, published by Penguin Putnam Inc., 1999.

Bunson, Matthew. *Angels A to Z: A Who's Who of the Heavenly Host*. New York: Crown Trade Paperbacks, 1996.

Burnham, Sophy. *A Book of Angels: Reflections on Angels Past and Present and True Stories of How They Touch Our Lives.* New York: Ballantine Books, 1990.

Burnham, Sophy. *The Ecstatic Journey.* New York: Ballantine Books, 1997.

Chiffolo, Anthony F., ed. *Pope John Paul II: In My Own Words.* Liguori, Missouri: Liguori, 1998.

Chinmoy, Sri. *God Is..., Selected Writings of Sri Chinmoy.* Jamaica, New York: Aum Publications, 1997.

Clark, R.T. Rundle. *Myth and Symbol in Ancient Egypt.* New York: Thames and Hudson Inc., 1959.

Concise Columbia Encyclopedia, The. New York: Columbia University Press, 1989.

Cowper, William. *Poems.* London: Everyman's Library, J.M. Dent & Sons Ltd., 1931.

Davies, Peter, ed. *American Heritage Dictionary.* Boston, Mass.: Houghton Mifflin, 1982.

Doniger, Wendy, ed. *Merriam-Webster's Encyclopedia of World Religions.* Springfield, Massachusetts: Merriam-Webster, Inc., 1999.

Ellwood, Jr., Robert S. *Many Peoples, Many Faiths.* Englewood Cliffs, New Jersey: Prentice Hall, Inc., 1976.

Fuller, R. Buckminster. *Inventions: The Patented Works of R. Buckminster Fuller.* New York: St. Martin's Press, 1983.

Gay, Peter, and the Editors of Time-Life Books. *Great Ages of Man, Age of Enlightenment.* Nederland: Time-Life International, 1966.

Godwin, Malcolm. *Angels, An Endangered Species.* New York: Simon and Schuster, 1990.

Goldsmith, Joel S. *The Infinite Way.* Marina del Rey, Calif.: DeVorss & Co., Publishers, 1947.

Good News Bible: Today's English Version. New York: American Bible Society, 1976.

Graham, Billy. *Just As I Am: The Autobiography of Billy Graham.* San Francisco, Calif.: HarperCollins Worldwide, 1997.

Gruen, Dietrich, et al. *Who's Who in the Bible.* Lincolnwood, Ill.: Publications International, Ltd., 1997.

Hewitt, Hugh. *Searching for God in America.* Dallas, Texas: Word Publishing, 1996.

Holy Bible, New International Version. Grand Rapids, Mich.: Zondervan Bible Publishers, 1978.

Holy Bible, The New Revised Standard Version. Nashville, Tenn.: Thomas Nelson Publishers, 1989.

Hope, Jane. *The Secret Language of the Soul: A Visual Guide to the Spiritual World.* San Francisco, Calif.: Chronicle Books, 1997.

Howard, Jr., Ph.D., David M., and Gary M. Burge, Ph.D. *Fascinating Bible Facts: People, Places & Events.* Lincolnwood, Ill: Publications International, Ltd., 1997.

Hughes, R. Kent. *1001 Great Stories & "Quotes."* Wheaton, Ill: Tyndale House Publishers, Inc., 1998.

Jacobus, Lee A. *A World of Ideas: Essential Readings for College Writers.* Boston, Mass.: Bedford

Books, A Division of St. Martin's Press, Inc., 1998.

Jones, Alexander, ed. *The Jerusalem Bible*. Garden City, New York: Doubleday & Company, Inc., 1966.

Keating, Thomas. *Awakenings*. New York: The Crossroad Publishing Company, 1991.

Kreeft, Peter. *A Shorter Summa*. San Francisco, Calif.: Ignatius Press, 1993.

Lang, J. Stephen. *1,001 Things You Always Wanted to Know About Angels, Demons, and the Afterlife*. Nashville, Tenn.: Thomas Nelson Publishers, 2000.

Lang, J. Stephen. *1,001 Things You Always Wanted to Know About the Bible: But Never Thought to Ask*. Nashville, Tenn.: Thomas Nelson Publishers, 1999.

Leeming, David Adams. *World of Myth*. New York: Oxford University Press, Inc., 1990.

Lewis, James R., and Evelyn Dorothy Oliver. *Angels A to Z*. Detroit, Mich.: Visible Ink Press, 1996.

Linn, Denise. *The Secret Language of Signs: How to Interpret the Coincidences and Symbols in Your Life*. New York: Ballantine Books, 1996.

Marks, Robert W., ed. *Ideas and Integrities*. Toronto: Collier-Macmillan Canada Ltd., 1970.

McDowell, Josh, and Don Stewart. *Handbook of Today's Religions*. Nashville, Tenn.: Thomas Nelson Publishers, 1983.

McKenzie, John L. *Dictionary of the Bible*. New York: Touchstone, 1995.

Miller, Gustavus Hindman. *10,000 Dreams and Their Traditional Meanings*. London: W. Foulsham & Co. Limited, 1995.

Myerson, Joel, ed., et al. *The Selected Letters of Louisa May Alcott*. Toronto: Little, Brown and Company, 1987.

Neusner, Jacob, ed. *World Religions in America: An Introduction*. Louisville, Kentucky: Westminster/John Knox Press, 1994.

New Book of Knowledge, Vol. 7. Danbury, Conn.: Grolier Incorporated, 1992.

New York Public Library Desk Reference. New York: A Stonesong Press Book, Webster's New World, 1989.

Ogden, Caroline. *God: A Beginner's Guide*. London: Hodder & Stoughton, 2000.

Parrinder, Geoffrey, ed. *World Religions: From Ancient History to the Present*. New York: Facts on File Publications, 1983.

Pegis, Anton. *Basic Writings of St. Thomas Aquinas*. Volume One. New York: Random House, Inc., 1945.

RavenWolf, Silver. *To Ride a Silver Broomstick*. St. Paul, Minn.: Llewellyn Publications, 1995.

Richards, Sue and Larry. *Every Woman in the Bible*. Nashville, Tenn.: Thomas Nelson Publishers, 1999.

Robinson, Jonathan, ed. *The Experience of God*. Carlsbad, Calif.: Hay House, Inc., 1994.

Schilpp, Paul Arthur, ed. *Albert Einstein: Philosopher-Scientist*.

Peru, Illinois: Northwestern University & Southern Illinois University, Open Court Publishing Company, 1970.

Schulberg, Lucille, and the Editors of Time-Life Books. *Great Ages of Man, Historical India.* Alexandria, Va.: Time-Life Books, 1968.

Stevenson, Ph.D., Jay. *The Complete Idiot's Guide to Philosophy.* New York: Alpha Books, 1998.

Toropov, Brandon, and Father Luke Buckles, O.P. *The Complete Idiot's Guide to the World's Religions.* New York: Alpha Books, 1997.

Trimiew, Anna. *Bible Almanac, Understanding the World of the Bible.* Lincolnwood, Ill.: Publications International, Ltd., 1997.

Walsh, James. *The Revelations of Divine Love of Julian of Norwich.* New York: Harper & Brothers, 1961.

Wangu, Madhu Bazaz. *Hinduism: World Religions.* New York: Facts on File, 1991.

Watchtower Bible and Tract Society of New York, Inc. *Life—How Did it Get Here? By Evolution or by Creation?* Brooklyn, New York: International Bible Students Association, 1985.

Watchtower Bible and Tract Society of New York, Inc. *My Book of Bible Stories.* Brooklyn, New York: International Bible Students Association, 1978.

Watchtower Bible and Tract Society of New York, Inc. *You Can Live Forever in Paradise on Earth.* Brooklyn, New York: International Bible Students Association, 1982.

Woodbridge, John, ed. *More than Conquerors: Portraits of Believers from All Walks of Life.* Chicago, Ill: Moody Press, 1992.

Internet Resources

Adhan. Encyclopaedia of the Orient: http://i-cias.com/e.o/adhan.htm

Adoration of the Trinity, Albrecht Durer:
   http://sunsite.dk/cgfa/durer/p-durer38.htm

Agni: http://www.hindunet.org/devatas/agni/

Al-Farabi—Great Teacher Series:
   http://theosophy.org/tlodocs/teachers/AlFarabi.htm

Altea, Rosemary: The Voice of the Spirit World:
   http://www.rosemaryaltea.com/index1.html

Alternative Religions: http://altreligion.about.com/?once=true&

Andrews, Lynn: http://www.lynnandrews.com/pages/frameabout.html

Anselm's Ontological Argument For God's Existence:
   http://members.aol.com/plweiss1/anselm.htm

Apocrypha. Cutting Edge Ministries: Ronald G. Fanter,
   http://pws.prserv.net/cuttingedge/Apocrypha.html

Arguments for God's Existence:
   http://www.owecc.net/stevecarden/descarte/argument.htm

Aristotle: http://www.blupete.com/Literature/
   Biographies/Philosophy/Aristotle.htm

Atheagoras: http://www.newadvent.org/cathen/02042b.htm

Atheism. Religious Tolerance.org: Author: B.A. Robinson,
   http://www.religioustolerance.org/atheist.htm

Bardo Thodel—the Tibetan Book Of The Dead:
   http://www.kheper.auz.com/topics/bardo/tibetan.html

Beatific Vision: http://www.catholic-church.org/grace/western/lap98tbv.htm

Being One with God, *InnerSelf* Magazine:
http://www.innerself.com/Magazine/Spirituality/being_one_with_god.htm

Beliefs and Customs of Wicca: http://wuzzle.org/cave/beliefs.html

Bernard of Clairvaux, Saint: 9th Edition of The Encyclopaedia Britannica—Vol. III:
http://www.ccel.org/b/bernard/bernard.html

Borysenko, Joan Ph.D. *Practical Paths to Wholeness in the Real World*:
http://www.joanborysenko.com

Bradstreet, Anne "Verses Upon the Burning of our House, July 18th, 1666":
http://www.library.utoronto.ca/utel/rp/poems/abrad8c.html

Britannica.com: http://www.britannica.com

Browne, Sylvia: http://www.sylvia.org/ home/aboutnovus.cfm

Burnham, Sophy. Papers:
http://gulib.lausun.georgetown.edu/dept/speccoll/ cl129.htm

Calvin, John. *Institutes of the Christian Religion*, A New Translation: by Henry
Beveridge, Esq.: http://www. smartlink.net/~douglas/calvin/

Catherine of Genoa: http://www.catholic-forum.com/saints/saintc35.htm

Catholic Encyclopedia: Volume I, II, VII, XIV, http://www.newadvent.org/cathen/

Celtic Deities and Myths: The Deities of Gaul:
http://www.eliki.com/ancient/myth/celts/

Celtic Religion and Mythology. Ceridwen's Cauldron:
http://users.ox.ac.uk/~arthsoc/Cauldron/celtic.html

Chopra, Deepak: http://www.who2.com/deepakchopra.html

Christianity, Latter-Day Saints:
http://lds. about.com/religion/lds/library/weekly/aa012899.htm

City of God: http://members.truepath.com/cityofgod/

Columbia Encyclopedia: Sixth Edition. 2001: http://www.bartleby.com/65/

Cosmological Argument:
http://www.faithnet.freeserve.co.uk/cosmologicalargument.htm

Crosby, Fanny. Biographies: The New York Institute for Special Education:
http://www.nyise.org/fanny/

Cyrus the Great: http://www.oznet.net/cyrus/cyrus_g.htm

Daily Bible Study: http://www.execulink.com/~wblank/index.htm

Defense of *Sola Scriptura:*
http://elvis.rowan.edu/kilroy/CHRISTIA/library/ sola-scr.html

Didymus of Alexandria: http://www. bartleby.com/65/di/DidymusA.html

Divination. Easton's Bible Dictionary:
http://bible.crosswalk.com/Dictionaries/EastonsBibleDictionary/ebd.cgi?
number=T1047

Eadie, Betty J. *Embraced by the Light*, The Official website:
http://www.embracedbythelight.com/index.html

Eckhart, Meister—passing beyond God:
http:// www.users.dircon.co.uk/~harrison/ eckhart.htm

Eckhart Society: http://www.op.org/eckhart/ meister.htm

Emerson, Ralph Waldo. Quotes:
http://www.chebucto.ns.ca/Philosophy/Sui-Generis/Emerson/quotes.htm

Encyclopaedia Britannica—Online: http:// www.britannica.com

Encyclopedia.com: http://www.encyclopedia. com

Encyclopedia Mythica: http://www. pantheon.org

Etymology of the Word "God": http://www. newadvent.org/cathen/06608x.htm

Extradimensional Nature of God:
http://www.godandscience.org/apologetics/xdimgod.html

Fenelon, Francois:
http://www.gospelcom.net/chi/GLIMPSEF/Glimpses/glmps108.shtml
Books: http://www.oxfordbooks.com/bs/fenelon.html.

Five Ways, The: http://www.blackwellpublishers.co.uk/religion/relgloss.htm

Francis of Assisi: http://www.travel.it/relig/saints/francis.htm

Galilei, Galileo: http://galileo.imss.firenze.it/museo/b/egalilg.html

Gandhi. Quotations: http://www.mkgandhi.org/epigrams/contents.htm

Gathas ("Hymns") of Zarathustra: http://www.avesta.org/gathas.htm

Gematria, Hebrew Numerology: http://www.inner.org/gematria/gematria.htm

Generation of the Primordial Water: http://www.weirdvideos.com/g5.html

Glossary of Theological Terms:
http://www.blackwellpublishers.co.uk/RELIGION/glossary.htm#beatific

Glossary of Theological Terms:
http://www.blackwellpublishers.co.uk/religion/relgloss.htm

God of History:
http://www.religion-online.org/cgi-bin/
relsearchd.dll?action=showitem&id=388

God: Invented in the Image of Man?:
http://www.godandscience.org/apologetics/invented.html

Hildegard of Bingen: http://justus.anglican.org/resources/bio/247.html

Historic Church Documents: http://www.reformed.org/documents/index.html

History of the Barbarians: Philosophy and Beliefs:
http://www.wizardrealm.com/barbarians/beliefs.html

Holy Living: http://www.ccel.org/t/taylor/holy_living/holy_living04.htm#Heading5

Imago Dei: http://www.counterbalance.com/theogloss/imago-body.html

Inspirational Prayers and Quotations: http://www.thecourse.org.uk/Poems.html

Irish Theological Association: http://www.theology.ie/

Ishmael: http://www.encyclopedia.com/searchpool.asp?target=@

Japan: the Land of Shinto:
http://www.trincoll.edu/zines/tj/tj4.4.96/articles/cover.html

Jefferson, Thomas. Quotes:
http://etext.virginia.edu/jefferson/quotations/download.htm

Julian of Norwich:
http://www.oldcity.demon.co.uk/norwich/historic/names/julian.html

Kepler, Johannes. Creative Quotations:
http://www.CreativeQuotations.com/one/1996.htm

King, Martin Luther, Jr. : http://www.smartlink.net/~fred/ml-king.htm

Koran, Basic Beliefs:
http://www.acs.ucalgary.ca/~elsegal/I_Transp/IO4_QuranBeliefs.html#Judgment

Law-Original Sin. Christian Apologetics & Research Ministry:
http://www.carm.org/dictionary/dic_l-o.htm#_1_118

Leibniz, Gottfried Wilhelm:
http://mally. stanford.edu/leibniz.html
http://www-groups.dcs.st-and.ac.uk/~history/Mathematicians/Leibniz.html

Light and Sound of God:
http://www.eckankar.org/light.html

Living in Peace, Ghandi:
http://gandhi.virtualave.net/
http://gandhi.virtualave.net/religion.html

Lutheran, The: Lorel K. Ewald: http://www.thelutheran.org/9701/jan-con.html

Manichaeism, General Information:
http://www.mb-soft.com/believe/txn/manichae.htm

Me and Jesus, the Journey Home, An Odyssey:
http://www.westarinstitute.org/Periodicals/4R_Articles/Borg_bio/borg_bio.html

Medieval Monks: http://www.kyrene.k12.az.us/schools/Brisas/sunda/ma/1xiao.htm

Mere Christianity Study Guide: http:// mcsg.org

Mesopotamian Gods:
http://www-relg-studies.scu.edu/netcours/hb/sess3/mesopgod.htm

Michelangelo. Sistine Chapel Scenes from Genesis:
http://gallery.euroweb.hu/html/m/michelan/3sistina/1genesis/index.html

Mighty Fortress is Our God, A:
http://www.cyberhymnal.org/htm/m/i/mightyfo.htm

Mormons, All About: http://www.mormons.org

Myths of Creation by a Supreme Being:
http://cgibin.rcn.com/bcccsbs/opt1.htm

Names of God in the Old Testament:
http://www.evangelbaptist.org/highschool/lessons/law/names_bookmark.htm

Names of God: by Lambert Dolphin: http://www.ldolphin.org/Names.html

Nature of God: http://members.aol.com/gwerner200/

New Age Dictionary: http://www.aznewage.com/dictionary%20a.htm

New Age Spirituality: Beliefs, Practices, etc.:
http://www.religioustolerance.org/newage.htm

New Frontier Magazine: http://www.newfrontier.com/

Orisa of West Africa:
http://home.earthlink.net/~ravenswan/theorisha.html

Philosophers: http://logossophia.freeservers.com/bios.htm

Ponticus, Evagrius: http://arts-sciences.cua.edu/ecs/jdk/evagpont/index.htm

Prayers of Saint Francis Assisi:
http://www.webdesk.com/catholic/prayers/francisofassisi.html

Proof for the Existence of God:
http://www.self-realization.com/prooffor.htm

Quotes from Scientists Regarding Design of the Universe:
http://www.godandscience.org/apologetics/quotes.html

Ramakrishna, Sri: http://www.ramakrishna.org/Rmk.htm

Raphael, *Disputa* (Dispute Over the Sacrament):
http://www.artchive.com/artchive/R/raphael/raphael_disputa.jpg.html

Realm of Existentialism:
http://members.aol.com/KatharenaE/private/Philo/Barth/barth.html

Reflection (Page 1) Drawn Towards God:
http://users.erols.com/peterbb/752.htm

Religion in Ancient Persia:
http://members.tripod.com/historel/orient/08perse.htm

Restoration of the Sacred Name:
http://www.revelations.org.za/NotesS-Name.htm

Samaj, Arya: http://www.aryasamajworld.org/

Schaefer, Dr. Henry F. "Fritz," III: http://www.leaderu.com/offices/schaefer/

Sikh Gurus: http://www.sikhs.org/10gurus.htm

Sikhism: http://www.sikhs.org/

Sina, Ibn (980-1037 A.D.): http://www.ummah.org.uk/history/scholars/SINA.html

Spiritual Journeys of Great Christians:
http://www.intouch.org/myintouch/mighty/portraits/index_77957.html

Stout, Timothy. *Great Scientists Who Were Also Creationists:*
http://www.innercite.com/~tstout/cs/pog_a.shtml

Structure of the Bible:
http://www.biblestudygames.com/biblestudies/structure.htm

Supralapsarianism & Infralapsarianism:
   http://www.gty.org/~phil/articles/sup_infr.htm

Tagore, Rabindranath 1861-1941: http://www.kirjasto.sci.fi/rtagore.htm
   Selected Quotations: http://www.schoolofwisdom.com/tagorequotes.html

Taylor, Hudson: A Heart for China's Millions:
   http://www.gospelcom.net/chi/GLIMPSEF/Glimpses/glmps047.shtml

Teilhard de Chardin, Pierre: http://www.sjsu.edu/depts/Museum/chardin.html

Teleological Argument for the Existence of God:
   http://members.aol.com/plweiss1/paley.htm

Ten Sefirot of the Kabbalah:
   http://www.acs.ucalgary.ca/~elsegal/Sefirot/Sefirot.html

Tertullian: http://www3.ns.sympatico.ca/mfblume/early.htm

Thomas Aquinas, Saint: by Catherine Fournier:
   http://www.domesticchurch.com/CONTENT.DCC/19980101/SAINTS/
   STTHOM.HTM
   Five Ways: http://members.aol.com/plweiss1/aquinas.htm

Verwer, George: http://www.om.org/verwer.htm

Von Braun, Wernher:
   http://www.hq.nasa.gov/office/pao/History/sputnik/braun.html

Why Milk and Honey?: http://www.uhmc.sunysb.edu/surgery/m&h.html

Williamson, Marianne: http://www.marianne.com/

Woman's Journey to God, A, Part 2:
   http://www.spiritsight.com/writing/joabor/part2.htm

Women's History Guide: http://womenshistory.about.com

World Civilizations Home Page: http://www.wsu.edu/~dee/WORLD.HTM

Yasna: *Forward to the Divine Songs of Zarathustra:*
   http://www.zarathushtra.com/z/gatha/dji/forward.htm